Food Cultures of China

**Recent Titles in
The Global Kitchen**

FOOD CULTURES OF CHINA

Recipes, Customs, and Issues

Qian Guo

The Global Kitchen

BLOOMSBURY ACADEMIC

NEW YORK • LONDON • OXFORD • NEW DELHI • SYDNEY

BLOOMSBURY ACADEMIC
Bloomsbury Publishing Inc
1385 Broadway, New York, NY 10018, USA
50 Bedford Square, London, WC1B 3DP, UK
29 Earlsfort Terrace, Dublin 2, Ireland

BLOOMSBURY, BLOOMSBURY ACADEMIC and the Diana logo are trademarks of Bloomsbury
Publishing Plc

First published in the United States of America 2023

Library of Congress Cataloging in Publication Control Number: 2022062281

ISBN: HB: 978-1-4408-7782-7
ePDF: 978-1-4408-7783-4
eBook: 979-8-216-17150-8

Series: The Global Kitchen

Typeset by Westchester Publishing Services, LLC
Printed and bound in the United States of America

To find out more about our authors and books visit www.bloomsbury.com and sign up
for our newsletters.

To those who confront food insecurity with resilience
and innovativeness

Contents

Series Foreword

Imagine a typical American breakfast: bacon, eggs, toast, and home fries from the local diner, or maybe a protein-packed smoothie, sipped on the go to class or work. In some countries in Europe, breakfast might just be a small cookie and a strong coffee, if anything at all. A South African breakfast might consist of a bowl of corn porridge with milk. In Japan, breakfast might look more like dinner, complete with rice, vegetables, and fish. What we eat varies from country to country, and even region to region. *The Global Kitchen* series explores the cuisines of different cultures around the world, from the history of food and food staples to main dishes and contemporary issues. Teeming with recipes to try at home, these volumes will delight readers by discovering other cultures through the lens of a treasured topic: food.

Each volume focuses on the culinary heritage of one country or one small group of countries, covering history and contemporary culture. Volumes begin with a chronology of major food-related milestones and events in the area, from prehistory to the present. Chapters explore the key foods and meals in the country, covering the following topics:

- Food History
- Influential Ingredients
- Appetizers and Side Dishes
- Main Dishes
- Desserts
- Beverages
- Holidays and Special Occasions
- Street Foods and Snacks
- Dining Out
- Food Issues and Dietary Concerns

Chapters are textual, and each chapter is accompanied by numerous recipes, adding a hands-on component to the series. Sidebars, a glossary of important terms, and a selected bibliography round out each volume, providing readers with additional information and resources for their personal and scholarly research needs.

Whether readers are looking for recipes to use for classes or at home, or to explore the histories and traditions of world cuisines, the *Global Kitchen* series will allow readers to fully immerse themselves in other cultures, giving a taste of typical daily life and tradition.

Acknowledgments

The world came under siege from the COVID-19 pandemic shortly after I signed the contract for this book. Lockdown and remote work upended people's lives, especially their foodways. Nowhere has the pandemic had a greater impact on foodways than it has in China, where the first outbreaks took place and where the stringent zero-COVID policy lasted for nearly three years, before it ended abruptly at the end of 2022. Amid the crisis, the food catering sector and ordinary people of China find themselves at a crossroad of tradition and the *avant-garde* in terms of what to eat and drink, where to get food, and how to prepare the daily meals.

This volume is intended for American high school and college students, as well as the general public. It is by no means an all-encompassing guide to one of the most complex and enduring food cultures in the world. Rather, I want to demonstrate not only the Chinese gastronomic richness and diversity but, more importantly, the historical and cultural context in which the Chinese food culture has evolved. I hope to show two driving forces behind the Chinese food culture. First, persistent food insecurity has driven the Chinese to be daringly innovative with ingredients and eagerly open to change. Second, traditional Chinese food is distinguished by both its environmentally influenced varieties and artistic renderings of the preparers; these traditions, however, are fading in the era of globalization and commercialization.

My work was delayed repeatedly by pandemic-related challenges. I would not have succeeded in completing the book if not for the support of devoted family, friends, and colleagues. I'd like to thank Kaitlin Ciarmiello, who, as a senior acquisitions editor, helped me conceptualize the project. I'd like to thank Kevin Downing, Editorial Director, Books, and Saville Bloxham, Editorial Assistant, both of ABC-CLIO/Bloomsbury, for their understanding and support. I owe special thanks to Maxine Taylor, Senior Acquisitions Editor at ABC-CLIO/Bloomsbury, for her patience, advice, and support.

I'd like to thank Zhigang Chen, Chie Soong, Fang Guo, and Mike S. DeVivo, who have inspired me in many different ways, not least of which is their culinary expertise. I'd like to acknowledge Xiaojian Fang, who not only impressed us with her renditions of the Yangzhou cuisine but also advised me on a couple of recipes in this volume. Finally, I want to thank my family, Beth, Galen, and Ethan, for letting me try my clumsy cooking on them, from which I gained deeper appreciation of food in family life.

Introduction

What is patriotism but love of the good things we ate in our childhood?
—*Lin Yutang*

We eat to live, and we live to eat. The Chinese, however, may have stridden a lot further in their quest to satiate hunger from life sustainment to moral commitment, and from epicurean pleasures to national pride. Sun Yat-sen (1866–1925), the founding father of modern China, hailed China's culinary sophistication as a triumph of the Chinese nation. In his *Fundamentals of National Reconstruction* (1953 [1924]), Sun asserted that China's food culture was still the most advanced and sophisticated in the world, despite lagging the West in science, industry, and civic engagement. Mr. Sun's assertion was echoed by his compatriots who have taken food for faith. When the Chinese ask a visitor's impression about their food, it is largely rhetorical since the query is meant to solicit expected affirmation of the superiority of their foodways.

A popular quotation circulating on the internet goes like this: "Fashion is in Europe, living is in America, but eating is in China" (Lin, 2000). Indeed, it is not far-fetched to say that the Chinese would go to the end of the earth, and beyond, in search of gastronomical satisfactions. In June 2021, China sent three astronauts to the core module of the Chinese space station. Live streaming of astronauts at work and at ease became an instant national sensation, and one highlight of life in outer space was the 120 different meals and beverages available to the astronauts. The meals included popular dishes such as Kung Pao Chicken and Yu-Shiang Shredded Pork (shredded pork sautéed with spicy garlic sauce). It is said that the meals not only were nutritionally balanced but also tasted almost like "the real thing" on earth.

Before returning to earth in the fall of that year, the astronauts, who were in their 40s and 50s, requested their first meals back on earth: all were their hometown favorites. Major General Nie ordered a famous beef noodle soup from his hometown in Hubei Province; Major General Liu asked for special green beans known to his native Heilongjiang Province; relatives of Senior Colonel Yang prepared a big urn of pickled green chili peppers, a hometown side dish that the colonel had requested from outer space. Indeed, as Lin Yutang reminded us, "[w]hat is patriotism but love of the good things we ate in our childhood?"

The Chinese believe that a good diet can enhance physical and mental health because it uses ingredients that complement rather than contradict each other and emphasizes seasonality of food that brings harmony with nature. Traditional Chinese diet and medicine are intertwined; so are their respective myth and reality, which have left an informative and sometimes controversial legacy.

Chinese cooking perfection is embodied in the concept of *xian*, the most complex and delicate flavor, a euphoric sensation to the tongue. The flavor was scientifically identified by Japanese chemist Kikunae Ikeda in 1908, who termed it *umami* ("a nice savory taste") and traced its association to a range of amino acids. Some have speculated that the pursuit of *umami* in some Asian food cultures was an effort, subconscious perhaps, to compensate protein deficiency in their traditional, starch-heavy diets. The Chinese treat gourmet cooking as a high art that must lead to "whole-body" euphoria, the highest attainment of which must showcase a harmonious combination of colors, aroma, and taste in a dish. Throughout history, however, most Chinese had no mind, nor opportunity, to savor epicurean pleasures as they were tasked with feeding themselves daily. The threat of food insecurity may have made eating, talking about, and imagining food the greatest Chinese pastime.

As China continues to experience economic prosperity, food has become the first choice for most Chinese to indulge in. Food is a favorable subject in China's burgeoning creative cultural industries. *A Bite of China*, a television series about the history and regional diversity of China's culinary heritage, became an immense success and was dubbed by a food reporter for *The Guardian* as perhaps the best TV food show ever. The virtue of humility is cast aside when it comes to gastronomical expertise. One's claim of aptitude in preparing or consuming a specific dish would most definitely elicit robust exchanges over ingredient quality, preparation methods, eating etiquette, health benefits, or regional superiority. The country turned to food for solace during the COVID-19 pandemic lockdown in the early 2020; cooking became the most popular pastime and distraction when people gathered online to share new recipes, cooking techniques, and joy of eating. Many emerged from the lockdown claiming to have become master chefs.

The Chinese are so confident about their culinary superiority that they can be hypersensitive about an outsider's opinions on their cuisines. In late November 2019, Michelin published its inaugural edition for Beijing, MICHELIN Guide Beijing 2020 Selection. The publication triggered an uproar in China mainly due to discrepancies between its selections and those by the Chinese, especially the Beijingers, in terms of the best restaurants in the capital. Michelin was harshly criticized for being negligent, even arrogant, by giving too much weight to Western-styled ambience and ratings by nonlocals. It was ridiculed for being nearly irrelevant to the Chinese as a gourmet guide in comparison to recommendations found on social media platforms such as *Douyin* (the Chinese version of TikTok). The 2021 Michelin edition did not fare much better among the Chinese, as shown by blog postings on *Zhihu*, a Chinese online hub for professional knowledge. By the same token, some in the Chinese diaspora are quite defensive toward critiques from "outsiders" (Wei, 2020) and are alarmed by non-Chinese who venture into Chinese food businesses, blaming them for committing "cultural appropriation" (Cheung, 2019; Chow, 2019).

Some say the Chinese have insatiable culinary obsessions, pointing to a popular motto attributed to Confucius, "Food and sex are basic human desires." This "motto" is but a vulgar and imprecise transliteration of one sentence in a debate between two philosophers, one of whom was Mencius, an intergenerational Confucian disciple. It had little to do with food or sex, however. Much more telling evidence of the Chinese obsession with food may culminate in a common greeting: "Have you eaten?" Today, it is a Chinese cliché similar to "How are you?" in American greetings, but its prevalence reflects the existential burden for the masses in history, when the Chinese were perennially under the threat of food insecurity. It is little wonder that this greeting is losing its popularity among the Chinese youths today, who have no experience with hunger.

The Chinese food culture has several interwoven characteristics. First, the Chinese have a reputation for being unabashed omnivores with little inhibition over ingredients and preparation. Part of their coping strategy against food insecurity is to be eager to embrace new ingredients. A constant influx of new ingredients and borrowing from other food traditions throughout history have made the Chinese food culture a "melting pot."

Second, the Chinese are truly believers of the motto "You are what you eat," and view food and health as being integral with each other. The elites and the masses alike, they are driven by an infatuation for cooking innovations. Cuisine preparation is regarded as an art in which both preparers and diners search for "spiritual attainment."

Third, Chinese food has unrivaled regional variations because of the vast territory and diverse environment, an unbroken tradition, and intense and continuous exchange with other food cultures. There are eight highly popularized regional cuisines today; this geographical typology, however, is a very recent and arbitrary rendition (Phillips, 2017) and cannot reflect the diversity of regional cuisines that are steeped in the intricate history of human adaptation to the environment.

How Many Regional Cuisines Are There?

The short answer: many. The more popular accounts include either four or eight regional cuisines, each roughly corresponding to a modern provincial level administrative unit. Both accounts include cuisines from Shandong, Jiangsu (Yangzi Delta), Sichuan, and Guangdong (Canton). The "eight cuisines" also include those from Zhejiang, Fujian, Hunan, and Anhui. There are efforts to add more to the list. While there are distinct regional culinary traditions that reflect environmental adaptation and cultural diffusion, there were no nationally recognized regional cuisines until the dawning of economic reform. of the popularized regional cuisines today are but pop culture renderings in the era of unabashed consumerism.

Fourth, to the Chinese, sharing food is the most important form of social engagement. While by no means a unique cultural trait, the Chinese certainly treat food sharing with utmost importance. Business is done more smoothly at a banquet, vogue and prestige can be achieved with exotic dishes, and neighborly relations are strengthened over a big communal dinner. It must also be said that lavish dinners and banquets are also venues of corruption and waste.

Communal dinner festivals became quite popular in recent decades in China. One of the largest and most famous was held before Chinese New Year (between late January and mid-February) in a residential neighborhood, *Baibuting* ("One-Hundred-Step Pavilion"), in Wuhan, Hubei Province. In mid January 2020, as rumors and fears began to spread in the city about a mysterious, pneumonia-like illness, the local government and the community itself were faced with the dilemma of whether to press on with the festival, which had been held every year since 2000. On January 18, 2020, the food festival commenced with approval from the municipal government. It came to host over 40,000 households that presented nearly 14,000 dishes. The event quickly became the target of nationwide condemnation as the COVID-19 pandemic became full-blown and forced Wuhan, a metropolis of over 10 million residents, to complete lockdown (Huang, 2020; Zhao, 2020).

The Chinese are among the most adventurous eaters in the world, but, at least historically, that ostensible bravado may be a result of food insecurity rather than gastronomic pursuits gone awry. Today, however, when the latent function of food exoticism is no longer valid, obsession with wildlife consumption means only a threat to animal welfare, damage of natural resources, and real concerns about public health. In late January 2020, a video surfaced online showing a Chinese travel influencer relishing a bat soup dish, just as Wuhan, China, was hit by the first known outbreak of the COVID-19 pandemic. While it turned out that the video was made in Palau in 2016 as a tourism promotion, the footage aroused an outcry in China and the rest of the world, especially since bats were suspected to be the original carriers of SARS-CoV-2, the coronavirus that caused the infectious respiratory illness that eventually led to the COVID-19 pandemic. The controversy over wildlife as food was amplified by the ongoing COVID-19 pandemic which had its first known outbreaks being associated with a so-called wet market, that is, a market where fresh meat and seafood, even live animals, as well as vegetables and fruits, are retailed and wholesaled by various vendors.

Intense clashes are taking place between the old and the new foodways centered on consumption of wildlife and pets. On China's lively internet forums, one mention of eating dog meat would ignite the fiercest virtual shouting match that one can ever expect to experience. Animal rights activists often intercept carriers of dogs destined for some communities where dog meat is a delicacy and rescue the dogs by purchasing them and placing them in rescue shelters. There have been calls, from both the government and the general public, to ban or boycott the annual Yulin Dog Meat Festival, the biggest and most notorious such "festivals" in China, but they have not deterred the commercial sponsors and the avid attendees.

This volume focuses on Chinese home cooking and family meals, and there are some notable differences between them and the American foodways. Traditional Chinese meals are starch heavy. Cereal grains or root and tuber products are referred to as "main food" (*zhu-shi*) because they were the main portion of meals, being eaten to satiate hunger while animal proteins were scarce, and vegetables were not filling enough. Meat and poultry, along with soy products and vegetables, are referred to as "accompanying food" (*fu-shi*) in the Chinese diet because their function is to help ingest the "main food." Often, an entire Chinese family meal can comprise a concoction of "main food" and "accompanying food," such as noodle dishes, stir-fried rice, Chinese dumplings (*jiaozi*), or wonton (*hundun*). Side dishes in the Chinese diet also play the role of helping ingest starch-heavy "main food," especially when the "accompanying food" is unavailable or inadequate.

China faces challenges with a number of food issues and dietary concerns. First and foremost, China continues to be confronted with food insecurity. Shrinking arable land and growing consumption of animal products have forced China to become a leading food importer and investor in overseas agriculture in the last several decades, arousing suspicion and resistance. Inadequate regulatory enforcement and unscrupulous business operations have posed serious threats to food safety. Dietary changes, mainly the increase of animal protein intake, coupled with increasingly stationary lifestyles, have resulted in a wide range of public health concerns. Some culinary customs and practices, such as high sodium intake, oily dishes, and excessive use of monosodium glutamate (MSG) by restaurants, have come under scrutiny over their health ramifications. The most controversial aspect of the Chinese food culture, however, is the lack of inhibition with food ingredients.

The Chinese have coped with food insecurity by being innovative in production and consumption, and by adapting to and altering the environment. Meanwhile, they continued to adopt new food ingredients and cooking or dining methods from other peoples, be they nomads from the Central Asian steppes or merchants from Europe by sea. The Chinese food culture is, as a result, anything but stagnant. It embraces changes, and it has evolved through time. Stir-fry, the most common cooking technique, for example, was a major innovation that did not become widely adopted until about a thousand years ago. At the same time, the Chinese food culture has demonstrated amazing continuity in its philosophy and perspective, and has been a centerpiece of the Chinese history and culture.

Further Reading

Cheung, Helier. "Cultural Appropriation: Why Is Food Such a Sensitive Subject?" *BBC News*, April 13, 2019. https://www.bbc.com/news/world-us-canada-47892747.

Chow, Andrew R. "A 'Clean' Chinese Food Restaurant in New York Is the Latest Flashpoint in a Debate over Cultural Appropriation." *Time*, April 10, 2019. https://time.com/5567450/lucky-lees-chinese-food-appropriation/.

Huang, Kristine. "Coronavirus: 10 New Cases Confirmed, 30 More Suspected in Wuhan after Thousands Attend Lunar New Year Banquet." *South China Morning Post*, February 5, 2020. https://www.scmp.com/news/china/society/article/3049173/coronavirus-10-new-cases-confirmed-30-more-suspected-wuhan-after.

Lin, Kathy. "Chinese Food Cultural Profile." *EthnoMed*, November 1, 2000. https://ethnomed.org/resource/chinese-food-cultural-profile/.

Lin, Yutang. *The Importance of Living*. New York: Reynal & Hitchcock (A John Day Book), 1937.

"MICHELIN Guide Beijing 2020 Selection." Michelin Guide, November 28, 2019. https://guide.michelin.com/mo/en/macau-region/macau/article/news -and-views/michelin-guide-beijing-2020-selection.

Phillips, Carolyn. "Dividing and Conquering the Cuisines of China." *Vice*, April 27, 2017. https://www.vice.com/en/article/z4dg4j/dividing-and-conquering-the -cuisines-of-china.

Sun, Yat-sen. *Fundamentals of National Reconstruction* (English ed.). Taipei: China Cultural Service, 1953 [1924].

Thring, Oliver. "A Bite of China: The Finest Food TV Ever?" *The Guardian*, September 2, 2012. https://www.theguardian.com/lifeandstyle/wordofmouth/2012/sep/12 /bite-of-china-finest-food-tv-ever.

Wei, Clarissa. "The Struggles of Writing About Chinese Food as a Chinese Person." *Vice*, April 18, 2017. https://www.vice.com/en_us/article/yp7bx5/the -struggles-of-writing-about-chinese-food-as-a-chinese-person.

Zhao, Yusha. "Controversial Baibuting Speaks up on Banquet." *Global Times,* April 25, 2020. https://www.globaltimes.cn/content/1186702.shtml.

Chronology

The Chinese civilization emerged from the vast and fertile river valleys, coastal plains, and interior plateaus of East Asia. Mutually perpetuating increases in food supply and population strained resources and subjected subsistence farmers to food insecurity. In addition to farming innovations and outmigration, the ancient Chinese coped with food insecurity by adopting an omnivorous and starch-centered diet that invigorated them to embrace new ingredients, cooking methods, and dining etiquettes. The cumulative outcome is a rich, varied, and innovative food culture. The evolution of the Chinese foodways can be broadly divided into several epochs: the classical epoch (ca. 30th–3rd centuries BCE), the early imperial epoch (3rd century BCE–6th century CE), the middle imperial epoch (6th–14th centuries), and the late imperial epoch (14th–early 20th centuries), before China entered the modern times (early 20th century–present). Much information for the classic epoch is based on archeological evidence, which makes precise chronicling difficult. Historical records during the early and middle imperial epochs are often vague and draw on legends or folklore, making it difficult to date food-related events more precisely. The Chinese food culture did not attain the level of refinement and diversity until the late imperial epoch, when ingredients, cooking techniques and many of the well-known dishes today began to appear. After the Opium War (1840), Western influence began to engender changes in Chinese foodways. Since economic reform commenced in the late 1970s, the Chinese food culture has been undergoing rapid transformations with profound cultural, economic, and environmental ramifications, in China and beyond.

Prehistoric Times

ca. 500,000 BCE
Meat roasting is practiced during the time of Peking Man (*Homo erectus pekinensis*).

ca. 20,000–10,000 BCE
Evidence shows dawning of Agricultural Revolution during the time of Upper Cave Man (*Archaic homo sapiens*) in Zhou-kou-dian area near Beijing.

ca. 10,000–9,000 BCE
Earliest known rice domestication takes place at Shang-shan in today's northern Zhejiang Province.

ca. 8,300–6,700 BCE
Common millet (*Panicum miliaceum*; also known as foxtail millet *Setaria italica*) and broomcorn millet (*Panicum miliaceum*) are domesticated and widely grown in the foothills of Tai-hang Mountains in northern China; dogs become one of the first domesticated animals.

ca. 7,000 BCE
The earliest known fermented rice wine is made in Jia-hu of today's Henan Province.

ca. 6,000–5,000 BCE
Domesticated soybeans are grown in the lower Yellow River Valley; pigs are domesticated and become a major source of animal protein; rice is fermented to make alcohol.

ca. 6,000–5,000 BCE
Early economies in continental East Asia transition from hunting, fishing, and gathering to agriculture; staple foods include grains steamed or boiled in pottery containers.

ca. 5,000 BCE
Archeological evidence indicates possible domestication of geese in today's Zhejiang province, making it the earliest known domesticated fowl. Fire-cooked food, including grilling, roasting, and pit cooking, is used in funeral and ancestor worship ceremonies; wheat is brought to East Asia.

ca. 4,500–4,000 BCE
Success in multi-cropping and animal husbandry improve food security; oxen is introduced.

The Classic Epoch (ca. 30th–3rd centuries BCE)

ca. 3,000 BCE
Millet and rice become the dominant crops for the north and the south, respectively.

ca. 3,000 BCE
Wheat and barley from the Middle East are widely adopted in the north.

ca. 3,000–2,500 BCE
Salt and plums become common seasonings and condiments.

ca. 2,500 BCE
Ginger is used in cooking; distiller's yeast is discovered.

ca. 2,500–2,000 BCE
Wu-gu (five grains)—millet, wheat, broomcorn millet, soybeans, and hemp (which is later replaced by rice)—become the most common grain crops.

ca. 2,000 BCE
The ruling elites use bronze vessels for cooking, dining, and ritualistic ceremonies. The earliest known noodles are made from millet.

ca. 1,600 BCE
The Shang court creates official positions charged with food preparations and sets strict rules for food rituals, including use of bronze utensils, rituals for consuming meat (with beef as the highest rated), and earliest records of chicken dishes.

ca. 1,600–1,100 BCE
Daily two-meal system becomes institutionalized.

ca. 1,549 BCE
Yi Yin, regarded as the primogenitor of Chinese cooking, establishes the concept and practice of seasoning and flavoring, especially in defining "the five flavors": sweet, salty, sour, bitter, and spicy.

ca. 1,500–1,100 BCE
The earliest known chopsticks made of bronze come into use by the end of the Shang Dynasty, mainly for fetching meats and vegetables from bronze vessels. Many bronze weapons are used as utensils, including knives, spoons, and forks.

ca. 1,200–1,000 BCE
Five condiments are used widely in cooking, especially in preparing court cuisines and ceremonial banquets, including salt, fruit plums (for their alpha hydroxyl acid), Sichuan peppercorn (prickly ash), wine, and sugar (maltose).

ca. 1,100 BCE
The concept of food and medicine integration is developed.

ca. 1,000 BCE
Cold drinks are popular in summer using ice collected in winter; the Western Zhou Dynasty (1,046–771 BCE) establishes an official position for managing the ice stockpile.

The Eastern Zhou Dynasty (771–221 BCE)
The ruling elites begin to have three meals daily, while the masses continue to have two meals. Medicated diets start to appear. They consist of ingredients that are believed to have health and medicinal effects and reflects the Chinese cosmic views of human–nature relations.

The Spring and Autumn Period (771–476 BCE)

Legendary inventor and builder Lu Ban invents stone mill (ca. 5th century BCE), which significantly improves grain processing and food quality. Tea is used in mixed drinks and as a spice for making stews, which is then the most common cooking method.

8th century BCE

China is the first in the world to make vinegar from grains. Official court positions are created for professional vinegar makers.

The Warring States (475–221 BCE)

Popular cooking methods are recorded in the encyclopedic *Lü-shi Chun-qiu* (*Master Lü's Spring and Autumn Annals*).

ca. 453–410 BCE

Tea becomes a beverage, likely first in the Yangzi Delta.

The Classical Epoch

Techniques in knife work, mastery of fire/heat, and seasoning evolve to become the core skills for cooking during this epoch.

The Early Imperial Epoch (ca. 3rd century BCE–7th century CE)

The Qin Dynasty (221–206 BCE)

Unique regional cuisines begin to emerge, including those of Shandong, Suzhou (Yangzi Delta), Sichuan, and Guangdong.

The Han Dynasty (206 BCE–220 CE)

With popularization of stone mills, wheat becomes much more popular, surpassing millet as the main staple in the north. It becomes customary to have three meals daily.

The Western Han Dynasty (206 BCE–9 CE)

The court establishes plantations in the south to produce tropical and subtropical fruits.

ca. mid-2nd century BCE

Prince Liu An invents *dou-fu* (tofu), the soybean curd, which makes soybeans more tasteful and easier to digest; soybeans become a key ingredient in Chinese food culture in the next two millennia.

ca. 126 BCE

The missions of Zhang Qian, the Han Dynasty's envoy to Central Asia, introduce many new food ingredients, including grapes, walnut, carrot, pomegranate, sesame, broad bean, celery, cucumber, green beans, lettuce, spinach, fennel, garlic, and watermelon.

The Eastern Han Dynasty (25–220 CE)

With advancement of iron metallurgy, the iron wok becomes a key cooking utensil and sets the foundation for the stir-fry technique. Three methods for wheat flour fermentation are developed, making wheat the most versatile grain in China at the time; the original forms of many contemporary flour foods, such as noodles, may be conceived during this period. Vegetable oil is invented using almonds and sesame; its variety and affordability are to increase in the ensuing centuries; the early form of wonton (*hun-dun*) appears.

Late Eastern Han Dynasty
Chopsticks become widely adopted as the individual eating utensil. *Hu-bing* (baked flatbread) is introduced from Central Asia and becomes the prototype of all Chinese baked breads.

3rd century CE
Vegetable oil (sesame and hempseed) is first used in cooking, and becomes affordable and popular during the Tang Dynasty (618–907)

The Western Jin Dynasty (266–316)
The prototype of stuffed dumplings (*Jiaozi*) is a popular food; tea becomes an exclusive beverage among the elites.

The South and North Dynasties (386–589)
Large immigration of nomadic groups in the north leads to a dietary shift to having more dairy, mutton, and beef consumption; tea drinking is fashionable in the courts of southern dynasties.

Mid 5th century
As recorded in *Hou-han Shu* (*The Book of Later Han*, 445), black pepper has reached China from South Asia.

Late 5th century
Chairs and high tables are introduced via the Silk Road and are set to reshape dining etiquette.

6th century
People begin to use wok-based "stir-fry" method in cooking.

ca. 544
Jia Si-xie, a court official of the Northern Wei Dynasty, completes *Qi-min Yao-shu* (*Techniques to Harness the People's Livelihood*), an encyclopedia of ancient Chinese agriculture that contains detailed accounts of Chinese foodways at the time. Noodles are described explicitly in the book.

The Middle Imperial Epoch (6th–14th centuries)

Early 7th century
Dining arrangement starts to transition from individual serving to group sharing as large dining tables are adopted.

Mid 7th century
Han-shi Jie (Cold Food Festival) merges into *Qing-min Jie* (Clear and Bright festival, also known as Tomb Sweeping Day). Tofu becomes an ingredient for gourmet cooking.

Late 7th century
A dairy-based ice confection, an ice cream prototype, is a popular snack for nobilities with ostensible nomadic influence.

Early 8th century
Black pepper becomes a popular, though expensive, spice in cooking.

Mid 8th century
Techniques for making cane sugar are introduced from South Asia (India); rock sugar becomes the major sweetener for Chinese food thereafter. China is to be the dominant cane sugar producer and exporter until the mid-19th century.

Mid to late 8th century
Stir-fry becomes a popular cooking method, which helps improve the flavor of vegetable-based dishes and promotes a vegetarian diet.

760–762
Lu Yu writes *Cha-jing* (*The Classic of Tea*), the first classic for tea culture that is infused by Confucian, Daoist, and Buddhist metaphysical views.

ca. 9th century
Champa rice, a high-yield rice variant from Vietnam, is introduced.

The Northern Song Dynasty (960–1127)
Mutton is served as the exclusive meat for the court.

Early 11th century
First restaurants appear in large cities, such as Kai-feng, the imperial capital, where the demand for dining out is high and active night life flourishes, providing impetus for normalizing three daily meals.

The Southern Song Dynasty (1127–1279)
Northern and southern cuisines further diverge, with the south eating more fish and the north more dairy. Vegetables become much more prominent food ingredients, and vegetarian diets develop, especially in Buddhist and Daoist monasteries. Snacks, mostly sweets, become popular in the Yangzi Delta region.

The Yuan Dynasty (1271–1368)
Large Muslim immigration from Persia, Central Asia, and the Middle East gives birth to the Chinese halal cuisine. Instant Boiled Mutton becomes a popular dish. The first roasted duck restaurant is founded in *Daidu* (Beijing). *Yue-bing* (moon cake) becomes the symbolic snack for the Mid-Autumn Festival.

The Late Imperial Epoch (14th–early 20th century)

14th–15th centuries
Meal sharing becomes the common dining arrangement across the social spectrum.

Early 15th century
Techniques are developed for making granulated cane sugar.

Mid to late 16th century

Many New World crops are brought to China, including maize (corn), potato, sweet potato, tomato, pumpkin, sunflower seeds, and squash via sea trade routes.

1570s

Chili pepper arrives in China.

Late 16th century

The Portuguese bring the first European foods to East Asia, including castella ("Nagasaki Cake"); Macao becomes a center for European–Asian food fusion, where local favorites such as the egg tart are created.

Late 16th century–early 17th century

Jiaozi (Chinese dumpling) becomes an official court food for the Chinese New Year.

The Qing Dynasty (1644–1911)

Beijing is the center of convergence of regional cuisines and the incubator of the so-called royal or court cuisine. Pork remains the favorite meat of the Manchu court, however.

1721

Chili pepper becomes a substitute to salt among the *Miao* (Hmong) people who concentrate in the southwest.

Late 18th century

Yuan Mei (1716–1797), arguably the most famous Chinese gastronomist in history, elaborates the concept and attainment of *xian* (*umami*) as the flavor above all flavors. In addition to the recipe classic, *Recipes from the Garden of Contentment* (1792), Yuan also writes the only biography of a chef in Chinese history.

1840s

A broader spectrum of European food cultures are introduced to coastal regions, especially Shanghai and Guangzhou, after the First Opium War (1840).

1860

First Western food restaurant, *Tai Ping Koon* (*Taiping Guan*) in China opened in Guangzhou by Chui Lo Ko.

1866

Martha Crawford, wife of American missionary Tarleton Perry Crawford, publishes a cookbook to help Chinese cooks learn to make Western food.

1900

The Russians open a beer brewery in Harbin, the first in China. The Chinese would not warm up to the foreign alcohol beverage until the second half of the twentieth century.

1903, August
Tsingtao (Qingdao) Brewery is founded by the Anglo–German Brewery Co. Ltd; its first beer, a German-styled pale lager, becomes available on the Chinese market the next year.

Modern Times (Early 20th century–present)

Republic of China (1911–1949)
Introduction of new, mostly Western, food ingredients, including MSG, curry, mustard, cocoa, coffee, butter, baking soda, and food coloring, spurs the modern food processing industry and modifies traditional cooking. Western and Japanese cuisines become popular in large cities and start to influence Chinese foodways.

1910s–1920s
Reproductions of royal cuisines become popular, especially in Beijing.

1920s
The so-called four regional cuisines, namely those of Shandong, Yangzi Delta, Sichuan, and Guangdong, are being formally promoted.

1927
Coca-Cola opens its first China bottling plant in Shanghai. It is to become the largest Coca-Cola plant outside the United States in 1933.

1948
Shanghai becomes the first market outside the United States to sell 1 million boxes (24 million bottles) of Coca-Cola.

1959–1961
China suffers three years of famine that cost millions of lives.

1979
After a 30-year hiatus, the first consignment of 3,000 boxes of Coca-Cola is shipped to Beijing from Hong Kong at the end of the year.

1980, June 20
"Eight major regional cuisines" are formally introduced in an article published in *People's Daily*.

1983
Beijing Maxim's, a branch of Maxim's de Paris, opens as the first upscale Western restaurant in Beijing during the reform era.

1987, November 12
Kentucky Fried Chicken (KFC) opens an outlet near Tiananmen Square, which becomes the first American fast-food restaurant in China.

1989, September 15
British Andrew Stow and wife open Lord Stow's Bakery in Macao, featuring their "Portuguese egg tarts," which later become a popular snack in Macao, Hong Kong, and Taiwan.

1990
In Mainland China, the first McDonald's opens in Shenzhen, and the first Pizza Hut opens in Beijing.

1992, April 23
The largest McDonald's in the world opens in Beijing with over 700 seats and 29 registers.

1995
Domino's Pizza opens its first store in Shenzhen, Guangdong Province.

1999, January
The first Starbucks coffee shop opens in Beijing.

1990s
Deep-fried crawfish becomes popular first in the south.

2002
SARS (Severe acute respiratory syndrome) breaks out in southern China and quickly spreads to other parts of China and beyond. Research shows possible connection of the virus to cave bats with civets, regarded as a delicacy in the Cantonese cuisine, as the intermediary carrier. The devastating epidemic leads to public debates over wildlife consumption and laws restricting such consumption.

2006
The Chinese government sets 1.8 billion *mu* (296.5 million acres) as "the red line," that is, the minimum amount of arable land for the country's basic food security.

2008
China becomes a net food importer in terms of trade values.

2018
Luckin Coffee, a Chinese coffee chain, opens its first stores in Beijing and Shanghai in January, and, by October, becomes the second largest coffee chain after Starbucks in China with 1,300 stores.

2020, January
The first outbreaks of the COVID-19 epidemic take place in Wuhan.

2020, January
Luckin Coffee announces it has opened over 4,500 stores, becoming the largest coffee chain in China

2020, March
Starbucks continues its planned expansion with at least 500 more outlets, as China reopens from the COVID-19 pandemic and becomes the bright spot for the coffee conglomerate's recovery.

2020, May 15
Popeye's, an American fast-food chain, opens the first of 1,500 planned Chinese outlets in Shanghai, drawing huge crowds of mask-wearing customers.

2020, June 18
Food and kindred products see the greatest spikes in the total sales of the e-commerce festival to a total of 48 billion RMB (US$6.8 billion), more than 10% of the total sales.

2020, June 29
Accounting scandals, starting at the end of January, sinks Luckin's market value and leads to NASDAQ suspension.

2021
The sector of ready-to-cook foods continues its astronomical expansion with 20% annual growth and more than 60,000 businesses, bringing new challenges to food safety, health ramifications, and changing food culture.

2022, September 13
Starbucks sets the goal of having 9,000 stores in China by 2025.

2022, September 26
Starbucks opens its 6,000th store in China and adds nearly another 100 by the end of 2022.

2022, October
Luckin Coffee makes a comeback and surpasses Starbucks in number of shops in China, though Starbucks China achieves higher revenues.

2023, January
Online retail platforms set new records for sales of ready-to-cook entrées prior to the Chinese New Year.

CHAPTER ONE

Food History

The Chinese take great pride in their culinary history, but it is perplexing that their forebears have left little systematic records, not to say scholarly works, on their food culture. Contemporary research on Chinese food history, as a result, must draw from journals that treated food in the contexts of historical events, social institutions, and health practice. Period personal accounts may also help restore the historical food scene, the most remarkable example of which was *Recipes from the Garden of Contentment* (1792) by Yuan Mei (1716–1798). These accounts were mostly from the high-brow foodie's perspective, however, which relished gastronomical pleasures but fell short of precise recording and systematic study of food as part of culture.

1.1. Chicken Stir-Fried with Chestnut, 18th century (*Li-zi Chao-ji*)

This was a dish popular among the elites in the late 18th century, as recorded in *The Garden of Contentment* (1792). Today's version of the recipe calls for simple ingredients and preparation and is suitable for home cooking.

Yuan's Recipe

Yield: Serves 3–4

Ingredients
1 whole chicken, cleaned
¼ cup canola oil
1 cup cooking wine
1 shot glass of first-drawn soy sauce in late October to early November
1 cup water
Bamboo shoots
Pinches of sugar

Preparation
1. Chop the chicken to 2-inch pieces.
2. Marinate in canola oil.
3. Boil chestnuts.
4. Simmer chicken to 75% cooked (145 degrees Fahrenheit).
5. Add chestnuts to chicken and simmer till chicken is full cooked.
6. Add sugar to flavor and serve.

Notes: Like many of the recipes in Yuan's book, there was a lack of details since Yuan himself was a foodie, not a chef. It is also likely that the chef kept the detailed recipe secret, a customary practice among all craftsmen. In addition, Chinese cooking is more an art than a science, which calls more for spontaneous inspiration rather than rigid precision.

Modern Version

Yield: Serves 3–4

Ingredients
9 oz. chicken breast
7 oz. chestnuts
1 long-stem bunching onion (or 2–3 spring onions), sectioned
1 thumb (approximate a 2-inch piece) fresh ginger, sliced
3 fresh garlic cloves, minced
3 cups peanut oil
¾ tbsp cooking wine
1 tbsp granulated sugar
½ tbsp salt
¾ tbsp soy sauce
1¼ tbsp starch
½ tbsp oyster sauce
¼ tbsp sesame oil
¼ tsp black pepper powder
¼ cup stock
½ tsp MSG

Preparation
1. Slice the chicken to ¾ inch cubes and coat evenly with the mix of half of the salt and ¾ of the starch.
2. Mix the remaining starch with 3 tbsp of water.
3. Stir-fry chestnuts in ¼ cup of peanut oil at 145 degrees Fahrenheit till golden brown, then remove from wok and drain the oil.
4. Deep-fry chicken with 2¾ cups of peanut oil till golden brown, then remove from wok and drain the oil, leaving a little in the wok.

5. Stir-fry ginger, onion, and garlic.
6. Stir in chicken and chestnut; add cooking wine, stock, sugar, oyster sauce, soy sauce, MSG, and the remaining salt; stir-fry for 3 minutes.
7. Mix in wet starch, then add black pepper powder and sesame oil; plate and serve.

Notes: Fresh and high-quality chicken and chestnuts are key to a successful rendition of this dish.

In recent decades, China's economic boom has spurred a quest for fine dining and exotic eating, as well as a keen interest in food history. On the one hand, the internet and social media provide fertile ground for free-wheeling renditions of Chinese food history, which either embellish or denigrate the culinary traditions. On the other hand, serious scholarship has produced volumes on China's food history in a more vivid and systematic fashion. In better understanding China's food history, let's take a quick look at three food-related Chinese words and critical questions that they may raise.

First, *fan* is the all-encompassing word for meals; it also refers to cereal grains and other starch food in a meal. *Cai*, on the other hand, means vegetables in more precisely but today refers to vegetable, meat, tofu, egg, seafood, and any mixture of them in a meal. Having a meal, the most important daily routine, is *chi* ("to eat") *fan*. Why, one may ask, do the Chinese not say *chi cai* for having a meal?

China's food history has been interwoven with sedentary subsistence agriculture. The Agricultural Revolution needed and nurtured a large population that created a magnificent civilization and, at the same time, exerted increasing pressure on the ecosystem and food supply. Food insecurity, as a result, became a persistent threat in China to this day, where mass famine and starvation frequently devastated the society. The Chinese appreciate not only "you are what you eat" but also "you eat what you can get." Ancient Chinese adopted a diet that emphasized starch food to strike a balance between the need for a large population and the sustainability of the food system. The diet was encouraged, even institutionalized, as a societal coping strategy to alleviate food insecurity. If and when possible, they would eagerly increase their intake from red meat, poultry, seafood, and vegetables (*cai*).

Second, the Chinese are always eager to introduce new ingredients, cooking methods, recipes, and even dining furniture to enrich their foodways.

While China was home to rice, tea, millet, and pigs, most of the key ingredients in today's Chinese diet were imported. The Chinese use three adjectives, *hu*, *fan*, and *yang*, to denote three historical periods when many of the foreign ingredients, especially fruits and vegetables, were brought to China. Those that came to China via the Silk Road during the Han Dynasty (206 BCE–220 CE) are mostly referred to as *hu*, including cucumber, pepper, garlic, walnut, cilantro, and sesame. The ones described as *fan* came during the 13th to 16th centuries, mostly from overseas trade that thrived along the southeast coasts, such as tomato, sweet potato, chili pepper, and peanuts. New ingredients that arrived with European expansion bear the adjective *yang* ("the sea"), such as onion, potato, and cabbage.

Third, food carries enormous social and cultural significance, and a shared meal functions as the lubricant to smooth any friction. "A (shared good) meal can resolve any problem," many Chinese would attest. The classic word for banquets is *yan-xi*, which originally described a seating arrangement of a long, shared mat (*yan*) topped with individual sitting mats ("*xi*"). The very emphasis on group sitting in describing a banquet shows group or communal dining had important social significance. Such dining rituals were always hosted, never "pot-luck," and the host, be he the emperor or the villager, would always try his or her best to ensure utmost epicurean satisfactions of the guests.

It is important to note that many of the identifying characteristics of Chinese foodways today, from ingredients and diet to cooking methods and dining etiquette, were actually developed in more recent times. For example, the signature Chinese cooking method, stir-fry (*chao*), was first mentioned in the 6th century in the classic agricultural manual *Qi-min Yao-shu* ("Essential Techniques for the Welfare of the People," 544 CE). Recipes that used the technique, as we know it today, did not appear until the Song Dynasty (960–1279) and became the leading cooking method only after the late 16th century. Meals, including banquets, were served with individual trays until the 4th and 5th centuries when the introduction of high stools and large tables made dish sharing possible and, thereafter, dining more social and efficient. The popular Chinese dining form of sitting around tables and sharing dishes, however, did not become a custom until the Song Dynasty (960–1279). The omnipresent round dining table, which was designed to seat eight comfortably, did not become the standard design until the Qing Dynasty (1644–1911).

Chinese food history may be divided into four epochs prior to the modern, post-imperial times based on major characteristics of the foodways resulted from broad changes in socioeconomic and environmental conditions:

The "classical epoch" spans about three millennia (30th–3rd centuries BCE) that include the late neolithic period, three dynasties (Xia, Shang, and Western Zhou), and the Eastern Zhou (Spring and Autumn and Warring States periods); the "early imperial epoch" extended from Qin to the so-called northern and southern dynasties (220 BCE–6th century CE), half of which was under the rule of the Han Dynasty (206 BCE–220 CE); the "middle imperial epoch" incudes Sui, Tang, Song, and Yuan dynasties (6th–14th centuries); the fourth epoch was the "late imperial epoch" (Ming–Qing dynasties, 14th–early 20th centuries).

Much of the remaining 20th century saw Chinese food culture going through a slowly accumulative transition. A sea-change has taken place in Chinese food culture charged by a fusion between the traditional and the new, the native and the foreign. Obsession with food has become a major source of national pride. Pursuit of culinary indulgence has provided inspiration to commercial ventures, creative cultural production, and serious scholarship. The much-disputed eight regional cuisines, very much a first product of pop culture and commercial promotion in the early 1980s, are but one of the examples of how the combination of these forces have deepened and embellished Chinese food history and culture.

The Classical Epoch (30th–3rd centuries BCE)

Continental East Asia was one of the early hearths of the Agricultural Revolution. Tribal societies in various regions on the East Asian continent thrived with early agricultural success which greatly improved food production and led to population growth. These tribal and regional cultures eventually merged into what came to be known as the Chinese civilization, which was deeply rooted in sedentary subsistence agriculture and a grain-heavy diet.

Archeological evidence shows that during the late Neolithic period, people in East Asia had developed various cooking methods, including stewing, steaming or boiling with pottery vessels, and grilling on open fire or over stone. Unsurprisingly, utensils were rudimentary, with pottery bowls and plates as well as bone and stone knives and chopsticks.

Food ingredients were not very diverse and were from both domesticated and wild plants and animals, including millet and rice; wheat started to appear as time went on. People used salt, plums, wild honey, bitter fruit, and several sweet herbs for flavoring and seasoning. Cooking was primitive, and meals were simple. One celebrated recipe passed on to later generations was pheasant soup that was served to the legendary Yellow Emperor (*Huang-di*, ca. 25th–27th century BCE). In a large geographic area with highly varied natural environments, there were distinct regional differences in terms of food ingredients, such as rice in the south and millet in the north.

One important aspect of the emerging prehistorical food culture was that food and dining were served to reinforce social order and coalesce the community. While prehistorical Chinese food rituals were not unique among their peers elsewhere in the world, their social and political functions were to become more and more prominent over time, eventually culminating in a distinct characteristic of the Chinese culture to this day.

Entering the Bronze Age during the legendary Xia Dynasty (ca. 2000 BCE), cooking improved in ingredients, cookware, and cooking methods; consequently, meals became more varied and sophisticated. The Chinese began to make breakthroughs with their foodways. First, food security improved with varied and more productive cultivars and breeds, which also provided expanded food ingredients. Second, bronze cookware enabled new and more efficient cooking methods; together with bronze dining and drinking utensils, they became symbols of status and power. With the rulers atop, each class of elites was allowed to manufacture and possess bronze cookware of specific number and size. It was during this time when chopsticks, made of bronze as well as animal bones, became widely used—mainly for picking food from large bronze cauldrons called *ding*, which stood on three or four legs and were heated from below for cooking food, especially meat.

Some characteristics that distinguish Chinese food culture today began to appear in embryonic forms during this period. Most traditional cooking methods other than stir-fry, such as stewing, simmering, braising, and marinating, were used. The rulers spared no efforts to conjure up the best food possible. The kings of Western Zhou (1047–772 BCE) enjoyed exorbitant meals dubbed "eight treasures," for example, which included (1) steamed rice topped with lard and meat source; (2) steamed millet topped with lard and meat sauce; (3) triple-cooked pigling (roasting, deep-frying, and three-day simmering) with sauce and vinegar; (4) triple-cooked ewe lamb; (5) thinly sliced beef, wine-marinated overnight, served with meat sauce, vinegar, and plum sauce; (6) five-flavored jerky made with beef, lamb, and wild herbivores; (7) baked pancake with rice and seasoned and cubed beef, lamb, and venison; and (8) dog liver roasted in dog caul fat.

Today, dog meat is still consumed in China, especially in some southern regions such as Yulin in Guangxi Zhuang Autonomous Region. Mounting public outcry against dog meat consumption seems to only serve as motivation for the locals to defend their inalienable food tradition with greater determination. During the classical epoch, however, dog was regarded as a major source of animal protein, together with sheep/goats, pigs, and fowl. Dog meat during this epoch was considered inferior to beef, mutton/lamb, or pork, however. Beef was exclusively for the royals, and slaughtering oxen for any other class or purpose was strictly prohibited, since oxen were the most valuable draft animal for crop cultivation.

Of course, the feast of eight treasures was fit only for the king. What was remarkable during the Shang and Zhou dynasties (17th–10th centuries BCE) was that food appropriation and consumption were strictly codified based on one's status in the societal hierarchy. For meat, for example, the king could eat beef, lamb, and pork, but the vassals could eat only beef. Among the bureaucrats, high-ranking officials could eat either lamb or pork, middle-level bureaucrats could eat pork, and low-ranking ones could only eat fish. Even for the elites, meat consumption was restricted to special occasions, especially sacrificial ceremonies for ancestors and deities. The commoners could only eat cereal grains and vegetables except for during sacrificial rituals, when they were allowed to have fish. Most people had two meals a day, which became a custom that persisted until the late imperial epoch; the kings and those in their inner circles, however, had three or more meals every day.

The Chinese had started making fermented alcohol drinks in prehistorical times. The wines were made from either millet or rice, with the former being similar to the Japanese *sake* and the latter being sweet. Only the elites could afford to enjoy alcohol beverages, but binge drinking was regarded by the likes of Confucius as an unruly and sinful act. Water was the preferred non-alcohol beverage. Also common were soups made of soy leaf or rice.

The main cooking utensil during the classic epoch was *ding*. This was exclusively used for ritual offerings and ensuing feasts. Its possession and use were also dictated by the social hierarchy. The king would have nine *ding* for ceremonies, feudal lords seven, minister-level officials five, and low-ranking bureaucrats, three or only one. *Ding* was mainly for cooking meat, and other cookware, either bronze or pottery, were used for steaming, stewing, or boiling grains, meat, and vegetables as well as for eating or drinking. Chopsticks were nowhere to be seen at this time. Rather, people ate cereal grain and vegetable with their hands, soups with spoons, and meat with knives.

Access to quantity and quality of food depended on one's social and political status. Elaborate rituals were institutionalized to reinforce the *status quo*. The elites dined while ritualistic music and dance were performed; they followed strict etiquettes to enforce the impression that they were the ones who were connected to the divine and, therefore, endowed with the good food. Court officials charged with food and health services were among the highest ranked and closest to the monarch. Yi Yin (ca. 17th–16th centuries BCE) may be the first of such officials and is said to be the father of Chinese food culture who set the foundation for the doctrines of "five flavors" and "mastery of fire," which remain the core concepts in Chinese cooking. It is noteworthy to point out that Yi Yin was also a shaman who possessed medical expertise. He was instrumental in promoting food–medicine integration that became deeply imbedded in the Chinese psyche. What was more, as a prime minister in the early Shang Dynasty (1600–1046 BCE), he offered a parity between societal governance and gourmet cooking.

The ancient Chinese identified "five flavors" in cooking: salty, sour, sweet, bitter, and spicy. The salty flavor came from salt, cured meat sauces, bean paste, and fermented soybeans. The sour flavor was originally obtained from sour plums and later from grain-based vinegar. Honey, fruits, maltose, sugarcane, and licorice provided the sweet flavor. Alcohol was said to be the main source of bitter flavor in cooking. Ancient Chinese spiced their food with ginger, peppercorn, cinnamon, black pepper, garlic, and green onion. The chili pepper was brought to China in the 1570s but was not widely used in cooking until more than two centuries later.

The second half of the Zhou Dynasty is divided into the Spring and Autumn period (ca. 771–476 BCE) and the Warring States period (475–221 BCE). Chinese food culture reached a new height from the previous centuries with technological innovations and intensified interregional exchanges. Extensive and large-scale public works improved food production and widened the scope of ingredients. Iron cookware began to appear, which inspired new cooking methods and seasoning techniques with greater use of animal fat, herbs, and spices. The north and the south began to show greater contrast in foodways, as freshwater fish and aquatic plants featured prominently in the warmer and more humid south.

Confucius (551–479 BCE), the most famous luminary of this fascinating time, felt consternation toward the rapid social and political changes during the Spring and Autumn period. He tirelessly advocated restoration of the social hierarchy as a remedy for uncertainty and change, and one of the means of doing so was to enhance food security, public hygiene, and social rituals. To Confucius, the essential need for the ruler is to obtain mandate from the masses, and the essential need of the masses was food security. Since food security was hard to ascertain, elaborate food rituals became imperative in enforcing social stability. Confucius elaborated on food preparation and dining etiquette that became guidelines for future generations. When speaking about quality of ingredients, for example, he advises:

"Know the origin or source of your food."
"Eat fresh and local; do not eat food out of season."

When speaking about food preparation, he emphasizes:

"Hygiene is essential in food preparation."
"The way you cut your food reflects the way you live."
"Don't eat when the sauces and seasonings are not correctly prepared."

When speaking about dietary health, he insists:

"Eat only at mealtimes; eat only until seven tenths full; control in portions promotes longevity."
"Don't eat food that smells bad; don't consume food that is not well cooked."
"Meat should be eaten in moderation."
"Eat ginger but in moderation so as to not increase the internal heat of the body."
"You need not limit drinking, but do not drink to the point of confusion."

Some of the modern transliterations attributed to Confucius may have been misconstrued by the Chinese themselves, however, who for millennia insist that their sage merely emphasized the deeply imbedded imperative that the desires for food and sex are the two most important in human nature. Some modern influencers have even gone so far to claim that Confucius was an obsessed foodie. A correct read of his words, however, shows that Confucius, known as being disinterested in material pursuit, was merely preaching for the food culture to follow the same code of filial piety and conformity as in any other aspect of the society to ensure stability and harmony.

Toward the end of the classical epoch, improved food security and food-related innovations brought China to the verge of major development in its food culture. Wheat, the wonder grain from West Asia, had not been popular in China because it was only eaten in steamed whole grain and was much less palatable than millet and rice. The invention and spread of the stone mill gave wheat a newfound popularity. Wheat, milled into flour, became extremely versatile and would replace millet to become the dominant starch food source in northern China in the coming centuries. Above all else, however, it was the inaugural unification of China that was to usher in a revolution to the food culture.

The Early Imperial Epoch (3rd century BCE–6th century CE)

The Qin Dynasty (221–206 BCE), short-lived but the first to unify major sedentary agricultural regions in East Asia, commenced an imperial history that continued for the next two millennia. China continued to confront food insecurity as a matter of survival and an imperative for good governance, as Sima Qian (ca. 145–86 BCE) wrote in his *Records of the Grand Historian* (ca. 91 BCE):

> "One cannot govern without the people; the people cannot be governed without food."

The sense of food crisis motivated the Chinese to be innovative and laborious in the search for more land, continued innovations, new ingredients, and ceaseless imagination with food. A unified China reached out to frontiers and opened to other cultures, intensifying exchanges and introducing new foods, which deeply influenced Chinese food culture as we know it today. Regional cuisines became more established, especially in the rapidly settling and environmentally more diverse south. Four classic cuisine traditions, that is, those of Shandong, Jiangsu, Sichuan, and Guangdong, began to emerge toward the end of this epoch.

1.2. Five-Flavor Rice Cake, Late 14th–early 15th centuries (*Qian-shi-gao*)

Prickly waterlily (*Euryale ferox; qian-shi*), an aquatic plant, was harvested for its edible nuts as early as 2,500 years ago. The flour of its dried fruit ("fox nut") was considered to have wide-ranging medicinal effects and was a popular ingredient in many local dishes in the Yangzi Delta. The use of prickly waterlily and other medicinal ingredients in this recipe is evidence that the Chinese, ancient or modern, have always intended to combine the benefits of food and medicine in their culinary experience.

Yield: Serves 20–30

Ingredients
2 lb. glutinous rice
6 lb. long-grain rice
1 lb. fox nut flour
1 lb. mix of ginseng, *bai-zhu* (*Atractylodes macrocephala Koidz*), China root
  (*Wolfiporia extensa Ginns*) and *sha-ren* (*Wurfbainia villosa*)
Granulated sugar, quantity to taste

Preparation
1. Finely grind all ingredients.
2. Sieve to get rid of coarser pieces.
3. Mix with sugar and boiling water.
4. Steam, cool, and serve.

The opening of the Silk Road during the Han Dynasty (206 BCE–220 CE) gifted the Chinese food culture with a slew of new food ingredients, preparations, and etiquette during four centuries of unification. The so-called Six Dynasties (220–589), including the devastating period of Invasion and Rebellion of the Five Barbarians (304–316), also witnessed unprecedented cultural exchanges between Chinese and nomadic cultures.

During the first half of this epoch, the Chinese experienced a phenomenal infusion of new ingredients, especially fruits and vegetables. Some of the regional ingredients became widely grown and consumed, such as bamboo shoot, lotus root, bottle gourd, persimmon, and loquat. The most remarkable, of course, were those that came through the Silk Road. New vegetables arrived, including cucumber, eggplant, cilantro, garlic, pepper, peas, and various beans; the Chinese embraced new fruits such as watermelon, pomegranate, and grapes. They also discovered ways to press sesame oil and later applied the technique to acquire soybean oil and canola oil. New agricultural innovations helped increase yield and production. Greenhouses came into use and provided some fresh vegetables even during the winter in the north.

Tofu (*dou-fu*) was undoubtedly the greatest food invention during the Han Dynasty. Legend has it that tofu-making was discovered after a botched alchemical practice, a mythical craft called *fang-shu*, by Liu An, the vassal king of *Huai-nan* (199–175 BCE). Like his peers, the king practiced *fang-shu* in search to yield pills that could extend youth and prolong life; instead, he gained eternal notoriety for one of the most important additions to the Chinese food culture. The Chinese had consumed

soybeans, a legume native to China, by steaming or dry-frying them, neither of which was quite palatable because of taste, texture, and digestive
problems. Tofu, in contrast, transformed soybeans from a humble dry
grain to one of the most versatile ingredients and a cheap, plentiful source
of protein for the Chinese and many other Asian peoples. Today, there are
infinite soybean food varieties, from soy milk to imitation meat, but the
original, white and bland gelatin-like bean curd, still dominates the soy
food world. It must be noted, however, that tofu remained an exclusive
food item and did not become widely present in the Chinese diet until the
Tang Dynasty (610–907).

There were many new cookware and resultant processing and cooking
methods. A variety of maltose sugars and alcohol became available and
were used increasingly in cooking. Chefs and cooks were empowered by
improved fire hearth and iron cookware. Food preservation methods
included pickling, marinating, and smoking. Cooking developed into two
specialized steps, namely, preparing the ingredients and making the meal.
Preparation was further compartmentalized into "the red counter" (meats),
"the white counter" (grains and other starch foods), and "the water counter" (fish, poultry, and vegetables). These changes had far-reaching ramifications for specialty cooking and food hygiene, which led to improved
cuisines. Lacquerware became the most common eating utensil.

Mutton and dairy products were more common in northern China,
where there were much greater interaction and exchange with nomadic cultures. In contrast, southern regions made the most of the warm and humid
environment and consumed far more fish and aquatic plants, as well as a
greater variety of vegetables. Regional cuisines continued to develop with
distinct ingredients, preparation methods, and unique flavors.

During this period, lavish party banquets were in vogue, as reflected in
many tomb murals and brick reliefs. These banquets not only served exorbitant entrées but also showcased strict etiquette. More elaborate banquets
usually had themes, such as hunting, full moon, bamboo groves, and
other enchanting scenarios. It goes without saying that most of these banquets were held by the wealthy and powerful, while the masses could
barely fill their stomachs. The decadent banquets coincided with a period
in Chinese history of change and uncertainty, and the elites tried to escape
reality by dwelling in the greatest Chinese cultural obsession: epicurean
decadence.

The second half of this epoch (4th–6th centuries) is characterized by
clashes among various groups, especially between sedentary and nomadic
societies in the north. Notwithstanding the devastating human toll from
wars and genocides, the intense cultural exchange during this period

which infused new ingredients, cooking methods and dining etiquette to northern cuisines. In the south, large refugee population from the north encountered indigenous foodways, which initiated a food fusion and rapid development of southern cuisines. It was during this time that the rise of Buddhism and revitalization of Daoism gave a great boost to a vegetarian diet throughout China, where the monasteries became centers for this new culinary adventure. Comprehensive food journals were compiled, among them was the epical classic of *Qi-min Yao-shu*. The ten-volume classic spans all fields of agriculture in all regions of China, with chapters focusing on foodways that include many recipes of the time.

The early imperial epoch was a transitional period that bridged the food culture of China in the classical epoch and the ensuing coming-of-age food culture in the middle imperial epoch. While many food-related traits were still at their nascent stages of development, they set up the foundation for the great maturity and prosperity that made the Chinese food that we still recognize and enjoy today.

The Middle Imperial Epoch (6th–14th centuries)

When China was reunified under the Sui Dynasty (581–618), its food culture was on the eve of breakthroughs after centuries of intense interactions with other cultures, especially those along the Silk Road. The ensuing Tang Dynasty (618–907), considered the apex of the Chinese civilization for its power and wealth, as well as its openness, drastically expanded the food horizon for the Chinese. It was during the Song Dynasty (960–1279), however, that the Chinese food culture reached unmatched sophistication nurtured by trade and commerce, urbanization, and, at least for the first half of the dynasty, high living standards. The Mongol Conquest and the resultant Yuan Dynasty (1271–1368) provided new stimuli to the Chinese food culture with enduring influence on northern cuisines. Food production increased and ingredients further diversified with prolonged periods of peace and stability, as well as diffusion from other cultural realms, during this epoch. Societal wealth incentivized gastronomical pursuits and culinary innovations. The Chinese food culture reached its second historical apex.

Many new food ingredients arrived via the Silk Road, such as the long-stem lettuce (*Lactuca sativa* L.) and, increasingly, from sea routes with growing oversea trade and commerce. China's contact with South Asia, mainly through efforts of introducing Buddhism during the Tang Dynasty, exposed China to more new food ingredients, such as spinach and sponge gourd, and to the valuable technology of making granulated cane sugar. In addition, imperial tributes that included exotic food items streamed into China, especially during the powerful Tang and Yuan dynasties. Carrot, for example, was brought to China during the Yuan Dynasty. A variety of wheat breads such as the renowned baked, unleavened, layered flatbread (*shao-bing*) were also brought to China and were refined quickly. Through the Silk Road there also came folding stools and high tables, the adoption of which started the transformation from dining with individual serving trays to dining around a communal table and shared dishes.

Fish and seafood were important in the south, as the regions became more settled and developed by both indigenous peoples and migrants from the north. Mutton and beef were the favored meats during this epoch, perhaps due to influence from the steppes and oases of Central Asia, especially in the court and at major cities in northern China. Pork was regarded as an inferior meat until Su Shi (Su Dong-po, 1037–1101), a renowned foodie, poet, and bureaucrat (in that order in terms of achievements) of the Song Dynasty, rediscovered its versatility with a recipe that produced a dish that still graces the menu of many high-end restaurants in China today: *Dong-po-rou* (*Hong-shao-rou*; braised pork belly). Pork would eventually become the go-to meat for the Chinese as a coping strategy under resource pressure, and new cooking methods generated countless tasty recipes.

1.3. Braised Pork Belly (Side Pork), Suzhou Style (*Su-shi Hong-shao-rou*)

This is one of the most famous Chinese dishes that dates its origin to the Northern Song Dynasty (960–1127). Hundreds of variations have derived from the original recipe since then. This version stands out because it requires fewer ingredients but demands expert heat control. Its heavy use of sugar reflects the culinary preference in the Yangzi Delta.

Yield: Serves 5–6

Ingredients
2–3 lb. pork belly (side pork)
½ cup dark soy sauce
½ cup rock sugar
1 cup cooking (yellow) wine
½ tbsp of Chinese (rice) vinegar *or* a dozen dry hawthorn flakes

Preparation
1. Cut the meat into 1-inch cubes.
2. Soak the meat cubes in cold water with ½ cup of cooking wine, 15–20 minutes.
3. Rinse the meat cubes and place them in a large pot topped with 2 inches of water.
4. Heat the pot on high; add the rest of cooking wine (or the hawthorn flakes) and the vinegar.
5. Continue for another 5–6 minutes after it comes to a boil, then skim off the froth off the top.
6. After 30 minutes of high heat (boiling) stewing, turn the heat to low and cook for one hour.
7. Move the meat to a clay pot on medium heat, add the dark soy sauce, and cook for 30 minutes.
8. Turn the heat to high, add the rock sugar, and mix gently to avoid breaking up the meat.
9. When the broth appears to thicken, transfer the entire contents to a deep dish and serve.

Notes: Experts of this dish emphasize the importance of fresh pork bellies that have more thin layers of lean and fat meat.

Improvement in cooking and dining were also noteworthy. During the Song Dynasty, adoption of bellows allowed more effective heat control during cooking, which was key to the stir-fry technique; steamers and hot pot were developed. Dining tables became larger and standardized for seating eight. During the Tang and Song dynasties, porcelain utensils replaced pottery, metal, and lacquer ones, and the fine porcelain from China came to be known elsewhere as "china."

During the Tang and Song dynasties, the Chinese fell in love with a great delicacy, *hui*: sliced raw fish served with sauces, which was very much like today's *sashimi*, the signature Japanese cuisine. Eating sliced raw fish dates back further, but it was not until the Tang Dynasty that the Chinese "sashimi" became a great delicacy and a main course at banquets. It might have been brought to Korea, where it is called *hoe* (pronounced "hwae"), and to Japan during the great cultural exchange between Japan and the Tang between the 7th and 9th centuries. It must be noted that the Chinese mostly used freshwater fish, especially carp, instead of saltwater fish. *Hui* eventually fell out of favor in China, as it might have caused frequent and widespread foodborne diseases due to lack of ingredient quality control and preparation hygiene.

During the Song Dynasty, one of the most important new crops that came to China was, alas, rice. The so-called *champa* rice, a rice variety from Vietnam, was brought to China in the 10th century as a tribute. Impressed by its drought enduring and early ripening qualities, the court promoted its adoption throughout China. It provided a huge boost to China's food security and rapid population growth.

New processing technologies yield new foodstuffs, especially seasonings and condiments. In addition to sesame oil, canola oil, soybean oil, and tea seed oil, which can endure high heat, also became available in cooking. These new cooking oils and the iron wok enabled stir-frying, which became a cooking method popularized during the Song Dynasty.

Tea started to gain popularity and became the leading nonalcohol beverage toward the end of this epoch. Historical records reveal that tea was introduced into the elite circles during the Han Dynasty, but it did not become a common beverage until the Tang Dynasty, when different types of tea and their brewing methods spread from the south to the north with booming interregional trade and commerce. During the Tang Dynasty, tea was consumed with ginger and salt, a tea-brewing method that is still used today in some remote, ethnic minority areas. By the Song Dynasty, the Chinese began to seek the unique and natural flavor of tea, which was processed into both loose tea leaves and cakes made of tea powder; the latter may taste similarly to the Japanese *matcha*.

Various alcohol beverages became available, in addition to the traditional rice wines. Grape wine was introduced from Central Asia and continued to be the most popular fermented fruit wine. Grape wine and its legendary drinking vessels were portrayed in a famous poem by Wang Han (687–735?) from the early Tang Dynasty:

A grape-wine so fine, a cup that gleams at night,
To drink on I'd love, but for the summons to fight.

The earliest evidence of distilled liquor (*bai-jiu*, a high-proof, colorless alcohol) dates to the mid Tang Dynasty, using wheat, barley, or millet and a dried fermentation starter (*qu*). The complex process became standardized during the Yuan Dynasty (1271–1368), perhaps aided by distillery technology brought from the Middle East. Since then, *bai-jiu* dominated Chinese alcohol consumption until modern times, when European styled alcohol beverages made inroad into China.

Fine dining during the Tang and Song dynasties was no longer limited to banquets sponsored by the powerful and the rich; public dining businesses, which were among the earliest restaurants in human history, emerged and flourished at times of economic prosperity and urbanization. Large Song cities, especially, Kaifeng, the capital, were world-class fine dining centers. A revolutionary change in Chinese urban culture was the opening of urban night life during the Song Dynasty accompanied by major changes in urban design and governance. The hustling and bustling night market attracted droves of customers for restaurants and dinner theaters catering to different clienteles, from exorbitant fine dining establishments to quick-bite street vendors. Northern, southern, or Sichuan regional specialties were featured prominently among the establishments. It was in this robust culinary environment that the Chinese chefs strived for, and to large extent achieved, the highest attainment in their creed: creating dishes with perfect combinations of color, aroma, and taste.

The Late Imperial Epoch (14th–early 20th centuries)

With the dynastic turnover from Yuan to Ming in the mid-14th century, China began to enter the late imperial epoch, which marked the third apex of Chinse culinary development. Over five centuries, long periods of stability and peace fostered sustained economic and social development, and the food culture reached maturity by synthesizing and standardizing prior culinary achievements in theory and in practice, and from preparation to etiquette. Waves of diffusion of new ingredients, driven mainly by European expansion, enriched and even revolutionized Chinese food culture: can one imagine Chinese food today without the chili pepper?

1.4. Free-Range Chicken Simmered in Mushroom Broth, 18th century (*Mo-gu-wei-ji*)

The use of white mushrooms (*Leucocalocybe mongolica*), which grow on the grassland of Mongolian Plateau, is evidence of exchange between sedentary and nomadic societies that brought new and innovative elements to the Chinese food culture.

Yield: Serves 3–4

Ingredients
4 oz. white mushrooms
1 whole chicken
½ cup canola oil
1¼ tbsp rock sugar

Sweet cooking wine, soy sauce, long-stem Chinese (bunching) onions, peppercorn

Preparation
1. Scald mushrooms through boiling water, then soak in cold water and clean with a toothbrush; rinse four times with clean cold water.
2. Stir-fry mushrooms over high heat and spray them with cooking wine several times.
3. Chop the chicken into square pieces and put them in a pot.
4. Bring the pot to a boil and skim off the froth; add sugar, cooking wine, and soy sauce; simmer for about 1 hour.
5. Add mushrooms to the pot and simmer for 20 minutes; add bamboo shoots, green onions, and peppercorn, cook for several minutes; serve.

Although the Ming Dynasty (1368–1644) failed to establish its rule over the Mongolian steppes, cultural exchanges between nomadic and sedentary regions continued to flourish and influence the Chinese food culture. The Manchu Conquest in the mid-17th century, furthermore, brought about a convergence of sedentary, nomadic, and hunting–fishing cultures that reshaped regional and national diets. In the meantime, southern China, especially the Yangzi Delta, the Pearl Delta, and Sichuan Basin, became the center of sophisticated and diverse cuisines.

1.5. Hibiscus Pork, 18th century (*Fu-rong-rou*)

The Chinese word for hibiscus, *fu-rong* (*fu-young* in Cantonese), usually describes egg dishes. Curiously, this recipe uses neither hibiscus nor eggs. The name may come from the shape of sliced pork, which often resembles flower petals. It is a famous Zhejiang dish characterized by its selective ingredients and elaborate preparation. The following closely follows the recipe in Yuan Mei's classic recipe.

Yield: Serves 3–4

Ingredients
1 lb. pork tenderloin
40 large shrimp, shelled
2 oz. lard
1 cup canola oil

½ shot glass soy sauce
1 shot glass cooking wine
1 teacup chicken stock
Steamed rice flour, Chinese long-stem (bunching) onion, and peppercorn, as needed

Preparation
1. Slice and dip the pork in soy sauce and let dry in open air for about two hours.
2. Cut the lard to dice size.
3. Place one shrimp and one dice of lard on each pork slice, and press them together with cleaver.
4. Cook through the pork combo in boiling water.
5. Heat ½ cup of canola oil, place the pork combo in a brass skimming spoon, and ladle hot oil over them.
6. Mix soy sauce, cooking wine, and chicken stock; bring to a boil.
7. Pour the mix over the pork combo pieces; add steamed rice flour, onion, and peppercorn; mix and serve.

Notes: Yuan's recipe was very vague in preparation. The modern renditions suggest coating the pork combo in wet starch to help keep the pork and the shrimp together before deep-frying it.

Many new crops arrived between the late Ming Dynasty and early Qing Dynasty. Maize (corn), sweet potato, and potato boosted starch food output, a major factor for rapid population growth and expansion of other agricultural sectors. New vegetables and fruits, especially tomato, cauliflower, broccoli, asparagus, chili pepper, and green beans, made the vegetable-heavy Chinese diet much more appealing. During the late stage of this epoch, Western foodways made direct inroads into China, engendering deeper changes in food culture.

The society began to indulge in fine dining as China settled in for a prolonged period of peace and prosperity. The elites carried out endless banquets which indulged in the best of ingredients, preparation, innovation, and ambience. This good time for dining inspired foodies to compile some of the most important works on Chinese cookery. The often dilettantish accounts by the *literati*, as a result, provide a glimpse of the culinary attainment of the time. The most important culinary compilation from this epoch is arguably *Recipes from the Garden of Contentment: Yuan Mei's Manual of Gastronomy* (2018 [1792]) by Yuan Mei, a most famous gourmet *illuminatus* who lived in the wealthy Yangzi

Delta region and spent much of his life enjoying gourmet cooking in the elite circle.

Behind the culinary achievements were many great chefs, who had access to both plentiful, quality ingredients and throngs of eager foodies. Unfortunately, like their brethren in other creeds, chefs were regarded as humble laborers and restauranteurs as lowly merchants. Their expertly takes on food preparation were not well recorded and passed on, and their names are long forgotten. As a matter of fact, Yuan Mei wrote the single biographical account in Chinese history about a chef who worked for him.

During the late imperial epoch, culinary craftsmanship reached the zenith of Chinese food history, culminating millennia of trials and errors. Regional cuisines began to establish geographical brand recognition. The south, wealthier economically and better endowed with a much wider range of ingredients, became distinctive with standard procedures in making their signature dishes. The Yangzi Delta's bland, sweetened cuisine(s) became synonymous to fine dining with ingredients of quality, freshness, and mutual accommodation.

While celebrating Chinese gastronomical achievements, one must be reminded that throughout Chinese history, the masses struggled with inadequate quantities of food and had little choice over quality of food ingredients and preparation. They were far removed from the fine dining scene. What they might have contributed was their resilience and ability of making the most out of whatever ingredients were available with little inhibition. This dichotomy in Chinese food culture may help explain the characteristics of Chinese food in the West, as well as the exotic and repulsive food preference by some in China, in the eyes of Westerners.

Despite its popularity around the world today, Chinese food was not automatically embraced by others as the East met the West in trade and commerce, and in cultural and social exchange. The early encounters with the Chinese, for example, did not enamor the Europeans with Chinese food. Legend has it that, during negotiations in Beijing in the aftermath of the Second Opium War (1860), the British officers did not even touch the royal banquet prepared in their honor by the Chinese officials. The saving grace came from their culinarily more enlightened French colleagues, who obviously devoured whatever on the table. In those days, Europeans often shunned local Chinese cooking and tried to stick to their own foods. One explanation was that Europeans were turned off by the exotic ingredients and flavors in southeast coastal regions such as Guangdong (Canton), where most Westerners resided; cultural bias may have also played a role.

In the 19th century, Western food began to gain a toehold among some Chinese elites and influence local food cultures in coastal cities such as

Shanghai or colonies such as Hong Kong. The Chinese might have otherwise been resistant to change, but they were never close-minded to foreign food, be it from Persia or America. Western food cultures filtered through barriers and influenced the modern Chinese foodways. Most Chinese did not consume much Western food and beverages sooner because either they could not afford them or lacked access to them for political reasons.

As China was transitioning from a feudal empire to a modern state in the early 1900s, roaring nationalistic sentiments found sustenance in the food culture, as Sun Yat-sen (Sun Zhong-shan) proclaimed in the preamble of his *Fundamentals of National Reconstruction* (1953). The reality was that Chinese food became a prime representative of inexpensive, run-of-the-mill ethnic food outside East and Southeast Asia. Fast forward to the present, the swelling Chinese urbanites and middle class are revitalizing their culinary heritage while embracing foods from all over the world, infusing new dynamics into every aspect of the Chinese foodways. Today's Chinese food culture is quickly evolving as a culmination of its gastronomical heritage, stimuli from globalization, rampant commercialization, and insatiable obsession with the fine and the exotic, endowed by the country's astronomical growth of wealth.

Further Reading

"Confucius on Dining Etiquette." *Ritual of the Table*, May 6, 2018. https://you.stonybrook.edu/babyface/confucius-on-dining-etiquette/.

John, Courtney. "9 Confucius Quotes on Eating Well." *Magnifissance.* https://magnifissance.com/selfcare/9-confucius-quotes-on-eating-well/ (accessed August 4, 2022).

Waley-Cohen, Joanna. "Celebrated Cooks of China's Past." *Flavor and Fortune* 14, no. 4 (Winter 2007): 5–7, 24. http://www.flavorandfortune.com/ffdataaccess/article.php?ID=625.

Yuan, Mei. *Recipes from the Garden of Contentment: Yuan Mei's Manual of Gastronomy.* Translated by Sean J. S. Chen. Great Barrington, MA: Berkshire Publishing Group, 2018 [1792].

CHAPTER TWO

Influential Ingredients

One of the most distinctive characteristics of Chinese foodways is its wide range of ingredients. Historically, there was little food taboo due to religious or ethical reasons, and food insecurity pressed the Chinese to be innovative, adventurous, and receptive to all edible sources of food. Traditional Chinese food, at the same time, was typical of sedentary subsistence agriculture, in which cereal grains were the staples of the diet. As a result, traditional Chinese diet is heavily dependent on cereal grains, supplemented by soy and vegetables. Chinese meals show a dichotomy of "main (staple) food" (zhu-shi), which consisted of cereals or other starch foods and provided the main portion of the meal, and "accompanying food" (fu-shi), which was in smaller portions, intended to help ingest cereal, and consisted of ingredients such as vegetables, soy products, red meat and poultry, and fishery and aquacultural products.

There is a Chinese saying: "Those living in mountains live off the mountains and those living near waters live off the waters." The Chinese have indeed made the most out of their environment in terms of foodways. With China's vast and diverse natural environment, there have been regional differences in influential ingredients. Furthermore, new ingredients discovered locally or brought in from overseas have added to the list of important regional food ingredients. For example, while rice has been a key ingredient in the Chinese diet, it is erroneous to describe the Chinese as a "rice-eating" people. People in northern regions may eat more wheat and other cereal grains than rice, which is not as important a crop in the north due to environmental constraints. The misconception about rice's omnipresent importance in Chinese diet may have to do with contemporary exposure of China, which has disproportionally concentrated on the southeast coast, where rice is the main staple. The warm and humid climate in southern China, at the same time, makes green, leafy vegetables more available to southerners, while their counterparts in the north traditionally had only a few choices, such as turnips, carrots, onions, cabbage, and napa cabbage, to enjoy in the winter. In the same token, freshwater fish is a regular accompanying dish in southern China while in the north it is much less available. Northern Chinese, on the other hand, tended to eat more mutton and beef than their brethren in the south.

Rice-Eating Chinese?

While rice is China's most important grain staple, wheat is a close second. It is estimated that the Chinese consumed about 145 million tons of rice and 125 million tons of wheat in 2019–2020. Rice cultivation dominates the warm and humid regions in the south, while wheat is the leading grain crop in northern China. It is reasonable to regard the northerners as wheat eaters. The southerners eat a lot more rice than their northern counterparts, but they also eat a lot of wheat in the form of noodles, wonton, pancakes, and buns.

Since the 1980s, China has undergone phenomenal economic growth, which has also stimulated far-reaching changes in Chinese food culture. Some of the prominent and essential ingredients in ancient times faded away in terms of their importance, both due to environmental changes and more available or productive alternatives, while new ingredients have been enlisted in Chinese cooking and food consumption. One notable change is that regional differences in influential ingredients have diminished significantly due to new cultivation techniques, population mobility, and interregional, even international, integration of the food supply chain. The Chinese anywhere now have access to most of the common Chinese food ingredients, and enjoy regional cuisines that, not too long ago, were exclusive to their respective geographical hearths. As living standards improve, alcohol, caffeine, and especially animal protein become much more prominent Chinese food ingredients. The increase in meat consumption has aroused strong reactions in the Western media, which sounded the alarm of an environmental and public health catastrophe with the rapid increases of meat consumption (Campbell, 2021; Rossi, 2018), and elicited retorts from the Chinese (Ku, 2021).

Notwithstanding political sensitivities associated with one's food culture, criticisms over China's increasing meat consumption are not justified because they are not only biased on cultural and social grounds but also not supported by facts. In 2018, according to data from Organization of Economic Cooperation and Development (OECD), China's per capita beef consumption was 3.62 kg versus the United States' 26.06 kg, and per capita consumption of poultry was 12.2 kg versus the United States' 50.1 kg. China did have higher per capita consumption in pork that year, registering 30.25 kg versus the United States' 24 kg. Indeed, meat is still "accompanying food" in the overall diet, and per capita meat consumption is still significantly lower than that of developed countries. At the same time, China has certainly experienced a rapid increase in meat consumption. Between 1999 and 2018, for example, China's per capita meat consumption increased 32% for beef, 30% for pork, and 59% for poultry. Considering China's population size, the steep upward trend does have profound ramifications on the environment and natural resources, as well as on public health.

The public health concerns may be even more prevalent because of China's socioeconomic dichotomy: the sharp contrast between the urban and the rural diets. Rural per capita annual meat consumption over the last 30 years has consistently been below that of urban by 15–35 kg. While annual per capita grain consumption in China has decreased, rural areas have maintained a higher intake of grains and remain on par with urban diets in terms of vegetable consumption, which is more typical of the traditional Chinese diet. Many observers of China's food culture and dietary changes have access to and firsthand experience with urban lifestyles, which have undergone the most drastic dietary transformation due to a much-improved living standard and traditional obsession with food. In discussing present influential food ingredients, therefore, it is important to keep socioeconomic and regional differences in mind.

Interactive graphics by National Geographic Magazine on the diet of selected countries ("What the World Eats," 2014), based on data from the United Nations' Food and Agriculture Organization (FAO), show that China's caloric intake in an average daily diet nearly doubled between 1962 (1,526) and 2011 (3,073). Forty-seven percent of the daily caloric intake is still derived from grains in comparison to the respective 22% for a U.S. daily diet. Meat counted for 3% of the daily caloric intake in 1962, and 17% in 2011. The trajectory of dietary changes indicates that the Chinese diet is becoming increasingly reliant on animal protein, but grains and other starch foods, as well as produce (vegetables and fruits), still occupy much greater portions of the Chinese diet in comparison to the American diet. Both changes and stabilities in the Chinese diet manifest in today's influential food ingredients.

Despite significant changes in their diet in the last two generations, the Chinese still place starch food as the centerpiece of a meal, which they refer to as the "main (staple) food." Starch-concentrated crops are mainly cereal grains but also include roots and tubers, especially potatoes from the Americas in recent centuries. The ingestion of starch foods, ideally, would be accommodated with plenty of the more flavorful "accompanying foods," such as vegetables, soy products, poultry, meat, or fish. Historically, with a limited supply of animal protein, the Chinese had to be innovative in making cereal grains and other starch food tasty by concocting a great variety of texture and flavoring, and pairing them up with the appropriate "accompanying foods."

Cereal Grains

In 2018, China produced about 20% of cereal grains in the world, comparable to its share of population in the world, 18%. Among the major cereal grains, China was the largest producer of rice (27.4%) and wheat (17.9%), and the second largest producer of maize (corn, 22.4%). With a slim margin for food self-sufficiency, China does not export much cereal grains. At the same time, China has become a major importer of maize and, especially, soybeans. In recent years, China has accounted for around 60% of the world's total soybean imports, mainly for animal feed, to satisfy the skyrocketing demand for meat of the 1.4 billion Chinese.

2.1. *Man-tou* (Steamed Bread)

This is the most common starch "main food" (*zhu-shi*) in northern China. The key to making good *man-tou* is to leaven and then knead the dough. Hard and prolonged kneading would provide the freshly steamed bread with a perfect *al dente*.

Yield: Serves 5–6

Ingredients
1 lb. of all-purpose wheat flour
1 cup of lukewarm water
1 teaspoon of yeast
1 tablespoon sugar (optional)

Preparation
1. Leave about 1 ounce of flour out for later use, and pour the rest of the flour into a mixing bowl, add yeast and sugar, then gradually add lukewarm water while mixing the ingredients.
2. Use hands to knead the flour mix into a smooth dough.

---

3. Keep the dough in the mixing bowl, cover it with a wet cloth and leave the bowl in a warm indoor place until the dough expands to twice the original size and is filled with beehive-like air pockets. The ideal temperature for leavening is the mid 80 degrees Fahrenheit, under which it will take approximately 2 hours in the summer, but longer in other seasons or when room temperature is significantly lower.
4. Place some unused flour on a chopping board (or any clean, hard surface), and knead the dough repeatedly until it becomes hardened. Return the kneaded dough to the mixing bowl and cover it with wet cloth again for 5–20 minutes of "secondary leavening," depending on room temperature (the higher the temperature, the shorter the leavening time).
5. Knead and elongate the dough, cut it into five pieces, and mold them into any shape of your liking.
6. Place the dough pieces in a steamer filled with cold water, cover it, and place it on the stove on high heat. After boiling, steam for 20–30 minutes.
7. Turn stove off and let the steamer stand for 3–4 minutes. Take the bread out and serve.

Notes: At the end of Step 3, if the dough tastes sour, dissolve a couple of pinches of soda ash (sodium carbonate) with hot water, wet hands with the solution, and knead the dough briefly to neutralize the sour taste.

It is interesting that, as the original home of soybeans, China today is the largest buyer of soybeans in the world. Of the five ancient grains recognized in the time of Confucius, proso millet (*Panicum miliaceum*), foxtail millet (*Setaria italica*), rice (*Oryza sativa*), wheat (*Triticum*), and soybean (*Glycine max*), though some have argued that it was cannabis rather than soybeans that completed the five ancient grains (Yeung, 2020). The first two have largely faded into obscurity over time. Low yield may be key to their demise, along with other factors such as environmental change, evolving cooking techniques, and adoption of new ingredients such as maize (corn) and potatoes. Scientific and technological innovations have also made a difference, as in the case of genetically modified soybeans.

Today, China's cereal consumption still contributes about 46% of the total calories to the daily diet. Rice and wheat are the main cereal grains consumed, counting for more than half and nearly 40%, respectively. As China's dietary structure changes, the government and some NGOs start to promote healthy diet and encourage greater proportions of produce, grains, and nuts. There is a distinct south–north dichotomy due to environmental, especially climatic, difference. Also important is a rural–urban contrast, in which the urban diet has lower caloric and weight intake of cereal grains than the rural diet.

Rice

As home for the earliest known domesticated rice, China is the leading rice grower in the world. Rice became more and more important in the Chinese diet as the Yangzi River valley and areas to its south, which were hot and humid in contrast to the north, became more settled and developed. By the Ming Dynasty (1368–1644), rice accounted for nearly 70% of the entire cereal grain supply (before the arrival of maize and potatoes). Despite rice's overwhelming importance as a cereal grain for billions of people in the world, its cooking and consumption have remained monotonous for thousands of years: the milled grain is mostly steamed and sometimes made into a congee (porridge). The saving grace for the bland rice is that its growing areas in the world are endowed with climates that would allow plenty of vegetables and fruits to grow and be "accompanying food" for rice, the main (staple) food.

Rice cultivation in China has been "a tale of two rices": in southern China, long-grain rice (*Oryza sativa* subsp. *Indica*) dominates, as it does in Southeast Asia and South Asia. It thrives in hot and humid subtropical and tropical climates and has higher yield. Roughly 70% of Chinese rice acreage is for long grain rice, which accounts for 80% of daily staples for southern Chinese. Short-grain rice (*Oryza sativa* subsp. *Japonica*), on the other hand, is a descendent of the rice subspecies first domesticated in China. It is grown mainly in the north and the northeast and accounts for a little more than 20% of China's total rice production. Rice has a much smaller share of daily staples in northern China, where wheat and coarse grains, such as maize, millet and sorghum, and potatoes, are consumed as popular staples.

Rice flour is a lot more versatile for combining with other food ingredients, and the most common concoctions are rice noodles and wrappers used in various southern cuisines. The third rice cultivar is the so-called sticky rice (*Oryza sativa* var. *glutinosa*). Unlike the other rice cultivars, sticky rice, because of its high glutinous content, is usually used as the key ingredient for desserts, sweets, and festivity foods such as *nian-gao* (New Year Cake), rice balls (*tang-yuan* and *yuan-xiao*) for the Lantern Festival, and many local specialties in the south.

Wheat

Wheat was one of the ancient "five grains" that reached China at least four to five thousand years ago. Until rotary millstones became popular during the Western Han Dynasty (206 BCE–9 CE), wheat was steamed whole, which yielded a coarse meal that was hard to ingest and, therefore, not favored by the Chinese. The fate of wheat completely changed after millstones became widely available and high yield new wheat cultivars were adopted. Since then, wheat has been the most versatile staple in Chinese cooking. Wheat cultivation is widespread in China with the North China Plain being the major producing region where five provinces, Henan, Shandong, Anhui, Jiangsu, and Hebei, accounted for about 80% of China's wheat production in 2019. Wheat is the dominant staple for much of northern China today.

There are literally thousands of foods using wheat flour: steamed, baked, boiled, and deep-fried. The most popular wheat-based food is none other than noodles. Noodles are loved everywhere in China; they are eaten as either the main course or a snack, and either hot or cold; they are stir-fried, boiled, steamed, or in soups. There are great variety of noodles based on their texture, size, or shape, and there are literally thousands of specialty noodle dishes. In the north, steamed wheat bread is widely eaten. Wheat flour is also made into wrappers for just about any fillings, and the most famous dishes with fillings are *jiaozi* (Chinese dumplings), *hun-dun* (wonton), and steamed buns (*bao-zi*). A most popular breakfast food is *you-tiao*, a deep-fried wheat flour dough often paired with soy milk, which is available just about anywhere in China.

Maize (Corn)

Maize (corn) arrived in China in the mid 1500s. For decades, its coarse texture turned off Chinese farmers and it was not grown widely. In the 1700s, however, maize, along with two other New World crops, potatoes and sweet potatoes, became the crop that would largely fill in the gap of food supply for the rapidly increasing population. Its environmental resilience and high yield made it the staple for the poor, especially those in the north, until recently, despite its inferior tastes and texture. In recent decades, with improved living standards, maize has been used mainly as an animal feed and an ingredient for processed food such as snacks, though some Chinese still enjoy corn meals and porridge made of freshly harvested maize as a side dish, and corn on the cob as a snack or side dish. Through China is the second largest producer of maize after the United States, its domestic production cannot meet its demand as a feed. As a result, China has become a leading importer of corn.

Other Coarse Grains

Coarse grains include all cereal grains other than rice and wheat, such as maize, barley, oats, millet, sorghum, and rye. None but maize play an important role in contemporary Chinese diet and overall grain consumption. They are used mainly as supplemental animal feed. As demand for animal feed grows rapidly, China is importing more coarse grains. The Chinese, especially those in the north, do consume millet and sorghum directly, albeit in small amount and infrequently, by steaming them or use their flours in a variety of specialty food.

Roots and Tubers

China produces nearly 20% of the world's root and tuber production. It grows nearly a quarter of the world's potatoes and about two thirds of the sweet potatoes. Potatoes have adapted well in China since they were brought over there about 400 years ago. As a matter of fact, the Chinese government has encouraged expansion of potato production in recent years because of their high yield and environmental resilience, which are important attributes for fortifying food security.

Much of China's potato production is consumed domestically both for humans and animals. The Chinese may eat whole potato and sweet potato steamed, and treat potato as a vegetable, either stewing it with meat or stir-frying it (see recipe). During the 18th century, the Qing court promoted sweet potato for its high yield in an attempt to cope with a huge spike in population. Farmers resisted it as the main staple, however, due to digestive problems such as heartburn and stomach acid reflex. It became the staple for the rural poor, especially in the hilly south central and southwest regions, until recent decades. As a snack food and a side dish, however, sweet potato has made a major comeback in recent years. Baked sweet potato is a popular street snack in the north.

2.2. Stir-Fried Potato Slices (*Chao-tu-dou-si*)

This simple recipe creates a popular, inexpensive entrée that is found at homes and in restaurants alike. Everyone improvises with this recipe, so there are countless renditions. The key to success is to cut the potato into evenly sized thin slices, which is a basic skill used in cooking schools for the challenging "knife work" training.

Yield: Serves 3–4 as a side dish, or 1–2 as a main course

Ingredients
1 large russet potato
1 stem bunching onion (*Da-cong*)
3 tbsp cooking oil
½ tsp salt
2 tbsp Chinese vinegar
1 tbsp of soy sauce
1 tsp Chinese or Japanese curry powder
1 tbsp sugar

Preparation
1. Skin and cut the potato to 2-inch-long slices, about ¼ thickness of typical French fries.
2. Rinse with water and drain the sliced potato.
3. Wash and chop the bunching onion.
4. Add cooking oil to a wok or deep pan, and heat on a stove.
5. When the oil is smoking hot, stir-fry the chopped bunching onion for a few seconds.
6. Pour the sliced potato in the wok and stir-fry in high heat for 1 minute.
7. Add salt, sugar, and curry powder, and continue to stir-fry for 2 minutes.
8. Put in the soy sauce, and stir-fry for 1 minute.
9. Put the vinegar in, stir-fry for 15–20 seconds.
10. Place the potato on a large plate; serve.

Notes: Be innovative with this simple recipe. Before Step 5, for example, stir-fry a dozen or so peppercorns for a few seconds and then ladle them out. The peppercorns add a unique and pleasant taste to the dish. Sliced green serrano or jalapeno peppers add some bite and refreshing taste to the dish. Avoid overcooking the potato.

There are other root and tuber crops that may have longer history of planting and consumption. One notable tuber is *shan-yao* (Chinese yam, *Rhizoma dioscoreae*), also known as the common yam, is considered to have great health and medicinal benefits, and is consumed as an ingredient in porridge, rice, or vegetable dishes. In southern China, taro (*Colocasia esculenta*) is also popular and is consumed either directly or as an ingredient in snacks or appetizers. There is also some production and consumption of cassava (*Manihot esculenta*) in Guangdong and Guangxi province where tropical climate is found.

Vegetables

There has been a persistent impression that the main ingredients of Chinese food are rice and vegetables. Notwithstanding its stereotypical nature, China produces about half of the world's vegetables according to the World Food and Agriculture Organization (FAO). Most Chinese can get by without meat in their meals for days, but the absence of fresh vegetables during the same length of time would prompt discomfort and complaints. The Chinese can boast to have the greatest variety of vegetable dishes in the world, though many of these dishes are concoctions of vegetables and animal or plant proteins such as meat, eggs, or soy products.

The Chinese concept of vegetables is all-encompassing, including all plants and fungi. If any part of a plant or fungus can be used to help ingest starchy "main" food, it would be regarded as a vegetable. Case in point, in the spring, many Chinese enjoy an ancient dish of stir-fried eggs and young sprouts from Chinese mahogany trees (*Toona sinensis*, also known as Chinese cedar or Chinese toon). Fungi are important and popular ingredients in Chinese food, popular because of their varied and delicate flavors. Wild mushrooms are found everywhere, and their varieties and culinary importance vary from place to place. Yunnan Province, for example, is renowned for its great variety of edible fungi. Traditionally, mushrooms were dried for preservation and off-season consumption. Today, however, horticulture technology and advanced logistics allow fresh mushrooms to be grown and consumed in all seasons and throughout the country.

There is a great regional disparity in terms of variety and quantity of fresh vegetables. The warm and humid south has an abundant supply of vegetables year-round, while the north sees far fewer choices. In addition to green vegetables, the southerners also enjoy aquatic plants such as the roots and seeds of lotus (*Nelumbo nucifera*), water chestnuts (*Eleocharis dulcis*), water spinach (*Ipomoea aquatica*), and jiao-bai, the stems of Manchurian wild rice (*Zizania latifolia*). In contrast, people in the north had to contend with napa cabbage, cabbage, turnips, carrots, onions, and potatoes as vegetables during much of the winter. Residents in northern cities used to stockpile several hundred pounds of napa cabbage in late fall as the most common and affordable vegetable for the winter and early spring. Piles of napa cabbage would be the most visible feature of winter landscapes in

Beijing and other northern cities. Winter stockpiling of napa cabbage has largely become a ritual of the past, however, as vegetable supply has drastically improved with the introduction of greenhouse technology, upgrade of logistics networks, and rising market demands since the commencement of the economic reform. Large-scale, commercial vegetable production in the north, especially in Shandong Province, can now supply much of the need and demand in the north in all seasons.

Consuming wild plants as vegetables is an interesting and enduring culinary practice in China. While it might have been a coping strategy to food scarcity and frequent famine, the practice has become a sort of popular ritual, as folks venture into the wild in search of previously unused plants and dine on them, risking digestive and health consequences. Called "wild vegetables (*ye-cai*)," these plants were eaten by the poor who had no other choices but now are sought after by the older generations of the urban middle class, perhaps out of nostalgia. With their increasing popularity, some of the wild vegetables have become commercially grown and may eventually shed the descriptor "wild" if they become common ingredients in China's growing repertoire of vegetables.

In addition to fresh vegetables, pickled vegetables are common both as a condiment and a side dish. Pickling vegetables was obviously a way to preserve the highly perishable ingredients, but evolved into a culinary art and a booming business. There is great variety of pickled vegetables in terms of ingredients, concoctions, and flavors. Some of the pickled vegetables invoke regional and even national pride. *Zha-cai* (*Cha Tsai*), a pickled spicy mustard stem originated in Sichuan Province, is arguably the most high-profile and popular pickled vegetable in China. In 2019, a Taiwanese financial expert caused an uproar by asserting on live television that the Mainland Chinese were so destitute that they could not even afford *zha-cai* (Zhuang, 2019). In 2020, Chinese and Korean netizens waged a fierce debate as to who invented *kimchi*, which the Chinese refer to as *pao-cai* (pickled cabbage).

Fruits

China is a major fruit producer. For example, in 2019, it produced three–quarters of watermelon in the world and produced the most apples, pears, peaches, grapes, strawberries; it was second in citrus production after Brazil. The Chinese not only consume much of what the country produces but also have acquired a taste for fruits from other places, such as raisins and Bing cherries from the United States or grapes from Chile. Most fruits are eaten fresh, but some are made into sugared or dried fruits as snacks, condiments, or nutritional enhancers in different dishes. Plums, for example, were made into a paste and used as marinade or condiment in ancient times.

Two fruits, common only in China, are regarded as "wonder fruits" in Chinese cooking. First, jujube (Chinese dates), the fruits of jujuba tree (*Ziziphus jujuba*) that is widely grown in northern China, is eaten fresh as a seasonal fruit. More commonly, however, it is dried and used as an important ingredient in a variety of foods, such as breads, porridge, soups, teas, and stews. It adds special flavors and is considered to have digestive (high fiber) and hematinic (high iron) benefits. The second wonder fruit, hawthorn (*Crataegus pinnatifida*), often in dried haw flakes, is used in meat stews, ostensibly to tenderize the meat and improve digestion. The fresh hawthorn, on the other hand, can be consumed fresh or candied as a snack. One of the most popular winter snacks in northern China is *bing-tang-hu-lu* ("ice sugar coated haws on a stick"). In the winter, haws are cued on a bamboo stick and then are dipped into melted malt syrup. The sugar coating hardens in cool breeze quickly, and the result is a tasty snack which dates its origin to the 12th century.

Animal Proteins

A misconception of Chinese dietary customs was that the Chinese preferred starch and vegetables, considered by some as being a healthier diet. It is true that traditional Chinese food centered on cereal grains and other starch foods, supplemented by soy products, vegetables, and limited animal proteins. Make no mistake, however; the traditional dietary structure was not rooted in health wisdom but in food scarcity. The Chinese, like their brethren in many other sedentary subsistence agricultural societies, ate little meat or dairy and made the most out of animals, domestic or wild, when they became available. They have also had a long tradition in aquaculture, from which they harvested fish, crustaceans, and mollusks to supplement a diet that was scanty in animal protein intake.

The Chinese love meat, but most could not afford having it regularly until recent decades, when China's economic reform brought about rapid improvement of living standards. The Chinese have since rushed to increase their meat consumption, which has serious health, environmental, and geopolitical ramifications. China's meat consumption jumped from about 55 million tons in 2000 to 89 million tons in 2018 (and a drop to 81 million tons in 2019 due to skyrocketing price increase caused by "African swine flu"). During the same period, China's meat production had parallel growth, from about 62 million tons in 2000 to 88 million tons in 2018. The obvious difference is that in two decades, China's meat consumption began to exceed its production and, as a result, China has become a major meat buyer in the world, importing 4.8 million tons of meat products in 2019.

Today, China accounts for about 18.3% of the world population and consumes over 25% of the world's meat. Some in the West have sounded alarms regarding the impact of China's meat consumption increases on the world's environment, but the fact is that China's per capita consumption is still about half of that of the United States or Australia. Rapid changes are taking place in the quantity, quality, and composition of China's animal protein consumption, which is leading to a transformation of the Chinese food culture.

Pork

The Chinese are known to be pork-eaters. China produces on average nearly 40% of the pork in the world but consumes about half of it. Pork counts for over 60% of China's total meat production and consumption. Pork was always one of the most popular meats in the Chinese culinary tradition, except during the Song Dynasty (960–1279), when mutton was preferred. It became the top meat in consumption during the late imperial epoch, when environmental constraints made the pig a much favored domesticated animal for its short life cycle, omnivorous diet, and adaptability to limited space. In addition, better neutering techniques and innovative cooking methods made pork much more palatable than it had been before, and it proved to be more versatile than other meats for various Chinese cooking methods.

In Chinese cooking, no part of a pig is wasted; all cuts and organs are made into a variety of dishes. The pig's offal, feet, and head, not widely consumed in the United States, are considered delicacies in China because of their strong flavors or unique textures.

2.3. Pork Head, 18th century (*Zhu-tou-rou*)

Some Chinese like pork head meat for its complex flavors and textures and have created elaborate recipes. The following is modified from one of two pork head recipes in Yuan Mei's *The Garden of Contentment* (1792).

Yield: Serves 8–10

Ingredients
1 pig's head, 5–6 lb.
6 cups sweet rice wine (10 cups if the head is 7–8 lb.)
1+ cup soy sauce

1 oz. granulated sugar
½ oz. star anise
30 Chinese long-stem (bunching) onion

Preparation
1. Clean the head and put it in a pot with sweet rice wine, onion, and star anise.
2. Bring the pot to a boil, then cool the broth by scooping some out of the pot with a ladle momentarily, then pour the cooler broth back into the pot and then bring to a second boil—repeat the process two hundred times.
3. Add sugar and soy sauce; cook fully.
4. Taste and season with soy sauce if needed.
5. Weigh the head down and add water till it is about one inch above the head.
6. Cover and cook on high heat for one hour, then simmer till broth is reduced to a sticky consistency.
7. Once the head is tender, immediately take off the lid of the pot to help retain fat inside the head.

Mutton and Beef

For much of Chinese history, mutton and beef were less important meats in Chinese cooking, albeit for different reasons. The environment was unfavorable for cattle ranching, and, as draft animals, oxen were protected. Sheepherding, on the other hand, required expansive grazing ground and ran into competition with crop cultivation. Sheepherding became sidelined as population pressure on arable land began to mount during the late imperial epoch.

Mutton and beef are considered less versatile meats in Chinese cooking, though they are the main meats for special (e.g., halal) and regional cuisines. The northern regions consume more mutton per capita largely because of its availability and traditional role in regional cuisines. Today, mutton and beef count for about 6% each of China's total meat production, but the demand for beef is growing rapidly along with increasing popularity of Western-styled fast food and fine dining. As a result, China is importing more beef to meet the demand.

Poultry

Chicken has always been a favored meat in Chinese cooking. Historically, however, chickens were raised mainly for their eggs and were considered an expensive meat for special occasions. The Chinese loved their "free-range" chicken, which Americans would describe as being "rubber chicken" and "gamy." Large-scale, industrialized poultry production has taken hold in China in recent decades, however. As a result, poultry has become most available and highly affordable, and its importance as a meat ingredient can only grow in the Chinese diet as the supply and price for pork and other meats fluctuate in an upswing trajectory. China now produces about 12–15% of the world's total poultry and remains the largest importer of frozen chicken.

In addition to chicken, China is the top producer and consumer of ducks and geese. Of the 7.2 million tons of duck and goose meat the world produced in 2018, China's share was 5.5 million tons (76%). The south raises and consumes most of the duck meat and boasts many renowned regional duck dishes. Even the most famous duck dish in the world, Peking roast duck, may owe its origin to Nanjing and the Yangzi Delta region.

China also consumes other fowls such as pigeon and quail, but they are considered specialty and exotic meats that are not consumed on regular basis or outside certain regions such as coastal Guangdong Province. Turkey, the second most popular fowl in the United States, is basically absent in production and consumption in China. One wonders if, and when, it will become popular in the land where people never hesitate to try out new edibles, especially when it is an American staple and favorite.

Other Meats

Large-scale consumption of animals that are more widely known as pets, especially dogs, is highly localized in China today. Dog meat demand shows clear regional concentrations in the south and southwest. Historically, dog meat supplemented pork, mutton, poultry, and beef, though dogs were raised not for food but for guarding and hunting, and as pets. Perceived in the West as being barbaric, dog meat consumption becomes increasingly controversial in China, as a fierce debate is raging on, and each side of the debate is as passionate as the other. Animal rights organizations are becoming more aggressive, while dog meat lovers are becoming ever more entrenched.

Many Chinese have an eager appetite for wild and exotic animals. Some wild animals have been domesticated and raised commercially for their meat, such as palm civets and bamboo rats (*Rhizomys*). Wild animal consumption periodically comes into the spotlight when there is a public health emergency, and the animals, not humans who traffic them, become the culprits. While more scientific research is needed, civets were initially blamed for the outbreak of the 2003 SARS (severe acute respiratory syndrome) outbreak. Some suspected the Chinese pangolin (*Manis pentadactyla*) to be the intermediary carrier of the severe acute respiratory syndrome coronavirus 2 (SARS-CoV-2), which caused the devastating COVID-19 pandemic. Wildlife markets, or the so-called wet markets, are usually unsanitary and breeding grounds for public health mishaps. Government efforts to regulate or ban them, at the same time, have not been fruitful.

Eggs

The Chinese love eggs, considering them healthy and nutritious as well as versatile and delicious. Each Chinese person eats about 300 eggs a year, making China number three in the world in per capita egg consumption (after Japan and Paraguay). China is by far the biggest producer of eggs, contributing about 35% of the world's total in 2018, and consumed most of the 466 billion eggs that it produces annually. Eggs are eaten scrambled, stir-fried, steamed, hard-boiled, mixed with vegetables, meats, seafood, fungi, starch foods, or combinations of any of them.

2.4. Steamed Egg (*Zheng-ji-dan*)

This is a dish that pleases infants and toddlers for its fluffy and moist texture, especially if they lack appetite. Seafood or sweet soy sauce adds flavors to the dish.

Yield: Serves 2–3

Ingredients
4 eggs
1 whole green onion
1 tsp of sesame oil
1 tsp of soy sauce
Pinches of salt
Cooking oil spray

Preparation
1. Oil-spray a bowl.
2. Crack the eggs into the bowl and add an equal amount of lukewarm water (8–10 tbsp).
3. Add minced scallion and salt to the bowl and mix the content well.
4. Cover the bowl with shrink wrap.

5. Fill a steamer with 2–3 inches of water and bring it to a boil on high heat.
6. Place the bowl on the rack and steam for 25–26 minutes.
7. Remove the bowl from the steamer, then remove the shrink wrap.
8. Drizzle soy sauce and sesame oil on top of the eggs; serve hot or warm.

While hen eggs count for most eggs eaten in China, duck eggs are also widely consumed in the south where ducks are common; so are goose and quail eggs, though to a lesser extent. In addition to being eaten fresh, duck eggs are often pickled. Salted duck eggs are a popular side dish for breakfast. One of the most notorious Chinese foods known to the West has to be the so-called "century egg" or "thousand-year egg," that is, duck eggs preserved in a mixture of clay, ash, salt, lime, and rice hulls for several weeks. The process produces dark, pungent eggs, which must be appreciated with an acquired taste. It is a popular appetizer or side dish in China, and over 3 million tons of them are eaten every year.

Fish and Aquacultural Products

Fish and seafood are among the most favored ingredients in Chinese cuisines and are major animal protein sources. While China's marine fishery catch counted for a little over 15% of the world total in 2018, China's freshwater fishery catch took nearly half (46.9%) of the world's total in the same year. China is also a dominant producer in farmed shellfish production and consumption. In recent decades, China has experienced a boom in aquaculture, amounting to 60–70% of the world's total aquaculture production.

Chicken and fish make a proper banquet, as a Chinese saying goes. Fish is a key ingredient in Chinese food, and fish dishes, in which the fish is usually prepared whole, are customarily a key main course at more formal or festive meals. Historically, freshwater aquaculture was highly developed in southern regions, where fish and other aquatic products were abundant and key ingredients in southern regional cuisines. In contrast, the northern regions did not have adequate access to freshwater fish, which were not as important ingredients as they were in the south.

The Chinese are not picky with the types of fish and are fond of what some Americans shun as freshwater "bottom-feeders" such as carps and catfish, which are usually cooked in heavy sauces to mask their earthy taste. The Chinese are patient with and skillful for the bony fishes, saltwater and freshwater alike, claiming they are more delicious.

In recent years, the crawfish, once an invasive species in Asia and China, has become a new food sensation. Starting from lower Yangzi valley, crawfish cooked in spicy and numbing (*ma-la*) Sichuan-styled sauce helped moderate the muddy taste of these freshwater crustaceans and made them a new gastronomical star as a main course, a snack, or an appetizer. The crawfish craze has swept through China, and the sudden fame has not only removed crawfish from the invasive species list but also driven large commercial endeavors to meet the seemingly insatiable demand.

Milk

Unlike many other food ingredients, China is not a major milk producer. It contributes only 3–4% of the world's total milk output. Dairy products are popular in regions with substantial nomadic herding or, increasingly, commercial ranching, such as the Mongolian Plateau, Xinjiang, or Tibet, but overall milk and dairy products are not prominent ingredients. The situation may be changing, however, as the younger generations drink more milk than their forebears and try to acquire a taste for cheese, butter, and other dairy products. There are specialty foods or dishes that use milk or dairy products as a key ingredient, such as the renowned Beijing yogurt, reflect historical influence from the steppes. The omnipresent custard tarts in Hong Kong and Macao, on the other hand, are a product of the European influence (Portuguese and British) in modern times.

Plant Protein

For much of history, the Chinese masses could not afford much meat and had little access to dairy products. To compensate for protein deficiency in their diet, the Chinese resorted to plant substitutes, and soybeans reigned supreme as a source of protein. *Dou-fu* (tofu), the whitish, bland soybean curds, is made by chemically destabilizing the soymilk micelles using bittern, the bitter and salty leftover from salt manufacturing. The process generates protein bonding while soybean curds are created from the enzymatic (rennet) hydrolysis of casein into para-casein. Through time, the Chinese created great varieties of soy-based foods as tofu became a beloved and versatile food ingredient in East and Southeast Asia ever since its legendary creation in the 2nd century BCE.

Nuts, Beans, and Seeds

The Chinese consume large amounts of nuts, seeds, and beans, which are important sources of plant-based proteins. Peanuts and sunflower seeds are the most popular snacks in China, and sesame seeds are widely used as a garnish or flavor enhancer. Various peas and beans are often eaten as fresh vegetables. Dry peas and beans are often cooked with rice and other grains as starch staples or made into flours. One of the best-known Beijing snacks, for example, is sweet pea pudding (*wan-dou-huang*). Soybeans are by far the most important bean in Chinese food, however.

Soy Products

The earliest known processed food from soybeans, the (Chinese) black soybeans, is a salted and fermented product of soybeans that has been used as a seasoning or condiment, and sometimes as a side dish, for over 2,000 years. Tofu became a popular Chinese food ingredient a millennium later, and took off to become one of the primary ingredients in Chinese food. One can use tofu and various soy products in every form of cooking: stir-fried, steamed, stewed, braised, or boiled (soups). They can be eaten alone or used as one of the ingredients in dishes. There are hundreds of derivatives of tofu, including *dou-jiang* (soy milk), *dou-fu gan* ("dry" bean curd), shredded or layered tofu, *fu-zhu* (soy skin), and deep-fried bean curd puffs. Soy products, especially dry bean curds that have a much firmer texture than tofu, can have different textures and be flavored to imitate various meats and fish. Fermented bean curds are arguably one of the most popular side dishes in China with many regional varieties. They are sometimes used as a seasoning or an ingredient in certain sauces. Buddhist monks in China, who are vegetarians, may have made the most important contribution to turning soybeans into delicate and varied foods.

Cooking Oil

China is one of the leading producers and users of edible oil in the world. Stir-fry, the most important Chinese cooking technique, depends on oil. The Chinese use cooking oil from different sources, but the most common traditionally are peanut oil, soybean oil, sunflower oil, and canola (vegetable) oil. Sesame oil is mainly used in salads and as a flavor enhancer. Olive, sunflower seed, and corn oils have also become more popular. As living standards improve, the per capita consumption of cooking oil has skyrocketed, and as a result, China has become a major importer of edible oil.

Many Chinese can now afford to use cooking oil liberally, which makes stir-fried dishes tastier. This newly found luxury may have its health consequences, however. Animal fat (mainly pork lard) remains of limited use in Chinese cooking.

Seasonings, Spices, Herbs, and Condiments

A mark of accomplishment in Chinese cooking is the ability to attain savory tastes in the dishes, which is done with superior preparation, including seasoning and flavoring masterfully. The Chinese have turned to all kinds of seasonings, herbs, spices, condiments, as well as fruits and vegetables such as Chinese chives, shallots, and onions, to season and flavor their foods. Some of the most common seasonings, such as salt and sugar, are also used as condiments. Some spices and herbs are hard to distinguish in terms of their use.

Salt is the most common seasoning and condiment. China is the top producer of salt and a major salt consumer. Its per capita salt consumption is among the highest in the world, partly due to the residual effects of the high-sodium traditional diet. High salt consumption has been called into question because of the health implications.

The Chinese have a long history in making and using sauces in cooking, and soy sauce may be the most famous. It occupies a special place in Chinese cooking for its effects in helping achieve savory and salty flavors. Soy sauce is used more extensively in northern Chinese cuisines, which tend to have more potent flavors and tastes. In addition, soy pastes and fermented soybeans (*dou-chi*) are also commonly used in certain regional cuisines. Oyster and shrimp sauces are popular in southeastern coastal regions.

Sichuan peppercorn and star anise are the most common and popular spices in Chinese cooking, but there are other widely used spices, such as curry, cumin, white pepper, Chinese cinnamon (*Cinnamomum cassia*), bay leaf, and dry orange peel. Five-spice powder (*wu-xiang-fen*), a powdery concoction of cinnamon, cloves, star anise, fennel, and Sichuan peppercorns, is very popular for braising and stewing. Black pepper, thought to have been introduced to China during the same period as Sichuan peppercorn, however, is not as common a spice in China as elsewhere, even though it is the most widely traded spice in the world. Cinnamon (*Cinnamomum verum*) or cassia (*Cinnamomum cassia*) is often used to achieve more subtle sweet taste, especially in meat stews, in southern China.

2.5. Sweet and Sour Soup (*Suan-la-tang*)

This soup may be the only item on the menu of Chinese American restaurants that is also popular in many parts of China. Its popularity may be due to its versatility as an appetizer, a side dish, or the last course in a typical daily meal or formal dinner. There are many regional and personal variations of this recipe, and adjusting the ingredients, both in types and quantity, can help enhance certain flavors and weaken others.

Yield: Serves 4–5

Ingredients
3–4 oz. raw tofu (¼ of a grocery store pack)
2–3 oz. lean meat (pork and chicken preferred for their milder taste and tender texture)
2 eggs
1 can chicken broth
½ oz. mung bean or rice vermicelli
8–9 dry wood ear
3–4 dry Shiitake mushroom
Condiments as needed: cooking oil, salt, ground white pepper, Chinese vinegar, green onion, fresh ginger, sesame oil, soy sauce, starch, cilantro, chicken flavored MSG (it is used as a flavor-enhancer and can be omitted)

Preparation
1. Rehydrate the mushrooms, wood ear, and vermicelli by soaking them in warm water (1–2 hours).
2. Cut the tofu, meat, mushrooms, and wood ear into thin slices, and cut the vermicelli to 2-inch pieces.
3. Mince the green onion and ginger; wash and chop the cilantro.
4. Crack and mix the eggs in a bowl.
5. Dissolve 3–4 teaspoons of starch in 1 cup of water.
6. Heat 3–4 tablespoons of cooking oil in a wok; stir in green onion and ginger to flavor.
7. Add the meat and stir-fry till its color turns darker.
8. Add mushrooms and cook till they soften.
9. Add the chicken broth and 1 can of water.
10. Bring the content in the wok to a boil, then add tofu, wood ear, and vermicelli.
11. Gradually drip dissolved starch into the soup till it reaches desired consistency.
12. Add drops of soy sauce to flavor.

13. Add salt to flavor.
14. Add vinegar.
15. Add egg and bring the soup to a boil.
16. Add white ground pepper, cilantro, and sesame oil to taste; serve.

In China, the most common herbs and vegetables for seasoning and flavoring are ginger, garlic, cilantro, bunching onion, and spring onion. In northern China, the long-stem *da-cong* (*Allium.fistulosum L.var.gigantum Makinois*), known in the West as "Welsh" or "bunching" onion, is preferred over spring onion for its more potent flavors. Minced garlic, ginger, bunching onion, and cilantro are also most popular condiments throughout China. There are some less omnipresent herbs and vegetables that are critically important for special dishes. Chinese chive flowers, for example, are a key ingredient in the sauce for the renowned instant-boiled mutton.

The Chinese are among those in the world who love spicy food. Modern science informs us that the pungent taste is a form of pain that may bring about a sense of euphoria. In search of this happy feeling, the ancient Chinese used ginger, brown mustard, garlic, scallion, and Sichuan peppercorn to spice up their food, which are still widely used to enhance pungency and other flavors in foods. One spice, edible cornel (*Zanthoxylum ailanthoides*), however, fell out of use after much better alternatives arrived in the late 1500s.

It was chili pepper from the Americas that allowed the Chinese to spice up and flavor their food more effectively and that empowered a revolution in the Chinese food culture. Today, China produces nearly half of the world's chili pepper. With the growing popularity of spicy food, chili pepper is becoming more prominently featured in more and more regional cuisines and favorite dishes.

Cooking (rice) wine is a sort of seasoning for flavor enhancement that the Chinese use for cooking meats and seafood. The Chinese also use monosodium glutamate (MSG) in their cooking both at home and in restaurants. Invented in Japan almost a century ago, MSG is said to enhance the savory tastes, but the debate goes on over its health effects.

MSG

A savory taste, termed *xian*, is the highest attainment in Chinese culinary art. It is achieved through pairing, flavoring, and seasoning foods. The Japanese discovered that this savory taste, or *umami*, came from naturally occurring glutamates in food and began to manufacture the sodium form of glutamic acid, known as monosodium glutamate (MSG), in the early 1900s. In the 1950s, MSG became popular in China as an inexpensive seasoning. Its alleged harmful side effects and peculiar association with American Chinese restaurants were debunked by the Food and Drug Administration (FDA) in 1995.

Today, Chinese vinegar, based mainly on fermented rice or sorghum, is the main seasoning, and sometimes the condiment, for obtaining sour flavor. It is also used as a food preservative, such as for pickled garlics. Sourness may be the most popular flavor in Chinese cuisines. The Chinese believe that the sour flavor helps digestion. There are regional sour flavored seasonings, such as a tomato-based sauce in Guizhou Province, or pickled napa cabbage (similar to the German sauerkraut) in the northeast.

The Chinese like sweet and sour dishes. In ancient times, plums and hawthorn were used as seasonings and condiments to attain the sought-after flavor. With their affinity for such a pleasant flavor, it should come as no surprise that the Chinese migrants in Southeast Asia are accredited for having invented ketchup.

Sweeteners are widely used in Chinese cooking. Some regional cuisines, such as those in the Yangzi Delta, are known for their sweet tastes. Sugar, in granulated or rock forms, is the top sweetener today. Malt is also used in cooking, though not in large quantities. Syrups and honey are two other important natural sweeteners.

The Chinese have little inhibition in adopting any edibles as food, and as a result, enjoy arguably the widest range of food ingredients in the world. A most notable missing category of food ingredients is dairy products, which reflects a civilization deeply rooted in sedentary subsistence agriculture in which dairying was not an efficient system for producing essential food sustenance. In modern times, the range and choices of Chinese food ingredients are expanding and changing, as living standard improves and global exposure increases.

Further Reading

Campbell, Charlie. "How China Could Change the World by Taking Meat Off the Menu." *Time*, February 1, 2021. https://time.com/5930095/china-plant-based-meat/.

"Kimchi Ferments Cultural Feud Between South Korea and China." *BBC*, November 30, 2020. https://www.bbc.com/news/world-asia-55129805.

Ku, Yuanzhi. "West Should Cut Its Own Meat Consumption If It's Serious About the Climate." *Global Times,* January 24, 2021. https://www.globaltimes.cn/page/202101/1213792.shtml.

Rossi, Marcello. "The Chinese Are Eating More Meat Than Ever Before and the Planet Can't Keep Up." *Mother Jones*, July 31, 2018. https://www.motherjones.com /environment/2018/07/the-chinese-are-eating-more-meat-than-ever-before -and-the-planet-cant-keep-up/.

"What the World Eats." The Future of Food, 2014. *National Geographic Magazine*. https://www.nationalgeographic.com/what-the-world-eats (accessed October 26, 2022).

Yeung, Jessie. "Cannabis May Have Originated in Northwest China, Study Suggests." *CNN,* July 16, 2020. https://www.cnn.com/2021/07/16/asia /cannabis-study-china-origins-intl-hnk-scn/index.html.

Zhuang, Pinghui. "Taiwanese Financial Expert Mocked for Saying Many Mainland Chinese 'Can't Afford Pickles'." *South China Morning Post*, August 9, 2019. https://www.scmp.com/news/china/society/article/3022190/taiwanese -financial-expert-mocked-saying-many-mainland-chinese?module =perpetual_scroll&pgtype=article&campaign=3022190.

CHAPTER THREE

Appetizers and Side Dishes

In 2017, the Chinese social media was abuzz over the news that a famous Sichuan appetizer was selected as "appetizer of the year" in the United States. The source of the news was an article published in the monthly magazine *GQ* by food critic Brett Martin in which he pitched his choices of the best in the culinary world of the United States. Among these "bests" was a Sichuan classic with an odd name, *fu-qi fei-pian* ("sliced lung of the husband and wife"), which was chosen by Mr. Martin as the "best appetizer of the year." Sometimes dubbed as "Mr. & Mrs. Smith" by some in the West, this famous snack/appetizer consists of "cold slices of beef tendon and tongue, tossed with sesame paste, Sichuan peppercorns, scallions, and chiles" (Martin, 2017). It is a signature appetizer in the vast and fiery repertoire of the renowned Sichuan cuisine.

3.1. Refreshing Sliced Celery (*Liang-ban-qin-cai-si*)

The Chinese pay special attention to the color esthetics of cold dishes and prefer a sweet and sour taste, which they believe would induce an appetite. This recipe creates a simple cold dish with a pleasant yellow–green color contrast and slightly sweet and sour palate.

Yield: Serves 4–5

Ingredients
3–4 stems of celery hearts (the tender inner ribs)
1 egg
1 tbsp rice (white) vinegar
½ tsp of cane sugar

pinches of salt
drops of sesame oil

Preparation
1. Wash and slice the celery hearts (¹/₁₀ inch in width) diagonally against the grain.
2. Lightly oil a small pan on medium heat, stir and pour the egg into the pan to cook it into a thin pancake, then slice it to similar size as the celery.
3. Mix the sliced celery and egg with sugar, salt, vinegar, and sesame oil; serve.

Notes: The Chinese celery, which has skinnier but stronger tasting stems, can be substituted with regular celery. Chinese vinegar works as well as the rice vinegar, though it may temper the vibrancy of the yellow–green color combination.

The most common appetizers in traditional Chinese food are the so-called *leng-pan* ("cold plates") or *liang-cai* ("chilled dishes"), because they are usually, but not always, served chilled or in room temperature. It may appear that appetizers have a somewhat indistinct place in the Chinese food culture, though they represent one of the three distinct traditional specialties in Chinese cooking along with those of staples (*zhu-shi*) and hot main courses (*zhu-cai*). Cold dish preparation has its own distinct and elaborate skillset, emphasizing arrangements and pairing of ingredients that make their presentation and flavors enticing. Family-styled appetizers usually feature vegetables and soy products, focusing on seasonality and freshness. It must be pointed out that the roles of appetizers are quite different between formal dining and daily meals. While appetizers are not a must-have for a casual or family meal, they are an integral and special component, like the overture to an opera, for meals on formal and special occasions, such as major holidays, weddings and funerals, and celebratory events.

Side dishes, sometimes referred to as "little dishes" (*xiao-cai*), have played an essential role in the Chinese food culture. On the one hand, many Chinese dishes are served with various accompaniments without which a main dish may not taste as good or "right" in some of the formal meals, holiday dinners, or banquets. For example, the classic northern hot pot, "instant-boiled mutton," requires several side dishes to make the meal complete. While thinly sliced leg meat is the centerpiece, the sauce is what makes this dish unique. It is an elaborate concoction of peanut or sesame paste, fermented bean curd, Chinese chive flower, sesame oil, soy sauce, cilantro, rice vinegar, and several other condiments. It brings the otherwise bland mutton slices to a level of savoring ecstasy. In addition, there are other essential side dishes, such as tofu, potato, leafy vegetables (especially napa cabbage), mushrooms, and small baked buns with sesame paste flavoring inside and sesame seeds as the topping. The last notable side dish is pickled sweet and sour garlic that helps remedy the overpowering gamy and greasy aftertaste of the main dish. Just like the case in the United States, many Chinese dishes can serve as either a main course or a side dish. It is noteworthy that both main and side dishes are meant to be shared in accordance with traditional Chinese dining etiquette.

For daily family meals, on the other hand, appetizers are not an essential component, especially if the family is poor or on a busy schedule. When served, they are usually simple and made impromptu, usually to the taste of the diners. There are two types of side dishes in Chinese food culture. The first is integral to a main course or an entire meal and, therefore, is essential for a complete meal, as in the case of instant-boiled mutton. The second type of side dishes, called "appetite enhancers" (*xia-fan-cai*), help improve or enhance flavors of the staple food (*zhu-shi*), usually bland cereals or tubers and roots. They represent a key component in the food culture rooted in sedentary subsistence agriculture. These side dishes are usually pickled, fermented, or otherwise preserved vegetables, soy products, or fish/seafood and eggs. Meat in this type of side dish would be a luxury item. To many Chinese, a meal would be less enjoyable or ingestible without their favorite side dishes.

3.2. Sweet and Sour Cucumber (*Suan-tian Huang-gua*)

The most common cucumber in China is what is frequently referred to as "Japanese cucumber" in the United States. It is dark green with a bumpy, ridged skin and tastes sweeter and refreshing in comparison to the slicing cucumbers in the U.S. supermarkets. It is consumed unripe, cooked or raw, when it grows to ¾ to 1 ft in length and ¾ to 1 inch in diameter.

Yield: Serves 3–4

Ingredients
3 medium-sized cucumbers
1 tsp salt

1 tbsp sugar
1 tbsp Chinese vinegar
Sesame oil to taste

Preparation
1. Wash and split the cucumber in half lengthways, then cut it across into thick chunks—do not peel.
2. Marinate the sliced cucumber with the salt for 10 minutes or so to extract its bitterness.
3. Remove the marinated cucumber slices with a slotted spoon to get rid of excessive juice.
4. Mix the cucumber with sugar and vinegar; garnish with a few drops of sesame seed oil.
5. Chill in refrigerator for 15–20 minutes; serve.

While appetizers and side dishes are discussed separately, it needs to be pointed out that there is little distinction among different components of daily family meals. What is regarded as a typical main dish can serve as an appetizer in small portions, snacks and side dishes can be served as appetizers, and *vice versa*. Conversely, typical appetizers and some side dishes can be consumed as full meals if one is not hungry or eats plenty of them. Appetizers can be either cold or hot, but most cold dishes, though not all, are exclusively served as appetizers. What is most remarkable about Chinese appetizers and side dishes is their seasonality and regional variations, evidence of adaptation to local natural environments.

How Important Is Pork in the Chinese Diet?

The Chinese character for "home" is comprised of two radicals: a "roof" and, underneath it, a "pig." Space-saving pigs were not the favored meat source until crops from the Americas, such as corn, reached China, which contributed to a skyrocketing population increase and shrinking per capita arable land. Pork is the most important meat in the modern Chinese diet. In 2019, pork accounted for 55.6% and 54.8% of China's total meat production and consumption, respectively, despite the impact of "African swine fever." China consumed 44.5% of pork in the world in 2019, although its per capita consumption was not the highest.

Appetizers: Cold Dishes, Small Plates, and Snacks

Like in other food cultures, Chinese appetizers are meant to entice dinners' appetite before the main course(s) of a meal and came to bear the
name that means "dishes that open the stomach" (*kai-wei-cai*). As such,
they tend to be light, refreshing, and small in portion. Daily family meals
either skip the appetizers or serve a couple of simple ones. For more formal meals, on the other hand, appetizers would definitely be served with
great attention to ingredients' quality, complementarity to the main
courses, and artistic arrangements. The most common appetizers are usually cold dishes served in small portions, and some can be interchangeable
as snacks. Vegetables are the most popular ingredients for appetizers since
they are inexpensive and light, seasonal and assorted. More formal appetizers are served on platters with an assortment of meats, seafood, soy
products, nuts, and fruits. Appetizers need to taste refreshing, which is
attained with use of ginger, garlic, Chinese vinegar, and sesame oil. There
are some appetizers that are popular throughout China, such as shredded
jellyfish in vinaigrette (*liang-ban hai-zhe*), but each region or even locale
features its own specialty appetizers.

3.3. Chilled Sour and Spicy Jellyfish
(*Liang-ban-suan-la-hai-zhe*)

The earliest records of human consumption of jellyfish dates to the late
Tang Dynasty (618–907) along the southeast coast. Jellyfish head (umbrella)
is dried and salted to preserve and rehydrated by soaking it in water. It is
the main ingredient for a popular cold appetizer, perhaps because its
slightly fishy taste invokes the sense of *xian*, and its chewy texture allows
prolonged enjoyment. This recipe is one of the many renditions of this popular appetizer.

Yield: Serves 3–4

Ingredients
1 dried jellyfish head
½ onion
1 small green chili pepper
1 small red chili pepper
1 tbsp cane sugar
Pinches of fresh ginger and garlic

A few Sichuan peppercorns and star anise if available
Chinese vinegar and soy sauce

Preparation
1. Soak the jellyfish head in water for 3–4 hours, changing water 2–3 times
   during the time to get rid of excessive salt and rehydrate the jellyfish.
2. Place peppercorn and star anise in a bowl; add 1 fl. oz. of Chinese vinegar, the cane sugar, and several drops of soy sauce, and stir well to
   make the sauce.
3. Clean and slice the onion, dice the peppers, and mince the garlic and
   ginger; add them to the sauce and mix well.
4. Chill the sauce in the refrigerator for 3–4 hours. When ready to eat, slice
   the rehydrated jellyfish and pour sauce over it; serve.

Archeological evidence shows that appetizers, in the form of cold
dishes, began to appear about two millennia ago at formal banquets of the
rulers and elites and eventually became the edible introduction of formal
meals. Today, formal meals must start with appetizers, usually cold dishes
that contain fancy or popular ingredients and display extravagant colors
and shapes. Appetizers, either hot or cold dishes, are a nonessential but
welcome addition to daily family meals, which include staple food (*zhu-
shi*) and accompanying dishes (*fu-shi*), either hot or cold or both, that are
served alongside of each other. Traditionally, appetizers would be a luxury
for most Chinese, who often found themselves on the verge of famine and
hunger; to them, there was little need to entice the appetite.

At the same time, appetizers are an important part in fine dining and in
the meals for those who are well off. Appetizers make a family meal more
special and enjoyable, since extra time and special ingredients are used to
prepare them. Appetizers also help build up the atmosphere at the dinner
table. Customarily, diners would drink high-proof Chinese liquor with
appetizers, which serve to line the stomach and lessen the impact of the
alcohol. Typical appetizers, usually small and light, accommodate rather
than hinder the distinct palates of liquor that the drinkers enjoy. With
wetted appetite and aired mood, the diners may find the main courses of
the meal more enjoyable.

Cold dishes can also be elaborate and expensive, as "Assorted Marinated Meat" shows. They require high-quality ingredients that can be
sliced and quartered and cut into various sizes and shapes, which means
there will be a lot of endpieces. While restaurants may find ways to utilize
these "food scraps," the labor and material costs make elaborate cold

dishes untenable for family daily meals or even casual restaurant dining. Most cold appetizers for daily meals, in contrast, can be made quickly using common ingredients and condiments, as shown in most of the recipes cited in this chapter, such as "Sweet and Sour Cucumber." Sometimes, snack foods and side dishes can be used as appetizers, too. One most common and popular appetizer throughout China, for example, is none other than roasted peanuts, though some may argue that it requires specific types of peanuts and good skill to roast the peanuts in order to transform this common nut into a presentable appetizer.

3.4. Assorted Marinated Meat (*Lu-shui Pin-pan*)

This Cantonese cold dish uses almost all parts of a goose and can serve 8–10 at a table as either a centerpiece appetizer or a formal entrée. The key to success is the braising master stock, which is used to flavoring the main ingredients. This recipe demonstrates the elaborate and exhaustive banquet-grade Chinese cold dishes. It is not meant for daily family meals.

Yield: Serves 8–10

Ingredients

Main ingredients:
1 lion-head goose (approximately 5.5 lb.; this is the largest domesticated goose, mainly raised in Guangdong Province)
8–9 oz. each goose liver, gizzard, feet, wing
8–9 oz. tofu (half of a container of tofu, often available in supermarket)
3 medium eggs
1 cup cooking oil

Master stock ingredients:
20 pints (20 16-ounce cans) of soup stock or chicken broth
5 oz. sea salt
7 oz. rock sugar
1.5 oz. MSG (can be omitted)
5 oz. rice cooking wine
5 oz. rose liquor (Chinese hard liquor with rose pads)
1 spice pack including: 1 oz. green onion; 1.5 oz. cilantro; 2 cloves garlic; ½ tsp each of star anise, Sichuan peppercorn, clove, licorice, orange peel, cardamom, amomum villosum, *luo han guo* (monk fruit); 1 tsp each of fennel, hot chili pepper, tsaoko, bay leaf; 2 oz. each of aromatic ginger ("sand ginger"), galangal ginger ("southern ginger")

Preparation
1. Clean and dissect the goose, separating and cleaning the feet, wing, gizzard, and liver.
2. Make the master stock by mixing and boiling all ingredients for 1 hour. It is for braising the main ingredients.
3. Braise the clean goose for 2 hours, then cool to room temperature.
4. Braise goose liver, gizzard, wings, and feet for 1 hour, then cool to room temperature.
5. Deep fry the tofu to golden, then braise for 10 minutes.
6. Boil and peel the eggs, then braise for 15 minutes.
7. Slice the tofu and place the slices at the bottom of a large plate.
8. Tease out big bones of the goose; slice and arrange the meat on top of the sliced tofu.
9. Slice the liver and gizzard into thin pieces, cut the wing and feet to bite size, and separately place each of them on top of the tofu.
10. Cut the eggs in half and place them on top of the tofu.
11. Heat the master stock and lace some of it over the main ingredients; serve.

Appetizers can be made with meat, especially organ meats, eggs, or fish and shellfish from both saltwater and freshwater, but the most popular ingredients for appetizers are vegetables and tofu products, which are relatively inexpensive, abundantly available, and not filling and heavy. The purpose of appetizers is to entice instead of overwhelming, not to say fulfilling, the appetite, after all. In the warm and humid south, aquatic plants are also popular ingredients for appetizers.

One notorious Chinese appetizer is a preserved egg, known in the West as "century eggs," "thousand-year eggs" or "millennium eggs." The traditional preservation process involves insulating the eggs in a mixture of clay, ash, salt, quicklime, and rice hulls for several weeks. The process turns the white into jelly-like and translucent dark brown and the yolk creamy and dark gray, and the flavor emanating potent sulfide and ammonia. The most popular Chinese names for this preserved egg are *pi-dan* ("rubber egg") for the white's rubbery texture, or *song-hua-dan* ("pine flake egg") for the pattern on the surface of the egg white that resembles pine branches. While chicken or quail eggs can also be used, the more popular ingredient for this peculiar delicacy is duck eggs. Ducks are a common fowl in the countryside in the warm and humid south. Many in China consider the texture and flavor of duck eggs as being inferior to that of chicken eggs, but they are preferrable for making salted or preserved eggs.

As an appetizer, century eggs are easy to prepare. The eggs are peeled and then sliced into eight equal pieces lengthwise (tip: it is easier to use a thread to cut it), arranged on a plate, and drizzled with Chinese vinegar, salt, and minced ginger: the appetizer is then ready to serve. The condiments help reduce the potent flavor and bring out a more complex taste. Some may also add soy sauce, sugar, and chili pepper paste to make the appetizer's flavor even more nuanced and delicate. Century egg porridge (see "Lean Meat and *Pi-dan* Porridge") is a popular Cantonese recipe that can be served as a snack or an appetizer. Most Westerners are turned off when being first exposed to the century egg, but some may eventually acquire a liking for it, just like many young Chinese have become fond of some of the stinky cheeses, which their parents and forebears were repulsed by.

3.5. Lean Meat and *Pi-dan* Porridge (*Pi-dan-shou-rou-zhou*)

This popular Cantonese dish can serve as a breakfast or brunch entrée; it can also be served as an appetizer or even a snack. It is becoming popular in other parts of China.

Yield: Serves 2

Ingredients
6 oz. rice (short-grain preferred)
4 oz. lean pork (or beef)
2 century eggs (*pi-dan* or *song-hua-dan*)
1 small piece of fresh ginger
1 head of scallion
½ tsp sesame oil
1 tsp salt
8½ cups water

Preparation
1. Rinse the rice and mix with the sesame oil; stir and let the mix soak for 30 minutes.
2. Mince the ginger and scallion.
3. Cut the eggs into ⅓-inch or so pieces.
4. Slice the meat into tiny cubes, mix with ¼ teaspoon salt, and marinate for 20 minutes.
5. Fill a pot with water and bring it to a boil, pour in the meat, and continue to boil for 5 minutes.

6. Pour in half of the egg pieces and ginger; boil for 2 minutes.
7. Pour the rice into the pot and cook for 40 minutes in low heat; stir against the inside of the pot every 5 minutes.
8. Pour in the other half of egg pieces and cook for 10 more minutes.
9. Mix in the rest of the salt and scallion; serve.

Notes: It is important to skim off the froth at the top of the pot when boiling the pork.

The flavors of appetizers vary greatly, but they tend to be served cold or chilled. Vegetables that taste refreshing with no or little cooking, such as cucumber, tomato, and radish, are preferred ingredients. A sweet and sour flavor is most popular because it can stimulate the taste buds and appetite. While in most regions, soups are served either as part of the main courses or as the last entrée, they are usually the first course in the dining tradition of Cantonese cuisine, so they are *de facto* appetizers. The Cantonese soups, which are often prepared with medicinal herbal ingredients, are said to possess a wide range of health benefits and to be particularly important to improve the digestive system. The proliferation of Cantonese cuisine in recent years may have promoted a soup-first dining habit, which makes soups into a more widely accepted appetizer.

3.6. Fresh Lotus Root Salad (*Liang-ban-xian-ou*)

Lotus (*Nelumbo nucifera*) is a beloved aquatic plant found throughout China, where 70% of the world's cultivated lotus is grown. It has been used for a variety of purposes, mainly for food and landscaping. While its seeds are a popular ingredient in beverages, fillings, and soups, it is its underground stem (rhizomes), commonly known as *ou* (lotus roots), that is the most popular food ingredient.

Yield: Serves 4–5

Ingredients
2 tbsp light olive cooking oil
3 fresh lotus roots, washed, peeled, and cross-sliced
4 scallion (green onion) stems, chopped
½ tsp salt
1½ tsp sugar
2 tbsp Chinese rice vinegar

Preparation
1. Add the cooking oil to a wok or fry pan, heat on medium, and then put in the scallions, the lotus root slices, salt, and half of the sugar (in that order) and stir-fry for about three minutes.
2. Add ¾ cup of water and reduce heat to low (or turn off the stove if it is electric), cover, and let it cook for five minutes.
3. Plate the content with a spatula (or skimmer) to avoid excessive liquid in the wok or pan.
4. Sprinkle the remaining sugar and then drizzle the vinegar on top; serve.

Notes: This dish can be served hot but tastes better, especially as an appetizer, if served cold, when it has a tangy flavor.

Side Dishes: The Accompaniments for Ingestion

Side dishes in Chinese food culture have a humble presence but crucial function: helping ingest starch foods or "main foods" that provide the bulk of each meal for commoners. Traditionally, meals for special occasions or for dining out always had multiple dishes served simultaneously, hence deeming "side dishes" unnecessary. In contrast, side dishes become crucial in the traditional diet for peasant farmers and the poor, which consists predominantly of grains or other starch foods that are difficult to ingest if eaten on their own. Unlike the case in the United States, side dishes are served not so much to supplement the main courses as to help ingest large portions of cereal grains ("main food") in the traditional diet. As a result, they tend to be tiny in portion but potent in flavor.

As in many food cultures, pickling and fermenting have been among the most important methods of preserving food. Pickled and fermented foods were particularly important side dishes to the Chinese because they were affordable and available for all seasons. As time went on, some of these humble side dishes evolved into sophisticated, stand-alone gourmet foods, and the most celebrated became trademarked and paved the foundation for large fortunes. People from all walks of life began to enjoy them as food enhancers for all occasions. Legend has it that Empress Dowager Ci-xi (1835–1908), the powerful woman who ruled China for nearly five decades, enjoyed the pickled vegetables from a proprietor in Jining, Shandong Province, so much that she ordered them to be sent to the court as annual royal tributes. That establishment is still in business today.

There is a great variety of pickled, fermented, or otherwise preserved foods with thousands of variations in terms of flavors and ingredients, but they are universally salty or pungent or both, for the purpose of making the bland staple foods more palatable. Today, the most popular food enhancers are usually pungent, as exemplified by the ever-popular *Lao Gan Ma* ("Old Grandma") hailed from the impoverished Guizhou Province in southwest China. The trademarked red chili sauce is now available in Asian supermarkets in the United States. As is known, pungency is not a taste but a pain, or a sensation similar to that from exposure to excessive heat. The utility of pungent side dishes might have been to stimulate ingestion of starch (main) foods to suppress the "heat" or "pain."

The enduring popularity of the so-called appetite enhancers is a testimonial to the challenges and resilience of the Chinese foodways. Many side dishes are interchangeable with appetizers and snacks. Traditional side dishes could have any food ingredients, such as meat, egg, and seafood. Salted duck eggs may be a good example. Two most common and important types of side dishes are pickled vegetables and fermented (soy) bean curds, both of which also serve as condiments in nearly all regional cuisines. Interestingly, these two most popular types of side dishes have not attracted non-Chinese, especially Westerners, perhaps due to their potency and exotic flavors, which makes eating them a vexing "acquired taste."

3.7. Scallion Tofu Salad (*Xiao-cong-ban-dou-fu*)

Tofu (*dou-fu*) is a basic and bland soy product. Flavoring it can be challenging, but success in doing so can yield satisfying dishes. This is an easy recipe for a tofu-based appetizer with many variations.

Yield: Serves 3–4

Ingredients
1 lb. box of tofu (available in supermarkets—get "medium firm," if possible, for this recipe; "silken" or "soft" types would also work)
Four scallion (green onion) stems, cleaned and chopped
Salt, white pepper, sesame oil, Sichuan peppercorn, and light olive cooking oil (which could be substituted with other cooking oil)

Preparation
1. Take tofu out of the box and slice it to half-inch cubes.
2. In a pot, boil 4–5 cups of water.
3. Put the tofu cubes in the pot and take them out with a slotted ladle (or a skimmer) when the water boils again. (Note: scald the soft or silken tofu in boiling water for about 30 seconds.)

4. Put the tofu cubes in cold water to chill them.
5. Transfer the chilled tofu cubes to a bowl with a slotted ladle.
6. Mix the tofu cubes with pinches of salt and white pepper powder, drizzles of sesame oil, and chopped scallion, to taste.
7. In a shallow pan, heat cooking oil and fry Sichuan peppercorn until aroma starts to emanate.
8. Drizzle the hot peppercorn oil over the tofu mix; serve.

Pickled Vegetables

Pickling seasonal vegetables was an important ritual and crucial strategy to supplement meals during the seasons when fresh vegetables were scarce. The necessity of food preservation encouraged efforts of perfecting pickling techniques that eventually became a culinary art. As a result, pickled vegetables have become a celebrated food specialty in Chinese cuisines, and each region has its own distinctly flavored varieties to boast about.

There are three general styles of Chinese pickles. The first, *xian-cai* (salted vegetables), is made from fermented vegetables in salty brine, and the most common ingredients are various mustards, turnips, and carrots. The second type, *jiang-cai* (sauce-flavored vegetables), is made from vegetables fermented in soy sauce or savory soybean paste. This method is a more sophisticated technique and uses a wide range of vegetables, fungi, nuts, and tubers as ingredients. It creates more delicate and varied flavors. The third, *pao-cai* (marinated vegetables), is made by marinating lightly boiled vegetables either in salt or in soy sauce along with any combination of seasonings, spices, herbs and vegetables such as chili pepper, sugar, vinegar, and garlic. The procedure may remind some of the Korean pickled cabbage wonder, *kimchi*, which indeed shares similar techniques with Chinese *pao-cai*.

In the north, where winter is long and seasonal vegetables can be scarce, pickled vegetables have been a more important side dish. Some of the most sophisticated pickles, however, were created in regions of the Yangzi Delta. One exception is Beijing, the capital of China for most of the last eight centuries. The capital city attracted various regional cuisines and other food specialties, including major pickle makers. It has been home to the most renowned pickle and sauce shop in China, *Liubiju*, which dates its opening to 1530 and represents one of the most prominent traditions in vegetable pickling.

3.8. Pickled Eight Delicacies, Beijing Style
(*Ba-bao-jiang-cai*)

This elaborate side dish of pickled vegetables and soy products is very popular, with various regional and period variations. The key ingredient is cucumber, which the Chinese consider as having the efficacy of treating hypertension, and the so-called yellow paste, which is derived from fermented soybeans and known to be rich in probiotics and amino acids.

Yield: Serve as needed

Ingredients
2 lb. cucumber ("Japanese" cucumber is preferred but can be substituted
    with other types)
1 lb. white turnip
2 lb. carrots
2 lb. celtuce (stem or "Chinese" lettuce)
2 lb. lotus root
2 lb. water chestnuts
2 lb. sunroot (sunchoke or earth apple)
1 lb. Thai chili
1 lb. peanuts
5 bulbs of fresh garlic
½ lb. ginger
75 fl. oz. soy sauce
2 lb. sugar
1 lb. salt
1 cup of Chinese hard liquor
5 bay leaves
5 oz. Sichuan peppercorn
5 oz. star anise

Preparation
1. Make the sauce: mix and boil soy sauce, sugar, bay leaves, star anise, and Sichuan peppercorn for 10–12 minutes, turn off heat, and let the sauce cool.
2. Wash and dry the vegetables, then cut them to ½ inch cubes (water chestnut can be quartered or halved depending on the size; Thai chili can be cut in half).
3. Marinate the cut vegetable in salt for 4 hours.
4. Clean and slice ginger, peel garlic, and place them with the marinated vegetables.

5. Prepare a crock pot (or an earthen water vat) large enough for the content; clean and dry the inside.
6. In the crock pot, layer vegetable mix with ginger/garlic/peanut mix alternately.
7. Pour the sauce into the crock pot.
8. Place a cleaned and dried rock to press the mix immersed in the sauce.
9. Dribble the Chinese hard liquor around the inside rim; cover the crock pot tightly.
10. The content is ready for serving after about 20 days.

Notes: Other than the cucumber and the yellow paste, all other ingredients can be substituted based on availability and preference.

The most popular pickled vegetable inside and outside China is *zha-cai* (pickled spicy mustard), a sauce-flavored pickle that was invented in the 11th century in Sichuan. Its main ingredient is a stem mustard (*Brassica juncea var. tumida*). The mustard is dehydrated either by wind or with salt, and remaining water is pressed out. Spices, especially chili pepper, and seasonings of choice are then added to the dehydrated mustard in tightly sealed urns for fermentation. *Zha-cai* has become one of the three most famous pickles in the world, along with cornichons (French pickled cucumber) and German sauerkraut. Its popularity in China is uncontested; anyone who has flown with Chinese airlines may remember that his or her in-flight meal or snack included a little packet of the salty and crunchy pickle slices. It is also used as a versatile ingredient in modern Chinese cooking, either as an ingredient or as a condiment. It is nevertheless best known as a side dish.

Fermented Bean Curd

There are hundreds of soy food products derived from tofu, the "cheese curds" from the coagulation of soy milk, and *fu-ru* (fermented bean curds) is one of the most popular and important of them. Fermentation not only makes the otherwise bland tofu flavorful but also solves storage and shipping difficulties that fresh bean curds are prone to. It is interesting that fermented bean curds are near nonexistent in other Asian countries, such as Japan, Korea, and Vietnam, where fresh tofu is eaten with great frequency and enthusiasm.

Like many other food items, there are many regional variations of fermented bean curds, but the basic steps of making them are similar. The basic ingredient is the firm bean curds. The dried curds are fermented using a yeast that contains hypercomplex bacteria which produces fungus spores that cause decomposition of the soy protein. The fermented curds are then salted in a sealed environment for about eight days. The third step, pickling, involves concocting special sauces with a mixture of alcohol and spices such as black pepper, peppercorn, star anise, ginger, and orange peels. It usually takes about a week for the pickled bean curds to be ready for eating, but it is said that the longer they are pickled, the fuller their flavors. It is imperative that each step is followed precisely in an insulated environment.

Different combinations result in different flavors, and there are three general types of fermented bean curds: the red, the white and the cyan. The differences among them go beyond the colorization. The red fermented bean curd is the most traditional way of making fermented bean curd, which gains its color from red yeast rice, that is, rice cultured with *Monascus purpureus*. The red curds are also popular as a seasoning or flavoring agent, especially for making braised pork belly, a favorite family dish that is also available in some restaurants. The white curds may have more delicate flavors and are more popular in the south. The most famous white fermented bean curds are from Guilin, Guangxi Zhuang Autonomous Region, which is best known for its stunning *Karst* landscape. The cyan curd is a "stinky" version of the fermented bean curds. Its potent smell and taste repulse a lot of people but attract equally as many. There are other fermented bean curds, some having long histories and others being new renderings. All in all, fermented bean curds are arguably the most common, popular, and varied side dish in China. Makers and merchants embellish the nutritional values of their high contents in protein, calcium amino acid, and B vitamins. Consumers may need to be reminded that the fermented curds are also high in sodium and purine, which can cause health problems in some people.

3.9. Garlic Spinach Salad (*Suan-rong-bo-cai*)

This recipe is a spin-off of a popular vegetable appetizer by substituting mustard oil, which is banned in the United States for cooking, with ground mustard to retain the sharp taste of the original dish.

Yield: Serves 2–3

Ingredients
1 bunch spinach
1 small carrot

2–3 oz. mung bean vermicelli (known as cellophane noodles or "rice noodles," if available)
1 scallion (green onion)
2 cloves of garlic
Slices of ginger
Salt, Chinese vinegar, sesame oil, peanut oil
Ground mustard

Preparation
1. Soak mung bean vermicelli in warm water for 10–15 minutes (this ingredient can be omitted).
2. Wash spinach thoroughly and cut to 2-inch sections.
3. Clean, skin, and slice the carrot (2 inches long, $^1/_{10}$ inch thick slices).
4. Blanch the cleaned spinach (scald in boiling water) for 30–40 seconds and mung bean vermicelli for 1 minute; rinse and cool.
5. Clean and mince scallion, garlic, and ginger.
6. In a bowl, mix ground mustard with a little water, then steam the mixture for 5 minutes.
7. Mix spinach, carrot, and mung bean vermicelli with mustard, garlic, ginger, and scallion; add salt, Chinese vinegar, sesame oil, and peanut oil to taste.

Notes: Mustard oil is banned in the United States for cooking due to its concentration of erucic acid that is suspected of being harmful to heart health.

Growing Importance in a Rapidly Evolving Food Culture

It is important to remember that the traditional Chinese diet was starch-heavy, and as a result its appetizers and side dishes have had very different functions and ingredients in comparison to their American equivalents. Unlike what Americans may find in a Chinese restaurant, foods using grain flours, such as eggrolls, dumplings, and noodles, are usually the main dishes of a meal but are rarely served as appetizers and side dishes.

The Chinese food culture has created a rich assortment of appetizers and side dishes fitting to all dining occasions. Appetizers are an integral component of formal meals and banquets but are often absent in family or working meals. They serve not only to "open up" the diners' appetite but also to brighten the social atmosphere at meals. They are also served as sides for alcohol beverages. As the Chinese experience continued improvement in living standards, appetizers are becoming the must-have start even at family meals, and new appetizers are being created at a fast pace.

Side dishes, on the other hand, have the most important function of helping ingest starch staples. This contrasts with the purpose and ingredients of typical American side dishes. As such, they must possess appetite invigorating effects, especially salty, spicy, and savory flavors. The Chinese have endeavored to perfect their pickling and fermenting methods, often using inexpensive and perishable ingredients, especially vegetables and tofu. Today, many traditional side dishes, such as pickled vegetables and fermented bean curds, may not be needed as the Chinese are eating much less starch staples and much more meat, seafood, and vegetables. These side dishes, however, are becoming even more popular. Their salty, pungent flavors are addictive to the taste buds and may bring nostalgia to a not-so-distant past. They will be with the Chinese for time to come.

Further Reading

Lydia. "How to Make Chinese Appetizers?" *Tell Me China*, April 5, 2021. https://www.tellmechina.com/how-to-make-chinese-appetizers.html.

Martin, Brett. "The Best New Steak of 2017, Plus 6 More Superlative Food Moments." *GQ*, April 21, 2017. https://www.gq.com/story/best-steak-and-food-moments-2017.

Pang, Kelly. "How a Chinese Meal Is Served." *China Highlights*, October 14, 2021. https://www.chinahighlights.com/travelguide/chinese-food/how-a-chinese-meal-is-served.htm.

CHAPTER FOUR

Main Dishes

Through much of history, eating was a luxury, even a privilege, for most people in the world. The norm was to have two meals, instead of three, every day. Ancient Chinese usually had their first meal at midmorning, then the second one in late afternoon or early evening. Food scarcity was obviously the main reason, since the aristocrats and the elites at the same time enjoyed having three meals a day; the rulers even relished four meals a day while prohibiting the masses from having more than two meals. A Western Han (206 BCE–9 CE) royal decree banishing a rebellious vassal king, Liu An (the one who invented tofu), included reducing his daily meals from three to two. There is an ongoing debate on when the three-meal day became the norm in China, but by the Song Dynasty (960–1279), it had become commonplace for most people to have three meals a day, enabled by great economic prosperity, robust urban development, and the emergence of active night life.

In some regions, the third meal evolved from mid-day snacks and became what was later known as the lunch. The tradition of having a good breakfast, a filling lunch, and a light supper was the outcome of coordination between daily meals and the lifestyle rooted in subsistence sedentary agriculture. Each of the three meals would feature typical main dishes that varied by region and seasonality. Overall, the meals were heavy on cereal starch and vegetables, supplemented by some form of protein such as tofu, eggs, or meat. The Chinese diet has been undergoing rapid transformation in the last several decades because of improved living standards and changing daily routines, which, first of all, have reshuffled the importance of the three meals.

Like other aspects of the Chinese food culture, there are great regional variations with the main dishes of each meal. The south's main starch source is rice, though wheat is also widely consumed. Wheat and coarse grains are the main staples in the north, with limited rice used in the main dishes. The south enjoys much greater variety and quantity of vegetables, as well as more abundant fish and aquatic products. The geography of main dishes is changing, however, as the regional differences are being blurred by population mobility, advancements in logistics, horticultural innovations, and improvement in processing technologies. Francization and fast food, as well as phenomenal growth of e-commerce, have also reduced regional exclusivity in terms of what people eat at their daily meals. Traditions developed in unique environments remain resilient, however, and many main dishes persist as regional specialties.

Breakfast

Breakfast provides energy for morning activities; this is especially true for traditional agricultural societies in which villagers have a morning of strenuous manual work in the field ahead of them. Today, convenience may be of greater concern: there is little time and limited ingredients for the folks to prepare an elaborate breakfast before heading out to work or school. Breakfast, while being the simplest meal of the day, needs to be adequate in quantity and quality in order to sustain the busy itinerary of the morning. In China, traditional home-made breakfast still varies from region to region, depending on both locally available ingredients and customary preferences. The northern breakfasts usually include steamed bread, noodles, or porridge made from corn meals or other coarse grains. Rice is favored in the southern breakfast, though wheat buns and noodles are also common. In Shanghai, for example, people used to mix the burnt, crusty rice left over from the previous day's supper with pork lard and salt in hot water for breakfast. Pickled vegetables and fermented bean curds are the most common side dishes for breakfast. Eggs and cured meats, especially sausages, are desirable but may not be always affordable items for rural and low-income folks.

Many city folks buy some breakfast items and bring them home to share, while others would grab something at street vendors or small eateries on their way to work. The most common, commercially made breakfast food has to be *you-tiao* (a deep-fried flour dough), which dates back at least one millennium. It is available everywhere in China with little variation. It is a common morning scene in big cities and small towns that street vendors deep-fry the elongated dough into puffed-up sticks in golden color, with customers eagerly waiting for their turn to get hold of the savory breakfast. In the north, people often eat *you-tiao* with soy milk, porridge, or *dou-fu-nao* ("tofu brain," or tofu pudding soup), with pickled vegetable sides. There may be other common breakfasts nationwide, such as stuffed buns, mostly steamed but sometimes pan-fried, and noodle dishes such as *Wuhan re-gan-mian* (Wuhan hot-dry noodle), *Chong-qing xiao-mian* (Chongqing noodles), and the famous *Lanzhou la-mian* (Lanzhou stretched noodles).

4.1. *You-tiao* (Deep-Fried Dough Sticks)

Research has concluded that frequent ingestion of *potassium alum*, the leavening agent for *you-tiao*, is harmful to health, but some worry that *you-tiao* without such a leavening agent may lose its classic fluffy texture. Or would it? The following recipe is one that does not use *potassium alum*, and people who have tried it swear that the healthier *you-tiao* is every bit (bite?) as good as the classic original.

Yield: Serves 8–10

Ingredients
8 cups all-purpose flour
2½ tsp salt
¼ tbsp baking soda (sodium bicarbonate)
1½ tbsp baking powder (sodium bicarbonate + an acidic ingredient)
2⅓ tbsp granulated sugar
3⅓ tbsp canola oil
2 eggs
2¼ cups water

Preparation
1. Put the flour in a large bowl.
2. In a separate bowl, mix salt, baking soda, baking powder, sugar, eggs, and cooking oil with the water.
3. Mix the liquid with the flour, using fists to knead the mix into a dough.
4. Cover the dough with shrink-wrap and let it leaven for 30 minutes, then knead the dough several times with fists.
5. Rob cooking oil evenly on a chopping board, on which to flatten the dough to about ¼ inch thick.
6. Cut the flattened dough into 1-inch-wide, 6-inch-long strips.
7. Use a chopstick to make an indentation on a strip, then top it with a strip without indentation.
8. Gently press the two dough strips together and stretch the combo strip to about 8 inches long.
9. In a wok, heat cooking oil to about 400°F.

10. Deep-fry the dough strip to golden yellow, turning it with chopsticks to ensure even cooking.
11. Remove the deep fried doughs (*you-tiao*, "oily sicks"), cool, and serve with soy milk, porridge, or on their own.

Notes: A critical step to making good *you-tiao* is pressing two dough strips gently together, which would make it easier to produce a less cooked, fluffy inside in contrast to the crispy outside.

Takeout breakfast has become mainstream in the last several decades, as the daily routines became busier and the increased income allowed extra spending for taste and convenience. There are distinct regional patterns of commercially made breakfast favorites, most of which evolved from humble street foods that became local cultural fixtures. It is interesting to note that for takeout breakfast, wheat flour is a lot more common throughout China, perhaps due to the versatility of wheat flour for a wide range of dishes. The following is a summary of the top five breakfast takeout dishes during the first five months of 2021 as reported by Ele.me Inc., an online food delivery service platform under e-commerce giant Alibaba Group.

The uniformity of leading breakfast foods, such as porridge, steamed buns, and *you-tiao* and soy milk, throughout the country should not come

Region	Top Breakfast Dishes
Northeast	Porridge, steamed stuffed buns, *you-tiao* and soy milk, burger and fries, noodles
North	Steamed stuffed buns, *you-tiao* and soy milk, pancakes, burger and fries, coffee
Northwest	Steamed stuffed buns, pancakes, porridge, *you-tiao* and soy milk, burger and fries
Southwest	Porridge, steamed stuffed buns, rice noodles, coffee, noodles
South	Porridge, rice noodles and noodle rolls, steamed stuffed buns, burger and fries
Central	Hot-dry noodles, hot pepper soup, porridge, steamed stuffed buns, rice noodles
East	Steamed stuffed buns, *you-tiao* and soy milk, coffee, pan-fried buns, pancakes

Source: http://www.199it.com/archives/1366308.html.

as a surprise, since these are tasty breakfast items that are not easy to make at home but can be mass-produced by professional vendors. The Chinese obviously want something tasty but not too heavy, while being nutritious and easy to eat, for breakfast. Pickled vegetables and fermented bean curds are still popular side dishes. Eggs are a favorite breakfast ingredient. Home-made pan-fried eggs are a staple for breakfast; tea eggs, either made at home or bought on the street, are another popular breakfast item: these are hard-boiled eggs with tea leaves and soy sauce and remain marinated in the broth until eaten. There is a lack of updated, quantitative data on popular dishes for home-made breakfast, but it is much more varied based on family habits, socioeconomic status, work schedule, and regional specialties. Again, breakfast is casual, and family breakfast is often makeshift as long as it has perceivably adequate nutrition to sustain a morning's regular activities.

Improved living standards and exposure to Western cultures have brought major changes to the Chinese breakfast. Western-styled breakfast orders are increasing at a faster rate than their Chinese-style counterparts. In the cities, milk has become part of the breakfast for kids and many adults. As data show, burgers and fries, regarded as being a typical Western style breakfast, have become popular among young, white-collar workers and school kids in the cities. Coffee and Western-styled pastries have also become popular for the same demographic groups. A close examination, however, reveals that the majority of Chinese still prefer their traditional breakfast. In 2021, for example, more than 87% of the orders for breakfast delivery were standard Chinese fare, such as steamed stuffed buns, porridge, and *you-tiao* and soy milk.

More and more people, especially the young, skip breakfast altogether even as they are being reminded it is the most important meal of the day. Many attribute this growing habit to overactive nightlife that often ends with filling night snacks and a morning rush to work with little appetite and time. On weekends, brunch has become popular for those who want to sleep in and then take their time to enjoy a more relaxed and substantial meal with family or friends.

4.2. Stir-Fried Rice Cake, Shanghai Style
(*Shanghai Chao-nian-gao*)

Glutinous rice cakes are very popular in some parts of East Asia. Stir-frying is one way to make the bland cakes more flavorful. The following is a Shanghai recipe with modified ingredients. Legend has it that the Korean elites fell in love with this dish and developed their own recipe, *tteokbokki*, which requires simmering instead of stir-frying the rice cake.

Yield: Serves 4–5

Ingredients
1 lb. rice cake, sliced and cooked (available in most Asian grocery stores)
6–8 shiitake mushroom, sliced
4–5 napa cabbage leaves, sliced into pieces about 2 inches long and 1 inch wide
6–7 oz. pork tenderloin, thinly sliced
2 scallion/green onion, chopped
2 cloves fresh garlic, minced
1 thumb fresh ginger, minced
3 tbsp cooking oil
2 tbsp soy sauce
1 tsp salt
1 tsp sugar
½ tsp starch

Preparation
1. Mix sliced pork with starch, ginger, and 1 tbsp each soy sauce and sugar.
2. Heat 2 tbsp cooking oil in a wok or pan.
3. Stir-fry the pork and put aside; clean the wok/pan.
4. Heat 1 tbsp cooking oil in the wok/pan.
5. Stir in rice cake, cabbage, and mushroom; stir-fry for 2 minutes.
6. Stir in cooked pork, scallion, salt, remaining soy sauce, and sugar; stir-fry for 2 minutes and serve hot.

Notes: The original recipe calls for potherb mustard (*Brassica juncea var. crispifolia; xue-cai or xue-li-hong*), which is widely grown in China and is an essential ingredient in many recipes from the Yangzi Delta. For easy stir-fry, make sure the rice cake slices are roughly ¼ inch thick, 1 inch long, and ½ inch wide.

Lunch

Traditionally, lunch was the family meal of the day when, ideally, everyone in the family would be at the table, customarily seated, and share the meal. For peasant farmers, a hefty lunch was a must for them to replenish the energy consumed in the morning and fill up for the afternoon's strenuous work in the field. Until a few decades ago, most rural Chinese and many urbanites worked near where they lived and would go home to eat lunch with their families. Few brought or bought lunch. One exception was during the wheat harvesting season in June in the north, when every moment counted in a desperate effort to get the crop harvested, processed, and put in storage before the rainy season arrived. Men and teenage boys stayed in the field day and night to harvest the crop with sickles, while women and girls brought meals to them several times a day.

4.3. Sweet and Sour Carp (*Tang-cu Li-yu*)

Carps are not a favorite fish for Americans but are very popular among the Chinese. Today, carps are a choice fish on the family dining table in southern China.

Yield: Serves 4–6

Ingredients
1 carp, 1–1½ lb., preferably a live one
1 small onion
½ green bell pepper
½ red bell pepper
1 thumb fresh ginger
3 scallions
4 tbsp cooking oil
3 tbsp wheat flour
3 tbsp corn starch
5 tbsp tomato paste
1½ tsp sugar
2 tsp vinegar
1 tsp water starch

Preparation
1. Scale and clean the whole fish, including the head.
2. Mince half of the ginger and one scallion; slice the other half of the ginger and one scallion.
3. Slice both sides of the fish at a 45-degree angle, with 1 inch between the slits.
4. Brush the fish with cooking wine and salt, and rub minced ginger and scallion on fish, especially inside the slits; marinate for 30 minutes.
5. Cut the green and red bell peppers, onion, and one scallion, sauté in wok with ½ tsp cooking oil.
6. Make batter by mixing wheat flour and starch and then gradually stirring in water until the mixture reaches a sticky consistency.
7. Rub ginger and scallion off the fish and coat it evenly with batter.

8. In a wok, heat cooking oil to medium high, then fry the fish until the batter hardens; turn heat down to medium and fry the fish for 3 more minutes; take it out and place on a large plate.
9. Mix tomato paste, sugar, and vinegar, adjust amount of each to taste.
10. In the wok, heat 1 tsp cooking oil on medium heat, sauté sliced ginger and scallion, add the tomato paste mix, stir until the sauce starts to bubble, then add water and starch and continue to stir for 1 minute.
11. Pour the hot sauce on fish; serve.

A typical family lunch varies across the socioeconomic spectrum and China's environmentally contrasting regions. The traditional family lunch shares two key characteristics that demonstrate the meal's traditional importance in daily life. First, the lunch was always freshly made. Second, the lunch often included several main dishes, making it more formal and enticing. Starch food was the staple and bulk of the meal, which henceforth are still called *zhu-shi* ("main food"). Rice was the favorite starch in the south, as was wheat in the north. Some poor rural folks also ate plenty of roots and tubers, such as potatoes and sweet potatoes, as staples. Vegetable dishes were key main courses for lunch, though in the north there was far less variety than in the south. Meat, mainly pork and poultry, eggs, tofu and, in the south, freshwater fish provide much needed fat and protein, though they were often absent from the lunch of the poor and the rural. Even for those who could afford to have meat, the quantity of it was usually small. Stir-frying mixed meat and vegetables was the perfect cooking technique to infuse the entire dish with enticing *xian* (*umami*) flavor.

It is impossible to identify representative traditional lunch dishes because of the regional diversity and socioeconomic disparity. Many well-known dishes can serve as main dishes for lunch, but it is rare to prepare dishes that are time-consuming or require exotic and expensive ingredients. Some of the favorable main courses for lunch are fried rice, stuffed buns and dumplings (*jiaozi*), and various noodle dishes. They are simple to make, tasty, and strike a balance among starch staples, vegetables, and meats.

4.4. Braised Noodles (*Zheng-mian-tiao*)

This is a popular "main dish" in northern China: it requires simple ingredients and is easy to prepare. Pork belly (side pork) is the preferred meat because it contains plenty of animal fat for flavoring, and green beans are choice vegetables because they can withstand long cooking time.

Yield: Serves 5–6

Ingredients
1 lb. young green beans (can be substituted with strong beans)
1 lb. fresh (wet) noodles
½ lb. pork belly (side pork)
4 cloves fresh garlic, peeled and minced
2 green onions (scallions), chopped
1 tbsp ginger, minced
2 tbsp cooking oil
2 tbsp soy sauce
1 tsp dark soy sauce
1 tsp sugar
1 tsp salt

Preparation
1. Wash green beans, tear off both ends, and break them into 2-inch sections.
2. Slice the pork into 1 inch long and ½ inch thick and wide pieces.
3. Heat cooking oil in a wok/deep pan and stir-fry pork with ginger, garlic, and green onion.
4. Add soy sauce, sugar, and salt; stir-fry for about 30 seconds.
5. Add green beans and stir-fry for about 1 minute.
6. Add water to the wok till all ingredients are submerged.
7. Cover wok and bring to a boil; pour half of the broth into a bowl.
8. Spread noodle evenly atop the pork and green beans; dribble broth in the bowl on top.
9. Cover and simmer until broth is almost absorbed completely by the noodle.
10. Mix meat, green beans, and noodle; plate and serve.

Notes: Do not submerge the noodles with the broth since it is the braising process that imparts the flavors into the noodles while retaining the noodles' *al dente* texture.

Midday napping, China's version of *siesta*, was an important ritual associated with lunch that the majority of the Chinese held dear. Until about two decades ago, the entire country would come to a standstill after lunch time. Though not enshrined in law, the time after lunch was officially designated time for napping; offices, public places such as libraries and most stores were closed, and people would nap at home or at their place of work. Nap time was adjusted with the season, from about one hour in the winter to up to two and half hours in the summer. Studies have shown that there are health benefits from taking a short nap or even some rest time after lunch, and people in general enjoy nap time. For the Chinese, however, the midday nap became an inalienable institution. Some suspect that their carbohydrate-heavy diet causes drowsiness; others consider midday napping a tried-and-true wellness exercise. Unfortunately, China's hopping on the globalization bandwagon means that it has to abandon and forgo some of its social and cultural traditions, and midday nap was among the first to go during the era of reform. Western-styled daily routines have most profoundly changed the lunch culture for the Chinese, especially that of the young and the urban.

4.5. Noodles with Fried Soybean Paste, Beijing Style (*Zha-jiang-mian*)

This is a signature Beijing main course. One can find it at street vendors and in hole-in-the-wall eateries, or make it at home relatively easily. The key ingredients are pork, yellow or sweet soybean paste, thick freshly made noodles, and one or more seasonal vegetables (the most popular including cucumber, turnips, shelled edamame, or bean sprouts).

Yield: Serves 4–5

Ingredients
1 jar or pouch of soybean paste, approx. 10–16 oz.
1 lb. pork ("Boston butt" is preferred; otherwise avoid overly lean cuts) or ground pork
1 lb. thick, freshly made ("wet") noodles
Vegetable toppings of choice, such as cucumber, turnips, shelled edamame, or bean sprouts
1 tsp minced fresh ginger
1 tbsp minced scallion
3 tbsp sugar (reduce to 1 tbsp if using "sweet" soybean paste)
2 tbsp cooking oil

Preparation
1. Dice the pork if using Boston butt.
2. Heat cooking oil in a wok, then fry the diced or ground pork till its color turns opaque.
3. Turn heat to low and add soybean paste to the pork.
4. Stir and mix the pork paste while it simmers; add squirts of water if the paste becomes too thick.
5. Add sugar, minced scallion and ginger, and two eggs (optional) to the paste; mix and stir.

6. When the paste turns to oily light yellow and exhumes a distinct aroma, turn off the heat.
7. Wash and shred the vegetable(s).
8. Follow directions to cook the noodles (similar to cooking spaghetti).
9. Top the noodles with the desired amount of paste and vegetables; serve.

Notes: The key to this recipe is the meat paste, which requires fattier pork. Some cuts of pork, such as pork shoulder, can produce fat in low heat and flavor the sauce nicely. Thick noodles, especially those made of bleached flour, provide a chewy texture that many Chinese prefer.

More profound than the abandonment of midday nap time, however, is the transformation of lunch from a family affair and home-cooking to a hurried routine and fast food. The rise of commercial catering and food delivery impose limitations to choices for the working lunch. Many people pack a lunch, but buying lunch is becoming increasingly common, especially among the young, because of freshness, choices, and affordability, as well as the increasing ease of mobile ordering and quick delivery. Pang (2021) documented some of the most popular types of lunch for the workers in China today.

The first type is affordable and flavor-balanced Chinese "fast food," that is, traditional Chinese dishes cooked in large volume and ready to order. They usually include a mix of a starch staple, some meat or animal protein, and vegetables. *Gai-fan* ("covered rice"), steamed rice topped with meat and vegetables of choice, is the top choice for a working lunch. Noodle dishes are also top choices for lunch, with great varieties and regional specialties, such as Lanzhou beef noodle (*Lanzhou la-mian*) or Wuhan hot-dry noodle (*Wuhan re-gan-mian*). In general, wheat flour noodles are common throughout the country, though in the south and southwest rice noodles are often local favorites.

The so-called "crossing-the-bridge noodles" (*Guo-qiao Mi-xian*) is an example of rice noodles' popularity in the south. Hailing from southern Yunnan Province, the essence of the dish is the broth made from chicken and pork bones. The fat on top of the broth holds the high heat in. The dish is consumed in two rounds. First, thinly sliced meat and tofu are cooked in the boiling hot broth for a few minutes, then are scooped out. Then rice noodles and vegetables are submerged in the still super-hot broth to cook. Then all the cooked ingredients are dipped into sauces, mixed, and ready to serve. With a century-old legend behind it, this rice noodle dish remains a quick, cheap, filling lunch. It was bestowed the honor of "an intangible cultural heritage of the City of Kunming" by the provincial government in 2008.

Another rice noodle dish is called *luo-si-fen* ("river snails rice noodle"), which was a local specialty in Liuzhou, Guangxi Zhuang Autonomous Region. The essence of this dish is a broth stock made from stewing river snails and pork bones together with a long list of spices. The yield is a pungent soup, fishy and spicy, in which rice noodles are served. It usually contains snail meat, pickled vegetables, soy products, fresh green vegetables, peanuts, and chili. Fresh cilantro and garlic, as well as extra chili, can be added by each eater to his or her own liking. Many find the smell and taste of this dish repulsive, but many more have joined the fan base. Its instant noodle version has become a multi-billion-dollar business, generating over 100 billion RMB or US$14 billion in sales revenue in 2020. The Chinese government even approved enlisting the dish as a National Intangible Cultural Heritage in 2021!

Noodles

China is the dominion of noodles. Archeologists have discovered 4,000-year-old noodles made from millet. Today, noodles are the most popular food in China with many regional variations. They can serve as main courses or as snacks; they can be eaten cold or hot, dry or soupy. The most famous noodle dishes include Beijing's noodles with fried soybean paste (*zha-jiang-mian*), Shanxi cut noodles (*dao-xiao-mian*), Lanzhou hand-pulled beef noodles, Wuhan hot-dry noodles with sesame paste, Sichuan *dandan* noodles, Shanghai plain noodles, and Guangzhou wonton noodles. Noodles are usually made of wheat flour, though rice noodles are common in the south and potato noodles (*fen-tiao*) are popular in some northern regions.

China tops all countries in total annual consumption of instant noodles and is in the top five in terms of per capita consumption. Instant noodles are omnipresent as a convenient and cheap alternative to other forms of lunch and are particularly popular among college students, office workers, low-income laborers, and travelers. Competition among businesses is fierce, and concerns abound regarding dietary health and even food safety (Zhang, 2022).

Stuffed buns (*bao-zi*) and dumplings (*jiaozi*) are at the top of lunch choices, be they homemade or mass-produced. Like *gai-fan* (covered rice) and noodle dishes, stuffed buns and dumplings are usually simple, affordable, and nutritionally balanced, and are suitable for mass production. There are many improvised and regional specialties of buns and dumplings, such as *Shanghai xiao-long-bao* (Shanghai steamed soup buns). Similarly, *Jian-bing Guo-zi* (pancakes made with mung bean flour and eggs) are popular in the north for both breakfast and lunch. For breakfast, it is folded and stuffed with *you-tiao* or *pai-cha* (a deep-fried, thin and crunchy dough sheet), as well as chili sauce, bean curd, and scallions. For lunch, though, some prefer to add meat to it. In recent years, a street food originating in Xian, Shaanxi Province, became a popular lunch food. *Rou-jia-mo* ("pancake stuffed with meat") is what it sounds: a thick pancake stuffed with braised and shredded meat. Called "Chinese Burgers" by foreigners, it is actually closer to the pulled meat sandwiches in America. It has gained a following in New York City in recent years (Mishan, 2014).

Many Chinese prefer to go out for lunch with colleagues. As a Chinese dining custom, they would order and share several entrées. Hot-pot is always a popular social lunch choice, and in recent years, a Sichuanese Street food, *ma-la-tang* ("numbing spicy hot"), has gained immense popularity among young workers. "Spicy Hot Pot," which is the officially sanctioned name, is a dish centered on a communal pot of boiling broth that is spiced up in classic Sichuan style. Skewers of uncooked foods, including a variety of meat, seafood, soy products, and some vegetables, are ordered; the diners would pick what they want and dip the skewers into the broth to cook them, then eat them next to the pot. Diners can order any kind of skewers in any number and at any time. Going *ma-la-tang* is a great way to have a quick lunch with colleagues or friends that presents many choices of ingredients and little inhibition.

4.6. Sliced Fish in Chili Oil (*Shui-zhu-yu*)

This recipe is unique because it is from a ready-to-cook dish. Originally a Sichuanese entrée, it has become popular throughout China. The ready-to-cook version is available in most supermarkets and requires minimum preparation.

Yield: Serves 4–5

Ingredients
1 store-purchased package including about 2 pounds of tilapia filet, preseasoned, and condiment packets: dry herbs including chili flakes and peppercorn, chili oil, sweet-sour sauce
1 bunch of fresh lettuce or napa cabbage

Preparation

1. Heat water in a pan, wash the lettuce leaves.
2. Scald lettuce leaves before water reaches boiling, then place them in a deep plate.
3. Empty the fish in the pan and boil for 10–12 minutes (per instruction on the package).
4. Heat the chili oil in a small pan or wok, then add content of the other two packets of condiments.
5. When aroma comes out, carefully pour the chili oil mix onto the fish and serve.

Supper/Dinner

Historically, the Chinese emphasized the health benefits of having a light and casual supper. For peasant farmers, who comprised the vast majority of the population, there was little to do but to go to bed after dark. Having a hefty supper and going to bed stuffed shortly thereafter would not be comfortable. For many, lunch leftovers would be served at supper, plus necessary freshly prepared light fare, usually in small servings. Soupy noodles, wonton soups, vegetables and tofu, and porridge were some of the typical main courses for supper. The tried-and-true conventional wisdom suggested that people should eat to no more than 70% full at supper.

Economic reform has led to socioeconomic transformations, including profound changes in the Chinese food culture. Today, supper is becoming the more formal and prepared meal of the day, necessitated by the same socioeconomic forces that drove the changes in American food culture, in which "supper" became "dinner," the big family meal of the day, when workers returned home after a day of hard work and could spend valuable time with their families during the height of industrialization. Supper is still not on par with the familial functions of traditional Chinese lunch, however, because family members often do not get to have supper together.

As supper becomes dinner, the big meal of the day, many traditional lunch courses have become common courses for the meal at the end of the working day. With a quick lunch and an evening of either more work or leisure activities, people need bigger, richer main courses than what traditional suppers had to offer. The supper today is usually multicourse meals no matter whether it is consumed by individuals or families, and whether eating in or dining out.

4.7. Lychee Pork (*Li-zhi-rou*)

This is a signature dish of the Fujian cuisine. Though called "lychee pork," there is no lychee (*li-zhi*) in the ingredients. The name came from the puffed shape of cooked spring onion. The unqualified name may also have been inspired by the fact that Fujian is one of the leading provinces of lychee production in China.

Yield: Serves 5–6

Ingredients
10 oz. lean pork
3.5 oz. water chestnut
4 scallions
1¾ oz. red vinasse (a paste of red yeast rice and glutinous rice)
¾ tbsp white vinegar
¾ tbsp soy sauce
1¾ tbsp granulated sugar
1½ tbsp fresh garlic
1⅓ tbsp (fava bean) starch
⅓ tbsp sesame oil
3¾ tbsp peanut oil
1¾ tsp MSG
4 tbsp chicken broth

Preparation
1. Wash the meat and dice to approximately 4 inch × 2 inch × 0.5 inch pieces, carve each piece diagonally, which produces an "oblique cross," then slice each piece into three smaller pieces.
2. Chop each water chestnut to 2–3 pieces.
3. Mix with hand the meat, water chestnut, red vinasse, and ⅔ of the starch.
4. Cut the white section of the scallion into ½ inch size.
5. Make a sauce by mixing soy sauce, white vinegar, sugar, MSG, chicken broth, and the remaining starch.
6. Heat peanut oil in a wok to about 400–420 degrees Fahrenheit.
7. Stir-fry the meat and water chestnut till the pieces are loose, about 2 minutes; take the contents out and drain extra oil.
8. With traces of cooking oil in the wok, stir-fry minced garlic and scallion white for 10–15 seconds, then stir in the meat and water chestnut mix.
9. Stir-fry for 10 seconds, place on a plate; serve.

As more and more people start to dine out for supper, typical supper courses made in bulk are becoming more varied and refined. Wonton (*hun-dun*), for example, is a good choice for supper or a night snack because it is a light fare with balanced nutrition and flavors. The versatile dumpling soup is a common street food, but the search for perfection has driven some to extreme endeavors to make a great delicacy out of the humble wanton soup.

A local specialty in Fuzhou, Fujian Province, called *rou-yan* ("meat swallow"), appears to be small wontons at first look. It is not quite the wonton as many know it, however, mainly because of its special wrapper. Meat swallow's wrapper is exhaustively made with a mix of freshly ground pork shank and sweet potato flour. The mix is pounded to a paste, then rolled into a very thin sheet. The filling is a pounded mix of high-quality meat and/or seafood with spices and herbs. The name "swallow" derives from the shape of the wonton dumplings. Some also say that the name *rou-yan* came from its exquisite taste and texture reminiscent of swallow's nest, one of the most exotic and expensive delicacies in China and other parts of East and Southeast Asia. Indeed, this is a dish that was for very special occasions, though nowadays it is also being mass-produced to meet the growing market demand. It is particularly suitable for a quick but tasty supper or night snack.

Folks in Wenzhou, Zhejiang Province, have outdone the original Fujian *rou-yan*. Located in the south of the Greater Yangzi Delta region, Wenzhou is known to be a wealthy area with a long tradition of overseas entrepreneurship. That wealth has translated into pursuit of culinary embellishment. Its version of *rou-yan* calls for making wrappers with fresh pork shank, too, but prefers pigs harvested on the day. It also uses lotus root flour in addition to sweet potato flour. The Fujian *rou-yan* wrapper uses sweet potato flour, with a 1:5 ratio between meat and flour. The Wenzhou *rou-yan*, in comparison, requires a 1 to 1 ratio between meat and flour, thence yielding a meatier texture and taste.

The chef would then use a special hammer in the shape of a wooden rolling pin to pound the meat and flour mix, beating them into a cohesive thin sheet. The locals claim that it takes two hours of rigorous pounding, adding pinches of salt in the process, at a temperature of 65 degrees Fahrenheit! One may wonder if most people would be able to tell the difference between Wenzhou *rou-yan* and its older Fujian cousin; it may be a task only the local gourmets would bother to take on for the bragging right. One thing is for sure, *rou-yan* is a perfect supper entrée and has gained an internet celebrity status that bodes well for the local economy. No wonder the Wenzhou municipal government hastily made its version of making *rou-yan* an "intangible cultural heritage" in 2016.

Night snacks are regarded as an extension of supper as well as a "night cap" food before bed. The Chinese cherish late night snacks, which sometimes were a necessity. During the pre-reform era, people who had to work past midnight were provided with either a small stipend or a snack by the government, with wonton or noodle soup among the most common. Today, night snacks have become an important part of night life throughout China, providing not only palate satisfaction but also a channel for socialization. The most popular night snacks are hot pot and Chinese variations of BBQ and kebobs. In many regions, especially those in the south, night snacks are almost must-haves for dining out and an essential activity at the night market.

4.8. Braised Shredded Chicken with Ham and Dried Tofu, Yangzhou Style, 18th century (*Da-zhu Gan-si*)

This is a renowned signature dishes from the Huai-Yang cuisine. Legend has it that it was invented to please Emperor Qianlong (1711–1799) during one of his imperial southern tours. It embellishes high-quality shredded *dou-gan* (firm tofu curds that can be thinly sliced and flavored) and local freshwater shrimp. It has many variations and is served for occasions from family dinners to state banquets.

Yield: Serves 6–8

Ingredients
15 oz. white *dou-gan*
1 oz. freshwater shrimp, peeled
2 oz. cooked chicken breast, shredded
2 oz. lard
1 oz. cooked and shredded Chinese ham
1 oz. pea sprout
¾ tbsp cooking wine, Shaoxing brand preferred
1 cup each chicken and pork bone
½ tsp salt
Pinches of MSG

Preparation
1. Cut *dou-gan* to 1/20-inch-thick slices, then cut the slices into thin shreds (close to the diameter of regular ramen noodles).
2. Soak the shredded *dou-gan* with water and salt, drain and repeat once, then rinse with water.

3. Clean the shrimp, add a little cooking wine, and steam to cook fully.
4. Heat 1.5 oz. of lard in a wok, add chicken and pork bone stock, stir in shredded *Dougan* and shrimp, then bring to a boil.
5. Add salt and cooking wine; stew at low heat for 10 minutes.
6. Turn heat to high, add half of the pea sprout, the remaining lard, and MSG.
7. Pour the entire content of the wok into a large soup bowl, top with shredded chicken and ham, garnish with the rest of pea sprout around the edge of the bowl, and serve.

Notes: Chefs often adjust the ingredients with the seasons to make the dish savory (*xian*): razor clam or other seafood in the spring, shredded freshwater eel in the summer, freshwater crab roe in the autumn, and wild vegetables in the winter.

Premade Main Dishes

A sea change is taking place in the Chinese food culture. Similar to what happened in the United States several generations ago, rapid economic development in recent decades has transformed the Chinese food culture from *de facto* "slow food" to practical "fast food." Burdened by their hectic daily routines, more and more working folks are switching from home-cooked dishes to premade, mass-produced ones. The premade dishes with fresh ingredients, termed *yu-zhi-cai* (ready-to-cook dishes), takes the lion's share of the growth.

China has undergone a most dramatic infrastructure growth in recent history. Nationwide cold supply chains, as well as food freezing and packing capabilities, allow traditional popular dishes to be mass produced and delivered to the end users, revolutionizing the preparation of just about any popular dishes. At the same time, the e-commerce market has exploded, enabling mass online ordering and rapid door-to-door delivery. Premade food had been around in China, since hot pot, kebob, and BBQ all required mass-produced, sometimes semi-cooked ingredients. The new ready-to-cook dishes, however, are expected to be freshly prepared by skilled professionals using special accommodations that cannot be substituted with prepackaged ingredients, which are often frozen or laced with preservatives. Most of the ready-to-cook entrées have the key ingredients paired and prepared, with some ingredients precooked or semi-cooked. They are ready for cooking at home with minimum preparation and additional ingredients. Many, especially those urban, young professionals, provide a growing market for these bulk-produced, ready-to-cook dishes (Ahuja et al., 2021).

With market demand emerging, ingredients aplenty, and infrastructure in place, the breakthrough came with the invention of the "lean kitchen," modeled after "lean manufacturing" that was perfected by Toyota. The lean kitchen is staffed by professional cooks who can guarantee the ready-to-cook dishes being freshly prepared and delivered. The business model sources most of the bulk ingredients, which allows it to save cost by reducing rent, waste, and labor expenses, and to adhere to high hygiene standards. While some gourmet *aficionados* insist that the often-frozen ready-to-cook dishes are no match to the "real thing," the masses seem to have concluded that they are close enough to be worth saving the time and energy that are required in preparing these dishes from scratch. Ready-to-cook meals may be poised to bridge the gap between the decline of traditional home cooking and the Chinese insistence on eating a balanced and well-augmented meal centered on hot main courses.

The fledgling ready-to-cook food businesses received a huge boost when the COVID-19 pandemic forced hundreds of millions of Chinese into lockdown in early 2020. Many, especially the white-collar young professionals, discovered ready-to-cook dishes and embraced them. Sales of ready-to-cook dishes have since skyrocketed. The total market value for ready-to-cook food sector grew from US$15 billion in 2017 to nearly US$40 billion in 2020 and continues to grow 18–20% annually. The sector is crowded with almost 70,000 businesses now, and has become a favorite for venture capital investment. Fierce competition among businesses and business models has created big winners and losers.

The sea-change in food culture has a profound impact on the daily meals in China. Time and effort saved in preparing the main courses inevitably lead to standardization; some of the popular main courses that are easier to mass-produce or prepare may come to dominate the dinner table, while individual cooking improvisions may diminish. As more and more people embrace the convenient alternative, one wonders if and when the art of traditional cooking would be lost forever.

There is no reason to bemoan the fading tradition, however, since the Chinese food culture, including all the popular dishes, has undergone many changes through time. The only thing that remains constant for the Chinese is the desire to eat well, that is, well paired ingredients, balanced nutritional value, and high-quality preparation. If bulk production can fit the bill, so be it.

Further Reading

Ahuja, Kabir, Vishwa Chandra, Victoria Lord, and Curtis Peens. "Ordering In: The Rapid Evolution of Food Delivery." McKinsey & Company, September 22, 2021. https://www.mckinsey.com/industries/technology-media-and-telecommunications/our-insights/ordering-in-the-rapid-evolution-of-food-delivery.

Mishan, Ligaya. "A Mystery of Chinatown." *New York Times*, September 11, 2014. https://www.nytimes.com/2014/09/17/dining/hungry-city-taste-of-northern-china-in-chinatown.html.

Osborne, Nicholas. "What The Chinese Eat for Lunch." China Educational Tours. https://www.chinaeducationaltours.com/guide/article-what-chinese-eat-for-lunch.htm. (accessed October 31, 2022)

Pang, Kelly. "What Chinese People Eat for Lunch—The Top 10 Meals in China." *China Highlights*, October 13, 2021. https://www.chinahighlights.com/travelguide/article-what-chinese-eat-for-lunch.htm.

Zhang, Lei. "The Rise and Rise of the Instant Noodle Nation." *China Daily*, March 26, 2022. https://www.chinadaily.com.cn/a/202203/26/WS623e6465a310fd2b29e536ff.html.

CHAPTER FIVE

Desserts

Many Americans like Chinese food, and there were over 23,000 Chinese restaurants in the United States in 2022 according to IBISWorld, a market research firm. Some sources even claimed that there were over 46,000 Chinese restaurants (Rude, 2016). Chinese food is the most searched ethnic food on Google Trends (Williams, 2020). Having enjoyed an exotically flavorful and relatively light meal, however, many diners may only find limited choices for desserts on a typical Chinese restaurant menu. Fortune cookies, an American invention (Lee, 2008), usually fill in as a modest but free dessert substitute. Some restaurants serve fresh seasonal fruits, such as citrus in winter and spring, and watermelon in summer and fall.

Assertions that the Chinese do not have good desserts often generate heated discussions at online forums. While some Chinese or Chinese foodies strongly refute such a notion, others view it as an objective observation and a fair inquiry. Desserts are such an essential dining component in American food culture that it is only natural for diners to take note of the lack of dessert choices after an otherwise enjoyable meal. Some try to probe the reasons for this perceived neglect and concluded that most Chinese restaurants are low-budget operations that have to forgo the untenable costs associated with substantial and elaborate dessert offerings.

Yet, Western visitors to China have also observed that desserts are not the essential last course of meals, no matter at a "hole-in-the-wall" eatery or at an upscale dining club. Unlike the Americans, the Chinese seem to treat desserts as if they were an afterthought. Can this gastronomic neglect be explained by the heavy intake of starch food and vegetables in the traditional Chinese diet? Such a diet, some insist, creates a "full" feeling that dissuades ingestion of a sweet entrée made of starch, sugar, and fat. Others have hypothesized that sugary foods were a luxury that, historically, few Chinese could afford to have regularly, and the lack of demand and affordability made dessert-making a neglected segment in an otherwise splendid culinary tradition. Yet another speculation attributes the seemingly disinterests in desserts among the Chinese to their not consuming much milk and dairy products traditionally, which put them in a disadvantage in making decadent desserts without being familiar with milk and butter, the wonder ingredients in making rich and savory desserts. Some people even assumed that the Chinese were not able to afford plenty of sugar, which not only prevents them from making good desserts but also helps explain that the limited offerings of Chinese desserts are often not sweet (and rich) enough!

5.1. Double-Layered Milk Custard (*Shuang-pi-nai*)

Legend has it that an old lady in Shunde, a coastal county of Guangdong, created this dessert in the mid 1800s. Made of water buffalo milk, egg white, and cane sugar, it is a custard that has two layers of "skin." The first comes from cooling the boiled milk and the second from the egg custard. It is a hugely popular dessert in Guangdong, Hong Kong, and Macao. The ingredients are few, but the preparation requires delicate skills.

Yield: Serves 3–4

Ingredients
1¾ cup whole milk
2 eggs
2 tsp sugar

Preparation
1. Pour milk into a bowl and tightly cover with shrink-wrap; steam for 10 minutes and let cool.
2. Separate egg white from the yolks and stir the white lightly.
3. Make a 3-inch slit in the milk skin along the edge of the bowl.
4. Pour most of the milk out of the bowl from the slit, keeping the skin intact.
5. Mix sugar and egg white with the milk.
6. Sieve the mix to get rid of bubbles and froth.
7. Pour the milk mix back into the bowl through the slit, letting the original skin stay on top.
8. Cover with shrink-wrap again and steam on medium heat for 10 minutes.
9. Turn off the heat and let the custard stand for 5 minutes; serve.

Notes: The original recipe called for milk from local water buffalo, which was said to have higher fat content. Some say whole milk actually yields a better taste.

It is true that the typical Chinese dining experience, be it a family meal or a lavish banquet, does not feature desserts as its Western, especially American, counterparts do in prominence and variety. The famous cookbook by Yuan Mei (1716–1797), *The Garden of Contentment*, a classic for "the way of eating," has no separate chapter for desserts in its 12 chapters of recipes (Yuan, 2019 [1792]). This is, however, a dietary preference rather than a culinary deficiency. The lack of investment in desserts, by American standard, may in part have to do with the Chinese view of food health. The Chinese gastronomical sensibility calls for balance and against excessiveness. The stomach needs rest after the main courses, so the last course of a meal is usually something refreshing in flavor and light in substance, such as a small bowl of savory soup or sweet congee; fresh and dry fruits would also fit the bill. In other words, it is not considered sensible and healthy to conclude a meal with heavy and rich desserts. Equipped with traditional wisdom and modern science, Chinese health experts have warned against consuming rich and large portions of desserts because they elevate blood sugar to unhealthy levels and force the pancreas to kick into overdrive. The sense of moderation may have made Chinese desserts "bland" and "dry" in comparison to some of the favorite American desserts, which helps explain why China's per capita sugar consumption is only about one third of that of the United States.

It is not correct, however, to think that traditional Chinese meals are completely devoid of desserts. Often, meals do have sweet endings, though they are usually light and refreshing tidbits served in small proportions, which are properly called *dian-xin* ("touch of the heart"). They can be cookies, sticky rice balls in broth (*tang-yuan* or *yuan-xiao*), steamed buns with sweet stuffing (*tang-bao*) or sweetened glutinous rice cakes (*nian-gao*). These sweet treats are enjoyed as both snacks and desserts, or, though not as common, as appetizers. Having sweet tidbits is not a required last course in a traditional Chinese meal, but many of the elaborately prepared sweets can be served as desserts. Like any other people, the Chinese love the sweet taste and have created countless sweet treats through time. One such sweet treat is potato (or sweet potato) in caramelized sugar floss (*ba-si tu-dou*). The simplest way to make this treat is, first, caramelize sugar in heated cooking oil, then, stir-fry sliced potato (or sweet potato) in the caramel; finally, dip the caramel-laden slices into ice water to solidify the fine sugar strands ("floss") on the potato slices.

5.2. Fried Sesame Balls (*Jian-dui*)

This is a deep-fried treat that can be traced back to the court of the Tang Dynasty (618–907). It was brought to the Pearl Delta in Guangdong, where today it is a popular snack, or *dim sum*, in Cantonese cuisine. It is also served as a dessert in some Chinese restaurants in the United States.

Yield: Serves 6–8

Ingredients
4 cups glutinous rice flour
½ cup granulated sugar
9 cups cooking oil (peanut oil preferred)
1 lb. red bean paste (approximate)
1 cup raw sesame

Preparation
1. Mix ¾ cup of rice flour with water, knead into small doughs, cook in boiling water, and place on a chopping board.
2. Mix the cooked doughs with the rest of the rice flour and sugar and knead until the dough feels malleable and pasty.
3. Stretch the dough into an elongated row about 1½ inches wide and cut it into pieces about 1½ inches long.
4. Flatten each dough with a rolling pin, wrap about 1 tsp red bean paste, and roll into a dough ball.
5. Place sesame in a deep dish; roll rice balls in sesame until they are coated with sesame.
6. Heat oil in a wok or deep frier to about 250 degrees Fahrenheit, slip several dough balls in, and turn them repeatedly with a pair of long chopsticks to allow them being cooked evenly.
7. When the balls turn into golden brown, take them out and serve.

Some in the West may have perceived the Chinese as being inwardly looking and resistant to change. This perception is not accurate as far as the food culture is concerned. The Chinese have always been open, even eager, to try the new in the culinary realm. The southeast coastal provinces of Guangdong and Fujian have been the most exposed to the outside world since the late imperial epoch, and their *émigré* comprise the bulk of the Chinese diaspora. There has been intense fusion between the cuisines of Guangdong and Fujian and that of Southeast Asia, because of economic and cultural interactions and similarities in their traditional food ingredients. It is widely known that Chinese and South Asian cuisines have had far-reaching influences on Southeast Asian food cultures. Southeast Asia, at the same time, has also brought new ingredients and dishes to China. Southeast Asian sweet snacks and desserts, for example, are quickly gaining popularity in China through tourism and addiction to sweets among the young Chinese, notably various versions of *cendol* (an iced concoction of rice flour jelly, coconut milk and palm syrup), *che ba mau* from Vietnam (colorful beans in shaved ice and condensed milk), and *bua loy kai* from Thailand (glutinous rice balls in coconut milk).

European culinary influence on Chinese sweets and desserts is most prevalent in port cities along the southeast coast, especially in formal colonies of Hong Kong and Macao. One example would be mango pudding, which bears British influence and is popular in Hong Kong and some Southeast Asian countries. Egg tart, hugely popular in Guangdong, Hong Kong, and Macao, was "invented" in Guangzhou in the early 20th century. It was inspired by the British custard tart but used lard and steamed eggs that were more attuned to local palates. It became very popular and influenced the development of the Macao version, which was also influenced by the Portuguese egg custard tart *Pastel de Nata* for its caramelized pastry crust.

The traditional inattention for desserts in Chinese dining may be changing as the country is becoming globally connected and eager to embrace new food cultures. *Avant-garde* Chinese restaurateurs are infusing traditional and innovative desserts to please, alas, the young, white-collar urbanites who can afford and do demand the sweet addition to their fancy meals, and who have quickly acquired a sweet tooth comparable to their Western counterparts.

5.3. Honey Cold Cake (*Feng-mi Liang-gao*)

This is a popular snack during the summer in northwest China.

Yield: Serves 8–10

Ingredients
8 cups glutinous rice flour
30 dried and pitted jujube dates

4 tbsp granulated sugar

Toppings: 1 oz. each: raisins, dried cranberries, dried mango, sunflower
seeds

¼ cup honey water

Preparation
1. Wash and soak jujube dates for 12 hours; steam and grind into a paste.
2. Wash and soak the rice for 12 hours, steam, mix with sugar, and grind
   to a paste.
3. Coat a baking sheet with cooking oil; place a thin layer of rice mix, then
   a thin layer of jujube paste; repeat to have three layers each of rice and
   jujube.
4. On top of the layers, spread dry fruits and sunflower seeds, then sprinkle honey water evenly.
5. Place in refrigerator until thoroughly chilled; slice and serve.

Meanwhile, increasing awareness about healthy diets has led to appreciation of light desserts in the United States, which are often found in
Asian confections and sweet snacks, and who's to say that ending a meal
with refreshing fruits is less pleasant! Treats that are considered of medicinal value are welcome, since the eaters can enjoy the dessert with less guilt
and even some delight for the sweet treat's health benefits. One such snack
in Taiwan as well as in Fujian and Guangdong, two of the southeast coastal
provinces, is the so-called *shao-xian-cao* ("grass jelly"). It is made by boiling a dried plant (*Platostoma palustre*), commonly referred to as "Chinese
mesona," with starch additives and salt. The product is a slightly bitter
jelly and is traditionally served with syrup and nowadays with fruits and
other toppings of choice. The grass jelly is also served as a dessert in
Guangdong and Fujian.

If the Chinese appear to have treated desserts nonchalantly, they have
certainly thrived in the use of sweeteners in cooking and in creating countless sweet treats. The Chinese have long used sweet ingredients in cooking,
be they fruits, honey, or, later in history, cane sugar or beet sugar. The
ancients regarded the sweet taste as being the best flavor, as recorded in *The
Rites of Zhou*, a classic that might have been compiled before the 3rd century BCE. The earliest known sweetener was maltose (*mai-ya-tang*), the use
of which could date back to one millennium BCE. Honey became widely
used in cooking, medication, as well as fermented alcohol beverages by the
time of Confucius (551–479 BCE), when sweet fruits and nuts, such as
chestnuts and jujube dates, were also used to sweeten food.

The Chinese employ three popular ways to make and enjoy the sweet flavor in food. In addition to desserts, sweeteners are widely used as both seasoning and condiments in many famous and beloved cuisines and dishes; sweet snacks are widely enjoyed outside regular meals. The Chinese have long discovered nuanced sweetening could greatly improve flavors of different ingredients and make their cooking more versatile. By using maltose and honey as condiments, for example, the ancient Chinese surmised that sweeteners could also be used as a thickener. This conclusion might have been important because the key to stir-fry is to avoid watery condition that would ruin the flavors of the dishes. In addition, sugar was a luxury, especially for the common folks, for much of their history. Sweetening food, therefore, was also a show of socioeconomic status.

5.4. Walnut Cloud Cake (*Yun-pian-gao*)

Legend has it that the origin of cloud cake in northern Jiangsu had to do with Emperor Qianlong (1711–1799), who bestowed the name upon a home-made treat but miswrote the first character as "cloud" instead of "snow." Today, two most famous styles of this sweet treat hail from Sichuan Province and Chaozhou (Teochew) of Guangdong Province. The thin, white slices are faintly sweet and retain the fragrant flavors of rose pedals, walnut, and glutinous rice. The following is a recipe from Meizhou (Hakka Chinese: Moichu), Guangdong Province, a major Hakka concentration.

Yield: Serves 6–8

Ingredients
8¼ cups glutinous rice flour
6 cups granulated sugar
5 cups walnut, shelled
½ cup rose syrup
½ cup all-purpose wheat flour

Preparation
1. Dissolve sugar in water and boil to make a syrup, stir, and let stand.
2. Scald walnut with boiling water, mix with rose syrup, then divide into three equal portions.
3. Mix rice flour with sugar syrup and divide the mix into four equal portions.
4. Line a rectangular container with the first portion of rice flour–sugar syrup mix, flatten, and press to firm.

5. Layer the first portion of the walnut–rose syrup mix on top and press to firm.
6. Repeat 4 and 5 to yield a total of four layers of rice-sugar mix and three layers of walnut-rose syrup mix.
7. Steam at 175 degrees Fahrenheit for 15 minutes.
8. Stir-fry wheat flour.
9. Take the cake out of the container, sprinkle wheat flour on top and let stand for about one hour, slice into thin pieces; serve.

Notes: The original recipe calls for walnut, but it can be omitted or substituted with other seeds or nuts, such as melon seeds or pine nuts.

Sugar cane was brought to China as early as one millennium BCE. The Chinese did eat it as a fruit by chewing on the peeled core to extract the sugary juice, which they still do today. The Chinese also developed pressing instruments to produce cane juice. Cane juice was limited in supply and highly valued as a banquet drink; even the nobles could not easily afford it. The cane juice was processed into solid or gelatin forms, which were called *sha-tang* (sand sugar) or *shi-mi* (stone honey). These primitive forms of cane sugar were consumed mainly as expensive candies and, quite rarely, sweeteners, and honey remained more affordable and available for sweetening food until the early Tang Dynasty (618–907), when sugar crystallization methods were brought to China from India. Granulated cane sugar became widely available after the Song Dynasty (960–1279), when Fujian and Guangdong became the centers of sugar cane growth and cane sugar production during the Ming Dynasty (1368–1644).

Today, nearly every edible sweetener is used in Chinese cooking: while cane sugar is most common, the Chinese also infuse their foods with brown sugar, corn sweetener, corn syrup, dextrose, fructose, fruit juice concentrate, glucose, honey, invert sugar, lactose, maltose, molasses, sucrose, and various syrups and sweet alcohol, as well as artificial sweeteners such as sucralose, acesulfame, and saccharin. The Chinese do not use sweeteners indiscriminately, though, and they insist that each sweetener has unique properties that would bring out specific flavors or textures of the main ingredients.

Careful selection and measured use of sweeteners for specific dishes is part of the art of cooking. Granulated cane sugar, for example, the most common sweetener in Chinese cooking, is said to enhance the *xian* (savory) flavor in foods and to suppress undesirable tastes in some ingredients. The melted sugar syrup becomes brown in color and is used to add coloring to some meat dishes, or to sugar-coat some ingredients such as roots, tubers, and fruits. Another common form of sugar available in Asian/Chinese grocery stores is the so-called rock sugar. Rock sugar is basically purified cane sugar that appears in large, rock-like crystals, which the Chinese consider as being superior to granulated cane sugar for cooking, especially in braising and stewing meat, because of its stronger sweetness, thickening ability, and, allegedly, more nutritious values.

In addition to sugar, other traditional sweeteners, such as honey, malt, fruits, and nuts, are limited in use. The Chinese chefs often create new dishes by making use of seasonal fruits, which would entail new color, texture, and flavor. Some fruits, such as raisins and apricots, are dried, sugared, or otherwise preserved for off-season use. Some fruits, such as jujube, haws (*Crataegus pinnatifida*), and goji berries (*Lyceum chinense* or *Lycium barbarum*), are used not only for their supposed health benefits but also their sweetening effect. Artificial sweeteners are used extensively in processed food and drinks, as well as in baking, but not so much in restaurant and family cooking.

Some regional cuisines are known for their sweet tastes, while others do not use sweeteners as much. Communities along the southeast coast, especially the Cantonese and the Fujianese, love savory and fresh tastes, and sweeten their dishes slightly to achieve this gastronomical feat. They often use seasonal and preserved fruits, such as pineapples, bananas, coconuts, and rambutans, all abundantly available locally. The wealthy Yangzi Delta region, on the other hand, reigns supreme as far as food sweetness is concerned. Some of the local dishes, such as pork spear ribs and wonton soup from Wuxi, a wealthy city on the Yangzi Delta, are too sweet for nonlocals to appreciate. In contrast, the poorer inland south has resorted to pungent spices and seasonings for flavoring, especially after the arrival of the chili pepper.

Historically, the northern cuisines, especially those for the elite, were known to emphasize sweet flavor. Over time, however, the south, especially the Yangzi Delta, became notorious for making their dishes sweet. One hypothesis has it that centuries of human and environmental disasters drove southward migration. Hundreds of thousands of northerners, including the nobles and the wealthy, fled to the Yangzi Delta. This story may not hold true, however, because there is not enough evidence to conclude that the northern diet was sweeter than its southern counterpart. An alternative theory is that the over-the-top sweet flavors of the Yangzi Delta cuisines may have to do with showcasing social status since sugar was an expensive ingredient during the late imperial epoch. Consumption of sweetened food may have satisfied both the sensory pleasure and social vanity at the same time. The Yangzi Delta, so well-off that it was dubbed "land of fish and rice," became China's most endowed economic region, which was in part reflected in the culinary transition to sweet food. It also helped that the Yangzi Delta during this period became the major trade hub of cane sugar from Fujian and Guangdong provinces to the rest of the country.

5.5. Honey Mito (*Mi-san-dao*)

This is a traditional treat in Shandong and Jiangsu provinces that gained popularity throughout northern China. Its heavy use of maltose creates a velvety texture.

Yield: Serves 3–4

Ingredients

For the wrappers:
⅓ cup all-purpose flour
½ tbsp peanut oil
1½ tbsp water
2 tbsp white sesame

For the pastry filling:
3 cups all-purpose flour
2½ tbsp peanut oil
½ cup maltose
½ tsp baking powder
¼ cup water

For the syrup:
¾ cup maltose
¾ cup granulated sugar
2 tbsp water

Preparation
1. Mix all ingredients for the wrapper and knead the mix into a ball; let rest for 15 minutes.
2. Mix all ingredients for the filling and knead the mix into a ball; rest for 15 minutes.
3. Roll both balls into elongated pancakes with a rolling pin.
4. Sprinkle some water on the wrapper pancake, then layer the filling pancake on it; the combo pancake should be about ⅓ inch in thickness.

5. Cut the combo pancake into ¾ inch square doughs, then make three stabs on each with a knife.
6. Deep fry to golden brown.
7. Melt all syrup ingredients on low heat, stir lightly.
8. Dip all deep-fried dough in syrup.
9. Cool and serve.

The latter theory may also be supported by correlating the socioeconomic conditions and cuisines of a region with that of others that have similar climates. The interior regions along the Yangzi River, including Hunan and Hubei provinces and the Sichuan Basin, are known for the overpowering pungent flavors of their cuisines. This culinary tradition is often attributed to environmental adaptation since spicy food stimulates perspiration, which is a relief of body heat in hot and humid climates. Regions along the Yangzi River all have hot and humid subtropical climate. The hot spicy cuisines in the interior south, however, emerged around the same historical period as the Yangzi Delta cuisines went sweet. It was likely that the takeover of hot spicy cuisines in the interior south was the coping strategy for the folks there to substitute the unaffordable salt with spicy seasonings and condiments. Surveys have shown that the "sweetest" region in China is the lower Yangzi River valley, especially its delta region. The least sweet region, not surprisingly, is the less developed interior regions along the Yangzi River valley.

Like anyone else, the Chinese are fond of sweet foods and have created countless sweet treats, ranging from elaborate court specialties to humble street snacks. Traditionally, sweets are more often served as snacks than as desserts (the last course of a meal) or appetizers since the Chinese did not like pairing sweet dishes or courses with the salty and savory ones. There are a great number and variety of sweet treats; their ingredients and preparation changed through time, but traditions persist, and regional specialties shine through as a reflection of environmental adaptation. The most important ingredients for desserts and sweet snacks are wheat and rice flours, lard (for Muslims, sheep fat), and sugar because of the absence of butter and cream in cooking. A popular sweet rice dish from the Yangzi Delta is *ba-bao-fan* (eight treasures rice), which uses glutinous rice, lard, and several dry fruits and nuts or seeds. Glutinous rice is widely used as a main ingredient in sweet snacks and desserts in the south, while wheat flour is more common in the north. Chinese sweet foods can be divided into three general and partly overlapping categories, as follows.

5.6. Eight Treasures Rice (*Ba-bao-fan*)

This is a tasty rice treat from Ningbo of northern Zhejiang Province. It can be served as a snack or a dessert, and it is often served as one of the entrées for New Year's Eve dinners. Its white dome shape, decorated with colorful dry fruits, serves as an auspicious symbol for families that gather to celebrate the coming of the New Year. This recipe is not to be confused with the congee served on December 8 of the Chinese calendar, which is called "Eight Treasures Congee."

Yield: Serves 4–6

Ingredients
6 cups of glutinous rice
1 tbsp pork fat or olive oil
¼ cup each: (1) dry cranberry, (2) raisins, (3) dry longan, (4) shelled walnut, (5) pine nuts, (6) dried apricot, (7) dried lotus seeds, (8) sugared cherry
16 oz. red bean paste
3 tbsp rose syrup

Preparation
1. Steam the rice for an hour, then mix with 1 tbsp pork fat (traditional ingredient) or cooking oil.
2. Steam the lotus seeds and slice the apricot.
3. Line a large bowl with shrink-wrap and place a sugared cherry at the bottom center.
4. Encircle the cherry with raisins and cranberries, then with longan, walnuts, pine nuts, and apricot slices.
5. Lay a thin layer of rice atop the fruits and nuts; place red bean paste at the middle arrayed with lotus seeds.
6. Put the rest of rice on top and flatten to be even with the edge of the bowl
7. Turn the bowl upside down, place it on a plate and steam on high heat for 10 minutes
8. Remove the bowl and sprinkle rose syrup over the top; serve.

Notes: The purists insist that pork fat (lard) is the best, but high-quality olive oil is acceptable. Rose syrups may be available in Asian supermarkets or online; they could be substituted with chrysanthemum or osmanthus syrups. Homemade syrup involves boiling fresh or dry flower petals with sugar and thickening it with a little wet corn starch.

The first category is processed specialty pastries and other sweets that are made with wheat or rice flours, lard, and a variety of syrups, fruits, and nuts. Called *dian-xin* ("touch of heart"), they are usually professionally made since their recipes require many ingredients and special skills, plus an assembly line with multiple workers. They are sold in grocery stores, food specialty shops, or concessionaires, and are usually expensive. These pastries are sometimes served as appetizers, desserts, or tea snacks and are often presented as gifts for special occasions. Some sweet food businesses have become "China Time-Honored Brands," a certification issued by the government. One such example is *Dao Xiang Cun* ("Village of Rice Fragrance"). It is the earliest pastry shop that made and sold Suzhou-styled pastries and is now a corporate franchise. In Beijing, there is a pastry business with the same namesake and certification but is described as being specialized in Beijing-styled pastries. Its pastry goodies are popular among locals and visitors alike and are brought back home as special gifts from the capital.

Some desserts and sweets in northern China celebrate the heritage of nomadic and hunting-fishing cultures. A popular pastry in Beijing, *sa-qi-ma* (*sachima*), is a Manchu treat that was originally used as a sacrificial food. Noodles made of wheat flour, animal fat, and eggs are deep fried and then mixed with a syrup of sugar, honey, maltose, and butter. The dried block was then cut into small cubes for eating convenience. Beijing yogurt is yet another example of a sweet and sour snack beloved by just about anyone who has tried it. Introduced by the Manchus and their Mongol allies after their conquest of China in the 17th century, the authentic Beijing yogurt is still made with only three ingredients: milk, granulated sugar, and the yogurt bacterium (*Lactobacillus delbrueckii subsp. Bulgaricus*).

Many processed and bulk-made pastries still feature local and seasonal ingredients. The Yangzi Delta is home to osmanthus blossoms in the fall. The locals not only get to enjoy the intoxicatingly fragrant season but also collect the flower petals for use in a variety of foods and beverages. One of the oldest and most beloved local delicacies, osmanthus cake, is a highly acclaimed sweet, powdery cake made with glutinous rice flour and dry osmanthus flowers. It is not highly perishable and has been shipped and sold in other places. It has been eaten as a sweet snack, or a dessert if served at the end of a meal, in many parts of China.

5.7. Osmanthus Cake (*Gui-hua-gao*)

Osmanthus fragrans, which literally means "fragrant osmanthus," is the city flower for Hangzhou, the capital city of Zhejiang Province. The fragrant smell from the small, pale-yellow flowers is so strong that street vendors would make bracelets and sell them to locals and tourists alike during the fall. The flowers are also used as an ingredient in regional snacks and drinks, and the osmanthus cake (or jelly) is one of the most popular with origins going back about three hundred years.

Yield: Serves 4

Ingredients
¾ cup rice flour
¼ cup glutinous rice flour
2 ¾ tbsp granulated sugar
2 tbsp sugared osmanthus
½ cup dry osmanthus

Preparation
1. Mix the rice flours and sugar well.
2. Add ⅓ cup of water; continue to mix.
3. Break up clumps in the mix thoroughly; sieve the mix several times if necessary.
4. Set the mix aside for 30 minutes.
5. Fill a pan with the mix, press and smoothen the top, and cover with cheesecloth.
6. Steam for 40 minutes.
7. After cooling, take the cake out of the pan.
8. Sprinkle dry osmanthus, then sugared osmanthus on top; serve.

Notes: There are countless recipes for this sweet treat, but the essential ingredients are rice flour, both regular and glutinous, and sugared osmanthus. Sugar is added to enhance the sweetness. If sugared osmanthus is not available, a concoction of dry osmanthus and honey can be used as a substitute. Some would make the mix with whole milk, while others like to add sesame as a topping.

There are distinct regional styles in making specialty pastries. The Yangzi Delta pastries are known for their flaky crust with heavy use of lard, while pastries in Beijing and other northern regions tend to be crunchy. Another example of regional differences is mung bean cakes. The Chinese like the taste of mung beans and claim they have special health benefits of detoxicating and reducing excessive body heat. Beijing style does not use any lard, which Yangzi Delta style does. The textures are as a result different: the latter has a smoother taste and easily melts in the mouth in contrast to the Beijing style; it is evidently not quite healthy according to modern standards!

Preserved fruits have long been used for snacking and cooking. Pickling fruits was traditionally more popular in the south, but maceration is more widely used to produce moist and flavorful candied fruits (*mi-jian*) that are enjoyed for many occasions. There are more than a dozen of major fruit processing techniques, with most mainly involve drying the sugared fruits under different conditions. The three leading producing provinces of preserved fruits are Jiangsu, Sichuan, and Zhejiang, which have long traditions of the trade. Preserved fruits from the Yangzi Delta may be the most renowned in China, featuring the pickled greengage from Hangzhou and the sugared Chinese bayberry from Suzhou. The southeast coastal regions, on the other hand, are known for their preserved tropical fruits, such as the sweet, salt, and sour dried plums from Guangdong, and dried plums cured with medicinal herbs from Fujian.

In the north, fruits are also dried so that to preserve them and to bring special flavors out of them. Dried fruits are often eaten as snacks, and a special treat is dried persimmons, which many prefer over the fresh ones. Dried haws are widely used in cooking as a tenderizing agent and in herbal medicine for improving the digestive system. Beijing claims to have the most famous candied fruits because of their supposed original court recipes and their use of a wide range of highly selective fruits. Like the specialty pastries, Beijing candied fruits are popular gifts in part because of the mystique and legends that they carry and, of course, their unique and tasty flavors.

China has a long history of making cold and icy treats. Some insist that it was the Chinese who invented the prototype of ice cream. Today, there are thousands of ice cream, ice milk, and popsicle treats, and each locale lays claims to its own specialties. They are usually not as rich as their Western counterparts, but they excel in unique and subtle flavors and textures.

Ice Cream

As early as 3,000 years ago, the Chinese started to stockpile ice for concocting cold drinks in the summer. Prototypical ice cream, a frozen dairy treat, was served in the court during the Tang Dynasty (618–907). Legend has it that Marco Polo brought a milk-based frozen confection favored by the Mongols back to Europe, which became the forerunner of what is today known as ice cream. The Chinese were left out of the modern ice cream craze, however, as dairy products became marginalized in their diet and industrial food technologies, especially refrigeration, did not reach China until recent times.

The second main category involves upscale restaurants that often make and serve their own desserts and sweet snacks at the premise. They range from steamed buns with sweet fillings to baked pancakes with layers of sweet ingredients, deep-fried sweet doughs, or puddings made with rice, tofu, or fruits. Traditional Beijing breakfast often includes a number of sweet entrées that can serve as desserts or be eaten as snacks any time of the day, including deep-fried cake (*zha-gao*) and deep-fried dough with syrup glaze (*tian you-tiao* and *tian you-bing*), donkey roll, kidney bean rolls, and *ai-wo-wo* (a steamed glutinous rice flour bun with sweet stuffing).

5.8. *Zha-gao* (Deep-Fried Cake)

This deep-fried dough is one of the three most famous snacks from Tianjin. It can be served as breakfast, a dessert after a meal, or just a treat for any time.

Yield: Serves 3–4

Ingredients
½ cup glutinous rice flour
¾ cup all-purpose wheat flour
4–5 oz. red bean paste (it can be substituted with the mix of ½ cup brown
    sugar and 1½ tbsp granulated sugar)
¾ cup hot water
Cooking oil, enough for deep fry

Preparation
1. Mix rice and wheat flours with hot water; stir with chopsticks till flours clump together.
2. Knead the flour mix into a smooth dough.

3. Coat palms with some cooking oil and knead the dough to about 1 inch thick.
4. Cut the dough into 1½ inch pieces (4–5 pieces) and divide the red bean paste (or the mix of the two types of sugar) into the same number of portions as that of the dough.
5. Flatten each dough and use it to wrap the red bean paste (or sugar mix); close, tighten and press the stuffed dough into 1-inch-thick cakes.
6. Heat enough oil to about 200 degrees Fahrenheit, slip in the cakes, and fry in medium heat until golden brown, fish out, and serve hot.

There are distinct regional differences in dessert characteristics due to differences in food traditions and available ingredients. Cantonese cuisine, for example, has contributed egg tarts and steamed egg custard buns, among many other sweet delicacies, to the Chinese dessert repertoire. One of the local favorites is the so-called "sugared water" (*tong-sui* in Cantonese), a sweet soup made by simmering rock sugar and any fruits or seeds that are considered having "cool-down" properties, such as mung beans or red beans, pear, papaya, silver or snow ears (a tree fungus), and lotus seeds. The soup is served lukewarm. The sweet and complex flavor is pleasant; the urge to consume it, however, may have more to do with its being perceived by the locals as a folk remedy for the long, hot, and humid tropical climate. *Tong-sui* is rarely available outside regions dominated by the Cantonese cuisine.

Third, China's street food may be the most innovative and popular venue for satisfying a sweet tooth. Street venders showcase their talents and skills by capitalizing on locally and seasonally available ingredients and making them into simple but uniquely enticing sweet treats that would lure endless stream of customers. Unlike pastry masters and restaurant chefs, these street vendors put their operations and products on full public display and are an intimate part of local cultures. The best of their creations have long made their way into fine dining and signature local delicacies.

5.9. Pea Paste Cake (*Wan-dou-huang*)

This was originally a street food in Beijing created during the Qing Dynasty (1644–1911) but was made famous after it was introduced to the court and became more refined in preparation and flavors. It is made of pea flours sweetened with granulated sugar. Pea paste cakes were a seasonal favorite of the spring but are now available all year round with refrigeration.

Yield: Serves 3–4

Ingredients
1 cup dry peas with skin removed
½ tsp baking powder
5½ tbsp granulated sugar

Preparation
1. Wash the peas, drain, and mix with baking powder.
2. Soak the peas in water (1 inch above the peas) for 5–6 hours.
3. Drain and wash the peas 4–5 times (to get rid of the baking powder taste).
4. Put the peas in a pot, pour in water until it is 2 inches above the peas, and boil.
5. Remove foam and turn to medium heat; continue boiling until peas start to break down.
6. Stir to help break down the peas, then sieve once to obtain a fine and thick pea batter.
7. Mix the batter with sugar and cook in low heat to yield a sticky, semi-solidified cake.
8. Place the pea cake into a tray, let cool to about 100 degrees Fahrenheit, then cover and place the tray in refrigerator for about 4 hours, slice to desirable size, and serve.

Notes: The folk recipe often used jujube or other dry fruits, but the court rendition emphasized the use of top-quality peas and sugar without any other ingredients. The essence of this treat is retaining the unique taste of peas by moderating the use of sugar, which is consistent with the Chinese preference for sweet foods.

Bing-tang-hu-lu (ice sugar coated haws on a stick) may be the most visible and beloved sweet snack in Beijing, Tianjin and several other northern cities. It is made with fresh, pitted haws strung up on a bamboo stick, then coated with caramelized sugar. The treat can only stay intact in low temperature in which the sugar can stay solidified. Traditionally, *bing-tang-hu-lu* was only available in the winter and was a signature festivity snack for the Chinese New Year. It is an extremely simple but surprisingly tasty snack that also adds a tinge of warmth to the otherwise bleak winter lull of the north.

In the north, sugared chestnuts and roast sweet potatoes are two universally coveted sweet treats in the fall and winter, mostly prepared and sold by street vendors. The Chinese began to enjoy roast chestnuts by the 12th century. Today, vendors stir-fry chestnuts in coarse sand or coarse salt to heat and cook them more evenly, then add sugar when the chestnut shells start to crack. Sugared chestnuts are ready once the nuts appear golden-brown. Roast sweet potato does not have as long a history since the tuberous root did not become a popular staple food in China until the 17th century. A tightly sealed, coal-burning portable stove, nowadays usually made from a converted oil drum, is used to roast sweet potatoes in low heat. When the sweet potatoes become softened but not burnt, they are placed on the top of the stove to be kept warm. Sugared chestnuts and roast sweet potatoes fill the chilly air with irresistible aromas in the winter, seducing thousands of passers-by to stop and satiate their taste buds.

Another street favorite is the malt sugar candy, which has a history of at least two millennia in China. While the popularity of malt sugar was first supplanted by honey and later by cane sugar, its unique flavor makes the candy a popular sweet treat known as *guan-dong-tang* ("candy from east of the pass"). It is usually made before the Chinese New Year, ostensibly to please the kitchen god, who is required to travel to heaven to report on the family's deeds. The happy deity would then be more likely to put in a good word for the family and bring back blessings for it in the new year. During the season, vendors used to walk the streets and alleyways to sell the elongated and opaque-colored candy bars coated with sesame seeds, with hordes of neighborhood kids in tow.

5.10. Tofu Pudding (*Dou-hua*)

Making tofu involves solidifying soy milk by adding a coagulant (bittern, which is more popular in the north, or gypsum) to it. The first stage of tofu-making yields a velvety curd called "tofu brain" (*dou-fu-nao*). Further solidification yields tofu pudding (*dou-hua*, "soy flower"), which is a soft curd that can be picked up with chopsticks. The two are very similar, though some soy connoisseurs would insist that tofu brain and tofu pudding are different. The bland tofu pudding is flavored with either savory or sweet sauces, and the sweet version, which is more common in the south, is a popular snack that is sometimes served as a dessert.

Yield: Serves 2

Ingredients
½ cup soybeans
⅔ tsp Glucono delta-lactone (GDL)
Toppings: syrup of choice, dry fruits, and dry nuts

Preparation
1. Soak soybeans in cold water for at least 6 hours.
2. Add 4¾ cups of water to the soybeans, and grind with a soymilk maker to make the soymilk.
3. In a large pot, bring the soymilk to a boil, then turn off the heat.
4. Sieve the soymilk with a cheesecloth to dispose of the soy pulp.
5. Cool the soy milk to about 175 degrees Fahrenheit.
6. Dissolve GDL in 2 tbsp of cold water; pour into a large bowl.
7. Quickly pour the soy milk into the bowl.
8. Cover the bowl with shrink wrap and let stand for 20 minutes.
9. Add desired toppings; serve.

Notes: GDL is found in honey and some fruit juices. As a food-grade additive, it is used as coagulant in this recipe and is available in some stores and from online retailers.

The Chinese food culture has created many sweet snacks and tidbits. These sweet foods, if served as the last course of a meal, would qualify as desserts. The missing formal course of desserts, at the same time, is rather a preference than an omission in the Chinese culinary tradition. The Chinese enjoy the sweet flavor no less than anyone else in the world, and the lack of desserts, as the West defines it, is more than made up by the variety, innovativeness, and popularity of sweet foods in the forms of snacks, appetizers, main courses and, indeed, desserts.

Further Reading

"China Launches the Festival for Time-Honored Brand to Boost Consumption." *Global Times*, May 13, 2021. https://www.globaltimes.cn/page/202105/1223334.shtml.

"Chinese Restaurants in the US—Number of Businesses 2005–2028." IBISWorld, February 24, 2022. https://www.ibisworld.com/industry-statistics/number-of-businesses/restaurants-united-states/.

Lee, Jennifer 8. "The Fortune Cookie's Origin: Solving a Riddle Wrapped in a Mystery inside a Cookie." *The New York Times*, January 6, 2008. https://www.nytimes.com/2008/01/16/travel/16iht-fortune.9260526.html.

Rude, Emelyn. "A Very Brief History of Chinese Food in America." *Time*, February 8, 2016. https://time.com/4211871/chinese-food-history/.

Williams, Caroline. "Most Popular Ethnic Cuisines in America According to Google." *Chef's Pencil*, February 26, 2020. https://www.chefspencil.com/most-popular-ethnic-cuisines-in-america/.

Yuan, Mei. *The Way of Eating: Yuan Mei's Manual of Gastronomy*. Translated by Sean J. S. Chen. Great Barrington, MA: Berkshire Publishing Group, 2019 [1792].

CHAPTER SIX

Beverages

In an ideal Chinese cosmic world, what we eat and drink, and how we consume them, should be in harmony with flow and balance of *qi*, the energy that drives the world within and without. Tea has long been the prime example of how to achieve such harmony in spirituality, medicine, and food culture. On the other hand, the Chinese have always enjoyed alcohol as much as anyone else. The Chinese are embracing all beverages, and the competition is fierce for their libations and wallets. While tea is still the national drink by tradition and affinity, they have demonstrated an insatiable craving for traditional high-proof liquor and have branched out to beverages relatively new to them, such as coffee, soft drinks, juice, and Western-styled alcoholic beverages: wine, beer, and liquor. With the rise in living standards and increase in global exposure, China is becoming a leading market and hotbed of innovations of beverages of any and all kinds.

Alcoholic Beverages

China is not one of the top countries in per capita consumption of alcoholic beverages in the world; that honor goes to Seychelles (20.5 liters), Uganda (15.5 liters), Czechia (14.4 liters) and Lithuania (13.2 liters); the United States ranked 40th in the world with a per capita alcohol consumption of 9.9 liters (The World Bank, 2018). China has been on a steep upward trajectory, however, in terms of growth in per capita alcohol consumption. In 2000, each Chinese individual 15 years and older consumed 3.8 liters of alcohol; this number almost doubled by 2018, when each Chinese 15 years and older drank 7 liters of alcohol. During the same period, per capita alcohol consumption in the United States increased only 0.7 liters (from 9.2 in 2000 to 9.9 in 2018).

Like other early civilizations, the Chinese began making and consuming alcohol at the dawn of civilization. The earliest alcoholic drinks were fermented fruit wines in prehistoric times, and manipulated fermentation allowed ancient Chinese to make alcohol from grains, called *huang-jiu* (yellow wine, because of its usual dark brown color), during the classical epoch. Rice wine reigned supreme until the Yuan Dynasty (1271–1368), when distillation technology yielded high-proof, clear liquor, referred to as *shao-dao-zi* ("burning knife") for its powerful effect, or *shao-jiu* ("burning alcohol"), which is now more often referred to as *bai-jiu* ("white liquor"). Many *bai-jiu* products reached 100–120 proof.

Traditionally, the Chinese refrained from drinking large amounts of beverages during meals due to the concern that excess liquid would weaken digestion. The exception to the rule was alcohol. The Chinese recognized that drinking alcohol on an empty stomach could induce drunkenness, and public intoxication was considered a disgrace. Social drinking usually involves the ritualistic game of finger-guessing, and the goal for the drinker-player is to stay sober and get others drunk by winning the game since the losers are required to drink their alcoholic beverage "bottom-up." Drinking alcohol at meals, therefore, is considered appropriate and even desirable because alcohol can loosen up the slightly buzzed diners, stimulate appetite, and make food taste better.

It is customary to start drinking alcohol at the beginning of a meal with appetizers, and the drinking continues with the main courses. Even when alcoholic beverages are consumed outside meals, the Chinese would have snacks and appetizers to buffer the effects of the alcohol and to delay, even avoid, getting drunk. In a short story by Lu Xun (Lu Hsun, 1881–1936), "*Kung I-Chi*" (1919), the tragic fall from grace of the protagonist Mr. Kung was in part portrayed by his not being able to afford a small serving of fennel-flavored fava beans, the standard and cheap snack for accompanying the yellow wine at the town's bar.

This does not mean that binge drinking has been uncommon in Chinese society. To the contrary, people seek to get drunk to achieve the euphoric sensation and to become uninhibited, especially during special occasions such as banquets and parties. Legends have it that ancient *literati* often searched for inspiration or escapism by getting inebriated. Li Bai (also known as Li Bo, 701–762), arguably the most famous poet in Chinese history, composed some of his best works when drunk on alcohol, including the well-known poem "Invitation to Wine."

Li Bai and his drinking buddies could take such large quantities of alcohol because they were gulping fermented rice wines and fruit (grapes and pomegranate) wines that were mostly single-digit proof. A few centuries later, during the late imperial epoch, sorghum-based, high-proof distilled liquor (*bai-jiu*) became widely available and overtook rice wines as the most popular spirit. The monopoly of Chinese liquor came under challenge during the last century from imported alcohol beverages, first beer and hard liquor, and lately wine. Today, Chinese alcohol consumption spans the spectrum of alcohol products, with clear socioeconomic, generational, and regional differences in popularity and growth.

Chinese Medicinal Liquor

A visitor may be startled to see Chinese liquor with immersed specimens, such as snakes or pilose antlers. One theory has it that the Chinese character for "medicine" derives from the character "alcohol" (*jiu*). The belief in alcohol's medicinal benefits inspired the Chinese to concoct elixirs by using liquor to dissolve the mythical properties of selected specimens. Each elixir targets specific health problems, for example, ginseng liquor for reinvigorating primordial energy and tiger bone liquor for rheumatism and arthritis. The continued popularity of medicinal liquor has to do with the animist belief that humans can acquire the desired qualities from wildlife by consuming them.

Traditional Chinese hard liquors, *bai-jiu*, are still the most popular alcohol beverage with many varieties and thousands of brands. Sorghum is the most important raw grain, though rice, wheat, millet, and other grains are also used. The dry fermentation starters, called *qu*, are mostly derived from wheat, barley, and peas. Experts have identified at least 12 aroma or flavor profiles for Chinese hard liquor, but three of them are most important in terms of the consumed volume and reputation ("Bai-ology"): the "sauce" aroma variety including the high-profile Chinese liquor *Mao-tai* (*Moutai*) from Guizhou Province, which is often served at state banquets; the "strong" aroma variety including famous brands such as *Wu-liang-ye* ("five grains liquor") and *Luzhou* from Sichuan Province; and the "light" aroma variety represented by *Fen* from Shanxi Province. The most famous of them can command a small fortune on the market, such as *Mao-tai* or *Wu-liang-ye*, thanks to both traditional reputation and market promotion. Taste, aroma, and quality vary, due to both crafting techniques and, as many connoisseurs insist, special properties in local water sources. Liquor can be served for any occasion, from daily family meals to state banquets, to which President Nixon and some of his successors would attest. Chinese hard liquor is rarely consumed straight; as a matter of fact, the

Chinese believe that drinking hard liquor straight is harmful to health, and liquor and food can complement each other.

Yellow wine, a rice-based alcohol beverage, dominated the drinking scene for centuries before it was upstaged by hard liquor. Today, it remains a popular alcohol beverage only in certain regions, such as the Yangzi Delta. The town's bar in *"Kung I-Chi,"* the aforementioned short story by Lu Xun, served only yellow wine. It can be served at room temperature, but purists prefer to have it warmed first, a custom that is reminiscent of the way some Japanese *sakes* are served. Much more common today, yellow wine is used as an essential seasoning in cooking meat and seafood. It is also used for concocting medicinal alcohol beverages.

European-style beer arrived in China in the early 20th century as Western colonial influence began to expand in China. Harbin Brewery, founded by a Pole from the Russian Empire in 1900, is the oldest beer brewery still in operation today. Tsingtao Brewery was founded in 1903 in Qingdao (Tsingtao), then a German colony. Tsingtao, a German-styled pale lager, has become the national beer and the best-known Chinese beer outside China. Beer became popular among city folks in the 1970s but was limited in supply and often not chilled due to lack of refrigeration. Beer production, variety, and consumption in China have skyrocketed during the reform era, and it is the favorite alcohol beverage for the younger generations. According to 2021 data, people under 40 consumed nearly 80% of beer in China. Beer is the top drink in clubs and bars, and in the summer; it is also commonly served at meals.

China is undergoing a sea-change in alcohol consumption. While hard liquor (*bai-jiu*) and beer remain most popular, wine is in vogue in recent years, especially among younger, well-off professionals under the age of 40 who, in 2021, consumed about 70% of all imported alcohol beverages, mostly wine. The so-called first-tier cities, that is, the 19 largest and wealthiest urban centers including Shanghai, Beijing, Shenzhen, and Guangzhou, alone consumed 55% of imported alcohol. In the early years of economic reform, Western hard liquors took up the lion's share of imported alcohol beverages, and drinking Remy Martin or Johnnie Walker Blue Label was a way to embellish one's socioeconomic status; in recent years, however, demand for wine has grown dramatically, making China the sixth largest wine market in the world with great potential to move up the ranking further. Both domestic viticulture (Shirouzu, 2021) and foreign imports have seen great growth. Some analysts have even projected that China would become the largest wine market by 2027 (García-Cortijo, 2019). The young, educated, and affluent are the vanguards in driving the new trend. Imported hard liquor and mixed drinks, however, are not as popular in China, perhaps because they do not pair well with any kind of food. They are mostly available in clubs, bars, and other trendy social venues frequented by internationals.

Tea

Tea, everyone knows, is the classic Chinese beverage. Indeed, tea (*Camellia sinensis*), a species of the *Theaceae* family, represents the Chinese civilization as silk and the Chinese writing scripts do. Tea is served in great variety and quality, from the minimally processed green tea to the fermented "tea bricks," and from *da-hong-pao* ("big red robe," a type of semi-oxidized Oolong tea) that can sell for half a million U.S. dollars per pound to the harsh, bitter tea served "free" at restaurants. To the Chinese, tea is the number-one beverage of choice to drink by itself and to pair with meals.

It is interesting that the British adopted the pronunciation *tea*, which was how the plant was called in the southern *Min* dialect in Fujian and Taiwan. The much more common name for the plant and the beverage is *cha*, which is the pronunciation of the Chinese character in Mandarin and most other Chinese regional dialects, including Cantonese. Some suspect Dutch influence on the British since the Dutch once dominated trade in East Asia, especially along the coast of Fujian and Taiwan, where the southern Min dialect was the *lingua franca* (Sonnad, 2018).

Tea was first domesticated in areas that include today's Yunnan Province, Tibet, northern Myanmar, and northeast India (Drew, 2019). Tea consumption had long existed in the Sichuan Basin and began to spread after the vassal state *Qin* annexed the region during the 4th century BCE. Tea drinking was still limited to the court and certain regions in southern China until the 4th century CE, when it became a popular daily drink. Tea consumption reached a new height in popularity and sophistication during the Tang Dynasty (618–907) throughout China, as reflected in the encyclopedic *The Classic of Tea* (*Cha-jing*, c. 760–780) compiled by Lu Yu (733–804), who is regarded as the Sage of Tea. In Lu's time, boiling (*jian*) was the main form of tea-making, which is similar to today's Japanese *sencha*, and tea leaves were dried and pressed into tea cakes for the convenience of preservation and trade. Loose tea leaves were rarely used until the Ming Dynasty (1368–1644), when brewing (*pao*) became the prevailing form of preparing for tea to this day. Tea cakes, or tea bricks, are still popular in nomadic areas such as Tibet, Xinjiang, and Mongolia.

Early consumption of tea was mainly in the elite circles, which might have contributed to the elaborate rituals of tea-making comparable to those of wine and coffee. Tea *aficionados* would zoom in on every detail, from the so-called *terroir* (the comprehensive growing environment) for tea plantations to the exquisite drinkware, from the best time of the day to pick the tea sprouts to the superior sources of water. In addition to the tea itself, water may be the most crucial ingredient, or "the mother of tea," for brewing the best tea. Spring water was considered superior, and it took none other than Lu Yu, the sagely tea master, to present the earliest rating of the top 20 springs as sources for making superior tea. The refinement, or snobbery, seems to have no limit for the tea connoisseurs. In one of the greatest Chinese literary classics, *Hong-lou-meng* ("Dream of the Red Mansion"), a young lady brewed tea for her best friends with melted snow water that she collected from the flower petals of Chinese plum (*Prunus mume*) and preserved in an urn buried underground.

6.1. Dragon Well Tea (*Long-jing-cha*)

This recipe shows how to brew the best-known green tea in China; it has three variations based on ways of handling hot water and tea input.

Yield: Serves 1

Ingredients
1 tsp *Longjing* ("Dragon Well Tea")
Hot water

Preparation
1. Prepare a glass with about 7 fl. oz. capacity.
2. Heat water to about 185 degrees Fahrenheit ("hot water").
3. Three ways of brewing:
   (1) Fill the glass with hot water, then put tea leaves in. The tea is ready for drinking when the tea leaves start to float up and down and the water becomes green.
   (2) Fill the glass to ⅓ full of hot water, put in the tea leaves, and shake the glass in slow circular motion a few times. When tea leaves are fully extended, fill the glass with hot water and serve.
   (3) Put tea leaves into the glass, pour enough hot water to submerge the tea leaves, and shake the glass in circular motion; as the tea leaves become extended, pour in hot water to fill the glass, and serve when the tea leaves become fully extended and start to float up and down.

Notes: Do not use boiling water (212 degrees Fahrenheit) to brew green tea. The unfermented and fragile green tea gets "cooked" in boiling water and produces a tannic and bitter taste. The desirable water temperature is between 176 and 194 degrees Fahrenheit (80–90 degrees Celsius). The optimum brewing time is about 15 seconds for the first time, and 3–5 seconds longer each subsequent time. Hot water can be added when there is about 30% of tea left in the glass; the same batch of *Longjing* tea leaves can be used for brewing for up to three times, and each time the water temperature can be slightly higher (5–9 degrees Fahrenheit). If the brewed tea does not appear to be clean, dump it and then add fresh hot water; this practice is called "washing the tea," which is used only when the tea leaves have impurities.

Originally, tea was a stand-alone beverage that was not paired with food. As tea became a common beverage, however, people began to drink it to quench thirst, help ingest food, and gain a boost of energy. Tea drinking began to show great disparity between those who could afford leisure and those who had to hustle and rustle. While the elites enjoyed artisan teas with the finest drinkware and ostentatious rituals, the masses were content with drinking tea as an upgrade from plain water, whatever they could afford and whenever they could take a break. Today, the disparity is still apparent, reflecting deepening socioeconomic gaps in China.

The diverse natural environment allows China to grow many different tea cultivars, and different regions have developed special processing techniques. The result is a tea culture that thrives on great variety based on environment, tradition, and seasonality. There are six classes of tea in China based on methods and extent of processing: green, yellow, white, Oolong, black, and fermented. Among them, green, Oolong, and fermented teas have the highest production and are the most widely consumed.

Green tea is made by briskly stir-mixing the freshly picked tea leaves and buds from the tea plant (*Camellia sinensis*) in heating vessels. The entire harvesting and processing is still done manually since the tea masters need to detect the desiccation level of the tea precisely. Green tea usually has a short shelf life (6–12 months) for retention of quality. Yellow tea can be considered a special type of green tea, and its production and consumption are limited. White tea may be even less processed than the green tea.

Among hundreds of green tea varietals, the most famous include *Longjing* ("Dragon Well"), the best known Chinese green tea, from Hangzhou, Zhejiang Province; *Bi-luo-chun* from the Yangzi Delta in Jiangsu;

Liu-an Gua-pian ("Lu'an Melon Seed"); *Huang-shan Mao-feng* and *Tai-ping Hou-kui* from Anhui; and *Xin-yang Mao-jian* from Henan province. Green teas from Sichuan Basin are also very well known, which present slightly stronger tannin and bitterness, to the delight of some tea connoisseurs.

Oolong ("dark dragon") is a type of semi-oxidized tea. The processing takes the steps of sun-withering and blanching, then drying by heat. Oolong production concentrates in Fujian and Guangdong provinces, and Oolong tea is more popular in southeastern China and in the Chinese diaspora, which was traditionally dominated by people who trace their ancestries to Fujian and Guangdong. Fujian is by far the leading producer of the best Oolong teas because of its unique *terroir*, especially the rocky cliffs of the Wuyi Mountains. The Oolong made with leaves from Wuyi varietals are referred to as "rocky teas" or "cliff teas," the most famous of which include *Da-hong-pao* ("Big Red Robe"), *Tie-luo-han* ("Iron Arhat"), and *Rou-gui* ("Cassia"). *Tie-guan-yin* ("Iron Goddess of Mercy") is the most famous in southern Fujian. The black tea, which the Chinese call "red tea," is more oxidized and is made with the Chinese varietal *C. sinensis var. sinensis* and is similar to black tea made from *C. sinensis var. assamica*. Black tea is not as popular in China, where most people prefer Oolong if they want to have some strong-flavored tea. Oolong is the tea for the Fujianese and Cantonese to enjoy their ritualistic *Kung-fu Tea* ("making tea with skills").

Fermented tea is the most processed type of tea, which can take months or years to make. It was invented in the southwest for long-term storage in a warm and humid environment, and for long-distance trade along the fabled "Tea and Horse Caravan Trail," an ancient trade route connecting tropical southern Yunnan province to Tibet and continental Southeast and South Asia. The most famous fermented teas are *Pu-erh* from Yunnan and the Tibetan brick tea. They can be stored for a long time; as a matter of legend, it is claimed that the longer the fermented tea stays in proper storage, the better in flavor and health benefits it would attain. *Pu-erh* became an extremely hot commodity around 2006, when a number of factors, including small investors escaping the stock market, commercial promotion, and short supply, generated a rush to buy and collect *Pu-erh*. During the "*Pu-erh* Rush," the bird-nest-shaped tea blocks became the most craved collector's item with skyrocketing prices. The hype was short-lived, however. The next year the *Pu-erh* market crashed, though the tea itself is still valuable and beloved by many.

Appreciation of tea requires focusing on the entire process of tea-making, from acquisition to preparation, and then to consumption. "The *Dao* (*Tao*) of Tea," the Chinese tea ceremony initiated by the intelligentsia, is both ritualistic and spiritual. Tea became affordable and widespread in the last several centuries and became a casual beverage that increasingly accompanied meals. Although the basic procedures of making and drinking tea remain intact, the ritualistic Chinese tea ceremony began to fade away in the 20th century. It is undergoing a renaissance in recent years, however, and is becoming popular again (Zuo, 2022). It is regularly performed at wedding ceremonies and during New Year's celebrations; it is also staged at commercial and tourist venues, such as classic Sichuan tea houses. Zen tea ceremonies are held at some large monasteries, while locals in Guangdong continue to enjoy traditional and authentic rituals of *Kung-fu Tea*.

6.2. Chrysanthemum Pear Tea (*Xue-li-ju-hua-cha*)

This simple concoction is said to help the liver and the eyesight (which Chinese medicine considers related), and "to improve oxygen absorption by the skin." It has no *tea* in it but should taste good and be rich in vitamins based on the ingredients. The Chinese use only the dried whole flowers of chrysanthemum for making beverages. Also, the Chinese prefer Asian pear (*Pyrus pyrifolia*) or Chinese white pear (*Pyrus bretschneideri*), though any pear should do.

Yield: Serves 2–3

Ingredients
1 pear
1 large chrysanthemum or 10 *hang-bai-ju* (*Chrysanthemum morifolium*—the most popular varietal for making chrysanthemum tea in China)
3½ tbsp goji berries
Rock sugar, as desired

Preparation
1. Scalp the chrysanthemum in boiling water; wash the goji berries.
2. Skin and pit the pear, then cut it into eight slices.
3. Put pear and rock sugar in a pot, add water, cover, and heat for 10 minutes after it comes to a boil.
4. Add chrysanthemum and goji berries and boil covered for 5 more minutes; serve hot, warm, or cooled.

Notes: The use of rock sugar is optional.

While any type of tea can be consumed anywhere, there is a regional pattern of preference. Among the six types of Chinese tea, green tea may be the most widely consumed throughout China and is traditionally the exclusive choice in the Yangzi Delta. It preserves the most refreshing and intricate palate of fresh tea leaves with minimal processing and is best to drink within the first year of production. Green tea is also used for some of the most elaborate forms of Chinese tea ceremonies. Oolong tea is a favorite in southeastern coastal regions, and its popularity is growing in other parts of the country and overseas.

For the tea purists, teamaking should require only two ingredients, the tea leaves and the water, but each should possess highest possible quality. Through time and in different places, however, other ingredients have been added to the tea. In northern China, especially in and around Beijing, for example, many locals enjoy tea infused with jasmine flavor, or the jasmine tea (*Mo-li Hua-cha*), a scented tea that southern Chinese and tea connoisseurs would shun. There are also beverages that are called "tea," which include any kind of herbal drink. Chrysanthemum (dry flowers), *goji* (berries of *Lycium chinense* or *Lycium barbarum*), and rose (dry flower buds) teas are but some of the most well-known and popular examples.

While each tea enthusiast would insist that his or her way of teamaking is superior, the reality is that most tea-brewing techniques are fundamentally similar, notwithstanding the specific takes that each recipe would bring about to the art of teamaking. Formal tea brewing requires specialized ceramic utensils to achieve the superior brew, but most people may not be able to tell the exquisite difference between tea made in the finest china or in glassware. Tea brewing must not use metal, paper, or plastic utensils since they may interfere with the pure tea flavor.

6.3. Mint Lemon Tea (*Bo-he-ning-meng-cha*)

This version of mint lemon tea is a version of the American classic with a Chinese twist.

Yield: Serves 2–3

Ingredients
1 lemon
1 tbsp goji berries
1 tbsp rock sugar
Fresh mint leaves

Preparation
1. Wash goji berries and mint leaves.
2. Rub salt on the surface of the lemon, then slice it into 6–7 thin pieces.
3. Put lemon slices, goji berries, and mint leaves into glasses (2–3 slices of lemon per glass).
4. Fill the glasses with boiling hot water.
5. Add rock sugar, if desired.
6. Cool and serve.

In the early history of tea drinking, salt, milk, and other ingredients were often brewed with the tea or added to the tea. These ingredients remain essential to teas in nomadic areas. Lightly salted milk tea, made with tea from "tea bricks" and sheep milk, or yak milk in Tibet, has been the favorite beverage of nomadic peoples for ages, providing life's sustenance not just to quench thirst but to bring warmth, energy, and nutrition.

The Chinese love tea, which plays a vital role in their lives no matter what kind. In the late 1970s, when China inaugurated its economic reform, the first private entrepreneurs in Beijing were those who sold "big bowl tea" in the street. The street vendors who sold cheap, low-quality tea in large porcelain bowls near Tiananmen Square became a pop culture sensation and tourist attraction of a changing time (Gosset, 2014). Today, tea drinking may be more associated with older adults, as the young and the kids may opt for the dizzying array of soft drinks, and professionals and urbanites go after coffee. But tea's place is deeply ingrained in the Chinese psyche, which has led to a boom of tea-flavored beverages, especially boba tea, which appear to be an effort of bridging the old and the new, the traditional and the modern.

Water

Edgar Snow, an American journalist, visited *Yan-an*, the *de facto* capital of the Communist-controlled areas in the mid 1930s, and was treated with a banquet. At the bumper meal, he noticed that only hot water was served. He not only asked for cold water, to the bewilderment of his hosts, but also speculated on the reasons for the seeming obsession of the Chinese with hot water (Snow, 1968). There are a number of theories and myths about this uniquely Chinese habit. Some point to the Chinese belief that cold drinks and hot food clash in the digestive system and thus should not be mixed, while others believe that hot water can better quench thirst, perhaps because it takes longer to drink the same quantity of liquid when it is hot, thence allowing the body to retain more water. Some hypothesize that the Chinese preference for drinking hot water had to do with the tea culture. The fact, however, is that drinking hot water was not a common practice, other than when making tea, during ancient times since boiling water was a luxury because most common folks could not afford the fuel. We may, therefore, deduce that the preference for hot water might have been a fad rather than a health-based preference.

The benefits of hot water gained a new myth in the mid-19th century. In 1862, a cholera outbreak in Shanghai spread to other parts of China but appeared to transmit faster in the north. Some assumed that this had to do with the southerners being more accustomed to drinking hot water, which somehow helped them ward off the extremely infectious disease. In modern times, public campaigns were launched to promote boiling water as a coping strategy to reduce harmful bacteria and to avoid foodborne epidemics, which may have furthered the myth of hot water's benefits.

Cold Drinks and Meals

The dialectic relationship of *yin* and *yang* transcends every facet of the Chinese culture, including its foodways. Cold (*yin*) and hot (*yang*) foods and drinks should not be consumed concurrently, due to their inter-inhibitive properties. Today, however, many Chinese, especially the young, carefreely consume cold beer, icy Coca-Cola, and other chilled beverages during hot meals.

Hot water remains the preference for those who want to use water as the beverage when eating. Its availability also meets a specific purpose since many prefer to make their own tea. Once upon a time, the thermos was a fixture in households and public places alike and an ever-popular wedding gift. It is quickly becoming a relic, however, with the ease of obtaining hot water from portable electric heaters or microwaves. The obsession with hot water due to perceived health reasons may also be waning, as the surging popularity of bottled water and soft drinks may have lessened hygienic concerns for people.

Soft Drinks

The Chinese love juice and have long made all kinds of juice using their local and regional fruits, vegetables, herbs, and grains. Fruit juice is a favorite beverage in China. Traditionally, fruit drinks were freshly made using seasonal fruits, sometimes vegetables, in small batches for home consumption or quick sales; the south, with abundant but highly perishable fresh fruits and vegetables, was known to have great variety of fruit juice. Modern food technology has made juice available and affordable, and there are numerous national brands as well as many regional specialty drinks, such as carrot juice from Xinjiang, sugar cane, kumquat or lychee juice from Fujian, haw juice from Hebei, apple juice from Shandong, and orange juice from Chongqing.

6.4. Osmanthus Plum Juice (*Gui-hua-wu-mei-zhi*)

Yield: Serves 7–8

Ingredients
3½ cups smoked plum (*Prunus mume*)
3½ cups dry hawthorn
2¼ cups dry osmanthus
2¼ cups licorice (*Glycyrrhiza uralensis Fisch.*)
Rock or brown sugar, as desired

Preparation
1. Soak the dry plums and hawthorn until they expand close to their fresh sizes.
2. Wrap all ingredients (excluding sugar) with cheesecloth.
3. Place the wrapped ingredients in a large pot filled with water; heat to boil.
4. Put in desired amount of sugar.
5. Cover and simmer for 2–3 hours until water reduces by about half.
6. Cool and serve.

Notes: Smoked plums may be available in Asian herbal medicine shops. Simmer longer and reduce water further to obtain a stronger flavor. Refrigerate leftover juice to prevent spoiling.

Modern, Western-styled soft drinks, characterized by their carbonation, were first brought to China by the Dutch traders in the 19th century. It was a mint or lemon flavored, carbonated soft drink that was appropriately called "Dutch beverage," which became particularly popular in large cities in the summer. The high profitability of these new drinks spurred local competition, which gave rise to several soda brands at specific locales in the 20th century, including *Bei-bing-yang* ("the Arctic"), a citrus-flavored soda from Beijing (1936), that competed against each other and the emerging global brands such as Coca-Cola. The latter withdrew from China after the Communists took over the mainland in 1949, after which the Chinese soft drinks remained mostly local and regional, nevertheless leaving enduring memories for those who came to age during this time.

Reform since the late 1970s have brought back American soft drink giants Coca-Cola and Pepsi Cola. Most Chinese were not used to the flavors of these foreign drinks at the beginning, claiming they tasted like herbal medicine or cough syrups. These strange-tasting bubbly drinks eventually gained popularity, in part because of their reputation as American pop culture icons, and in part because of their addictive potency.

As soft drinks from Taiwan and Hong Kong swept across the land, traditional mainland brands also joined the fray in the competitive marketplace. Interestingly, many Chinese soft drinks came back to life but have largely remained regional. Travelling through China, one would encounter numerous unique local soft drinks. International brands such as Coca-Cola and Pepsi Cola take the lion's share, about 80%, of the more than US$100 billion market sales, in part because of the popularity of American fast-food chains where Coca-Cola and Pepsi Cola are exclusive suppliers of beverages. Chinese brands, meanwhile, have turned to public financing and mass production to compete for a larger market share. *Nong-fu Shan-quan* (Farmer's Spring), *Kang-shi-fu* (Master Kang), *Wang-lao-ji* (*Wong Lo Kat* in Cantonese), and *Wa-ha-ha* are among the top Chinese soft drink producers that distribute nationally.

Soft drinks flavored with milk, cream, tea, or coffee have become extremely trendy in China, especially with the youth demographics. Boba milk tea, a concoction of tea, tapioca balls, and condensed milk, has gained enormous popularity among young people in mainland China since it was invented in Taiwan in the early 1980s.

Coffee

Coffee did not reach China until around the time of the first Opium War (1839–1842). It remained a beverage mostly for Western expatriates and a few Chinese elites. Legend has it that a French priest in Yunnan planted the first coffee plant at the beginning of the 20th century to satiate his personal thirst for the aromatic and bitter-tasting beverage.

Coffee consumption remained minimal until well into the reform era. Coffee's image as an exotic and bitter beverage did not win it many converts at first. By the late 1980s, improved living standards and exposure to Western lifestyles prompted more and more young Chinese to try coffee, and an all-out media campaign by Nestlé made a breakthrough in the Chinese market for its instant coffee.

In 1999, Starbucks opened its first outlets in mainland China. It did not fare well for the first 10 years mainly because it was too expensive even for the young, white-color professionals. The lifestyle imagery that Starbucks sells, however, must have impressed potential Chinese customers. In the aftermath of the 2007–2008 financial crisis, the enriched and expanding professional middle class made a dash for the bitter brew that bore the halo of Americana. In the ensuing years, one new Starbucks outlet was opened every 15 hours in China! In 2021, there were 5,400 Starbucks in China with US$905 million total revenue and 17 million members. On September 26, 2022, the company opened its 6,000th coffee shop in China and has presence in 240 Chinese cities. Starbucks has set its sights on opening 3,000 more shops in China by 2025.

6.5. Matcha Latte (*Mo-cha Na-tie*)

Mixed nonalcoholic drinks have become very popular among the Chinese youth, and this recipe, inspired by Starbucks, is easy to make and sure to please.

Yield: Serves 2

Ingredients
3 tsp (green tea) matcha powder
1 cup milk
1 tbsp condensed milk
Ice cubes, as desired
2 tbsp hot water
Whipped cream, for topping
Fresh mint, for garnish

Preparation
1. Pour matcha powder into a bowl, add hot water, and mix until the powder dissolves completely.
2. Mix milk and condensed milk; heat in microwave for 1 minute (approximately 140 degrees).
3. Gradually add matcha solution into milk while mixing them well.
4. Put ice cubes into glasses, pour in the mix, top with whip cream and mint leaves; serve.

Notes: Whipped cream is optional, especially if whole milk is used.

The lucrative coffee market has attracted many competitors, both international and domestic, but Starbucks had never encountered real challengers until Luckin, a Chinese enterprise, jumped into the fray. In 2019, it announced that it aimed to overtake Starbucks and become the number one coffee brand in China. Accounting scandals and temporary delisting from Nasdaq in 2020 appeared to doom the company, but it somehow survived and ended up with more than 6,000 shops by the end of 2021, surpassing Starbucks. With its first outlet opened in 2017, Luckin took advantage of the coffee craze and adopted a most aggressive corporate strategy to expand, including providing new members the first cup of freshly ground coffee for free. Luckin invests heavily in R&D to develop new products that suit the Chinese palate and provides a long list of new coffee drinks that are sweetened and flavored, such as its coconut-flavored latte.

It is estimated that there are more than 300 million regular coffee drinkers in China, with a gross market revenue about US$60 billion in 2021; some have projected the Chinese market would reach a revenue of US$160 billion by 2025. While instant coffee continues to count for 90% of China's coffee sales, the future seems to point to freshly ground coffee and coffee-flavored drinks that the young generations enjoy both as a beverage and as a medium for socialization, just like boba milk tea has become.

Other Beverages

For millennia the Chinese had limited choices of beverages. Similar to its historical peers, China's alcohol production and consumption accompanied its dawn of civilization with fermented fruit wines. Beyond alcohol beverages, tea has reigned supreme in China in the last 1,500 years, evolving from an exclusive beverage into the national drink that spans in quality and rituals as widely as the society itself. Hot water and soups also served as beverages, either independently or with meals. It is fascinating to see how the Chinese culture has transformed in terms of beverage preference and consumption during the four decades of economic reform. Driven by globalization and dramatically improved living standards, the Chinese have enriched their beverage experience with new and continuously updating alcohol and soft drink beverages. Tea is still the national drink that older adults cling to, while coffee continues to gain popularity among the young. Bottled water has become the affordable and convenient, and for the most part, safer source of water. It is mixed soft drinks, however, that may be poised to make gains in an enormous and competitive market.

6.6. Job's Tears Haw Juice (*Yi-ren-shan-zha-zhi*)

The Chinese consider "Job's tears" (*Coix lacryma-jobi*), also known as adlay millet, as possessing the property of reducing dampness in the body. In the same vein, they believe dry haws capable of improving digestion, and sun-dried mandarin orange peels of coalescing these properties. This beverage combines these three ingredients and is representative of how the Chinese enjoy beverages that have purported health benefits even if they may not taste the most pleasant.

Yield: Serves 4–6

Ingredients
½ cup dry haws
3 oz. Job's tears
2 pieces of dry mandarin orange peels

Preparation
1. Wash the ingredients clean and soak them in 10 cups of cold water.
2. Boil for two hours.
3. Add some rock sugar shortly before removing from heat source.
4. Cool to room temperature and serve.

Notes: Refrain from this beverage if having stomach acid reflux problems; while this beverage helps digestion, it may cause diarrhea to those who have a weak digestive system.

Further Reading

"Bai-ology." *Drink Baijiu.* https://drinkbaijiu.com/bai-ology/ (accessed November 5, 2022).

Drew, Liam. "The Growth of Tea." *Nature* 566 (2019): S2–S4. https://doi .org/10.1038/d41586-019-00395-4.

García-Cortijo, María, Emiliano Villanueva, Juan Castillo, and Yuanbo Li. "Wine Consumption in China: Profiling the 21st Century Chinese Wine Consumer." *Ciência e Técnica Vitivinícola* 34 (2019): 71–83. https://doi.org/10.1051 /ctv/20193402071.

Gosset, David. "The Revival of Chinese Tea." *China Daily Europe,* May 2, 2014. http:// www.chinadaily.com.cn/a/201405/02/WS5a2a3378a3101a51ddf8f677 .html.

Lu, Xun. "Kung I-Chi." *Selected Stories of Lu Hsun.* Beijing: Foreign Languages Press, 1960, 1972. http://www.coldbacon.com/writing/luxun-calltoarms.html#Kung.

Shirouzu, Norihiko. "Red China: Up-and-Coming Wineries Gain Recognition." *Reuters,* November 2, 2021. https://www.reuters.com/world/china/red-china -up-and-coming-wineries-gain-recognition-2021-11-02/.

Snow, Edgar. *Red Star Over China.* "Part Two: The Road to the Red Capital." New York: Grove Press, 1968.

Sonnad, Nikhil. "Tea if by Sea, Cha if by Land: Why the World Only Has Two Words for Tea." *Quartz,* January 11, 2018. https://qz.com/1176962 /map-how-the-word-tea-spread-over-land-and-sea-to-conquer-the-world.

"The 2007 Pu erh Tea Market Crash: The Boom and Bust Revisited." *Teasenz,* May 17, 2017. https://www.teasenz.com/chinese-tea/2007-pu-erh-tea-market -crash-boom-bust-crisis-recession.html.

The World Bank. "Total Alcohol Consumption Per Capita (Liters of Pure Alcohol, Projected Estimates, 15+ Years of Age)." *The World Bank Open Data,* 2018. https://data.worldbank.org/indicator/SH.ALC.PCAP.LI?end=2018&most _recent_value_desc=true&start=2000&view=chart.

Zuo, Mandy. "Hit TV Show Brings Back Forgotten Ancient Chinese Ceremony Involving Intricate Calligraphy and Patterns in Whipped Tea." *South China Morning Post,* June 19, 2022. https://www.scmp.com/news/people -culture/trending-china/article/3182152/hit-tv-show-brings-back -forgotten-ancient.

CHAPTER SEVEN

Holidays and Special Occasions

Holidays and special occasions are often associated with rituals that reinforce shared identity and renew ties among families, social networks, and communities. Food featuring special ingredients and dishes is often the centerpiece of festivities and, therefore, provides the best window to appreciate the holidays and special occasions. In the United States, for example, turkey is the signature ingredient of various recipes for Thanksgiving and corned beef is the special food for St. Patrick's Day, a holiday celebrating the Irish heritage.

The Chinese pay great attention to holidays and special occasions, and the celebration is always centered on food. The Chinese pair each holiday with food items that are specific for the occasion either in seasonality or in cultural significance, such as *yue-bing* (moon cake), a special pastry, for the Mid-Autumn Festival ("Moon Festival"). Foods for special occasions have regional variations, and different regions may have different foods for the same national holidays or special occasions. One ongoing debate among Chinese netizens is whether *jiaozi* (Chinese stuffed dumplings) should be regarded as the national dish for the Chinese New Year. Many southern Chinese insist that, first, their New Year's dinner does not feature *jiaozi*, and second, the classic favorite is a northern Chinese dish that is neither special nor particularly tasty to many in the south.

There are two types of holidays in China, namely those that are steeped in tradition and history and those that honor modern social and political events. The former are usually associated with seasonal and agricultural cycles and are more fastidious with specific dishes, reflecting the deep cultural roots in nature worship, food insecurity, and close-knit community, all of which are attributable to the Chinese sedentary subsistence agriculture.

Special occasions are ritualistic ceremonies that bring people together to start or reaffirm their relationships with each other or with their environment. Weddings are a prime example of a universally celebrated special occasion, but in China there are many others. Traditional cultures tend to have many rituals featuring communal feasts and special dishes.

Cultural and social holidays change with time. Some of the traditional holidays began to fade away in modern times; others, however, are still being celebrated and even become sanctioned by the government. Today, there are seven officially designated national holidays, each with paid time off (Chinese Language Institute, 2022). There are other holidays that grant half a day to one day off as a holiday to certain groups of the population, such as International Women's Day (March 8, half a day) and International Children's Day (June 1, one day). Ethnic minorities enjoy holidays specific to their cultures and traditions, such as the three-day celebration of *Eid al-Adha*, one of the most important holidays in Islam, in Xinjiang where Muslims are the majority.

Among the seven national holidays, New Year's Day, May Day, and the National Day are modern and imported holidays. The other four, in contrast, are rooted in cultural and historical heritage and are celebrated with specific dining rituals and distinct foods, including the Spring Festival (*Chun-jie*, the Chinese New Year), *Qing-ming-jie* (Bright Light Festival), *Duan-wu-jie* (Dragon Boat Festival), and *Zhong-qiu-jie* (Mid-Autumn Festival). Food and dining for each of them are centerpieces of celebration.

The Spring Festival (*Chun-jie*; the Chinese New Year)

The Spring Festival is China's most important traditional holiday, which generally falls between late January and mid-February of the Western (Gregorian) calendar. It marks the beginning of a new year on the Chinese agricultural calendar. Today, the Spring Festival entails a weeklong official holiday, starting on New Year's Eve and including three official holidays, one two-day weekend, and two more paid days off that are to be swapped with two weekend days. Traditional celebrations, however, start on the 23rd (northern China) or 24th day of December on the agricultural calendar (it is not a lunar calendar) and continue for about two weeks. Before the New Year's Day, folks would conduct house cleaning and present offerings to the kitchen god (Newman, 2018). A special treat for this occasion is *guan-dong-tang*, a malt candy, which is meant to enamor the god of family's fire hearth who is on his way to heaven to report on the deeds of the family during the past year. Of course, most likely the kids eat the candy while adults are busy shopping for special food ingredients in preparation of the most important meals of the year.

7.1. Braised Pork Ball in Brown Sauce, Yangzhou Style (*Hong-shao Shi-zi-tou*)

This is arguably one of the best-known dishes from the Huai-Yang cuisine. Dubbed as "lion's heads," the large and succulent pork balls can be steamed or braised. Some believe that this dish had already become one of the four signature dishes of the Yangzhou cuisine by the 6th century, when the city thrived on its location at the intersection of the Yangzi River and the Grand Canal. The recipe is a braised version and requires some rare and expensive ingredients. It is a fitting entrée for a bumper family holiday dinner.

Yield: Serves 4

Ingredients
½ lb. pork tenderloin
½ lb. pork belly (side pork)
3.5 oz. pork rib meat
1 egg white
1 fresh lotus root (red lotus preferred)
1 tbsp freshwater crab roe
2 tbsp freshwater crab meat
½ tbsp shrimp roe
2 oz. bok choy heart
1 cup cooking oil
Seasonings and spices to taste: rice (yellow) cooking wine, MSG, salt, cane sugar, Zhenjiang (black) vinegar, soy sauce, dark soy sauce, scallion, ginger, star anise (4–5), corn starch (1 tbsp)

Preparation
1. Grate the lotus root and set aside.
2. Scald the bok choy heart in boiling water until it softens, set aside.
3. Mince the pork into the size of rice; put the minced pork in a large mixing bowl.
4. Add grated lotus root, mix in a clockwise circular motion.
5. Add minced scallion, ginger, soy sauce, salt, sugar (1 tbsp), egg white, cooking wine, and starch, continue to mix in clockwise direction.
6. Add crab and shrimp roes, and crab meat, continue to mix in clockwise direction.
7. Add 7–8 drops of vinegar to the mix, continue to mix till the mixture becomes "gooey."
8. Use the mix to make four large meat balls.
9. Heat cooking oil in a wok to 250 to 350 degrees Fahrenheit, then fry the meat balls.

10. Take the meat balls out when their surface becomes light golden; drain oil.
11. Put meat balls, star anise, MSG, dark soy sauce, and ⅓ tbsp sugar in a pot with 4 cups of water and bring to a boil.
12. Turn heat to low, simmer until liquid appears to be reducing, then take the meat balls out.
13. Dissolved ½ tsp starch with water and add it to the pot to thicken the liquid and make a gravy.
14. Put the meat balls in a deep plate lined with the bok choy heart, top with gravy; serve.

Notes: This recipe is created based on the advice from Ms. Xiaojian Fang, a native of Yangzhou and a terrific cook. The steamed version of this recipe merely calls for skipping steps 9 and 10.

Hundreds of millions of migrant workers from rural and small-town areas, however, would spend at least two weeks back at home, leaving the cities with empty streets and closed services. The preparation heats up as it gets closer to the new year when people pay visits with gifts to relatives and close friends. The holiday season is marked by days of feasts, with the biggest and most exuberant being the New Year's Eve dinner and the New Year's Day banquet.

On New Year's Eve, families would gather to watch the New Year's Eve Gala, a national television variety show designed specifically for the occasion. A dinner featuring family favorites would be the highlight of the New Year's Eve. The family dinner invariably features tasty dishes that help immerse everyone in thanksgiving for the passing year and usher in the new year. Customarily, people stay up late to wait for the ringing-in of the new year (*shou-sui*); the dinner usually starts late, as a result, and lasts into the night. Family members may enjoy the food with alcohol and other beverages, chat and reminisce, and get ready to set off fireworks just before midnight. Importantly, the New Year's Eve dinner must have ingredients and entrées with names that are symbolic or homophonous of good fortune, such as fish (material surplus), chicken (good luck), and certain vegetables. An algae, known as *fa-cai* (*Nostoc flagelliforme*; "hair vegetable"), which appears like dark hair when dry, is a very popular ingredient in special New Year's Day dishes not as much for its purported nutritional value but for its sounding akin to "good fortune" (Fong, 2019).

Recent nonscientific surveys show that fish and, to a lesser extent, chicken entrées are the two most popular main courses for New Year's Eve dinners. Usually, whole fish and chickens are used, but the recipes vary greatly from region to region and from family to family. Pork, the most popular meat in modern times, is also well-represented in dishes that usually require elaborate preparation, such as braised pork ribs, belly, or knuckle (ham hock). Ducks and geese are common in many southern regions while beef and mutton dishes are popular in the north. In recent years, hot pot has also become the entrée of choice because of its versatility in terms of ingredients and flavors, and the celebratory atmosphere it creates when diners can join in the foray with relatively little formality and inhibition.

7.2. Braised Yellow Croaker, Family Style (*Hong-shao Huang-hua-yu*)

Yellow croaker, known for its tender and flaky texture, is a Chinese favorite. Overfishing and environmental pollution have decimated its population along the coast of East Asia, which in turn makes it even more precious and reserved for special occasions. Braising is the most popular way to cooking it since it is usually sold frozen. Fresh yellow croakers are best when steamed.

Yield: Serves 6–8

Ingredients
1 yellow croaker (about 1 lb.)
4 tbsp cooking oil
1 scallion
1 piece ginger
2 cloves garlic
1 tbsp soy sauce
1 tbsp cooking wine
1 tsp white vinegar
1 tsp sugar
7–8 peppercorns
3–4 star anise
1 tsp salt

Preparation
1. Clean the fish: get rid of the scales and the inside but keep the head on.
2. Slice the fish three times and brush soy sauce on both sides.
3. Mince scallion, ginger, and garlic.
4. Heat a wok, pour in cooking oil, and stir in scallion, ginger, and garlic till aromatic.

5. Turn heat to low and brown both sides of the fish.
6. Pour in peppercorn, star anise, salt, sugar, white vinegar, and cooking wine, and stew 1–2 minutes.
7. Pour in cold water but do not submerge the fish; bring to a boil, and turn heat to low.
8. Stew till little broth is left, about 15–20 minutes.
9. Turn heat to high for a minute or so to rid of excessive broth, place fish on a plate; serve.

As living standards improve and social changes take place, more and more families would prefer to dine out on New Year's Eve to uphold the dining ritual without exhaustive dinner preparation. The culinary industry has capitalized in this relatively new trend, but a reservation at top restaurants is hard to come by.

A bumper family banquet would be the highlight of the Spring Festival, with more good meals in the following days in the extended family and social networks. The season's celebration is capped off on the fifteenth day of the month, known as the Lantern Festival. In addition to viewing artsy lanterns in public places and guessing the riddles written on them, this day is marked by dumplings made of glutinous rice and stuffed with sweet fillings, which are called *yuan-xiao* in northern China and *tang-yuan* in southern China, respectively.

Lavish holiday meals are becoming more common in recent decades, as the living standards improve. It is taken for granted that the most important social meal of the year should feature expensive and exotic ingredients, meticulous preparation, and, above all, auspicious dishes either phonetically or ritualistically. It is expected that everyone in a multigenerational family be present at the dinner. Dining etiquette is strictly observed; seating and food serving are based on seniority in the family and, in the past, gender. Dishes served as main courses must be in even numbers, and *eight* is the most auspicious number. Certain ingredients are must-haves in the banquet dishes, especially the whole fish and chicken, since a meal won't be counted as a banquet if either fish or chicken is missing, as a popular Chinese saying goes. These holiday food ingredients and dishes are served more for their homophonous connotations that entail health and good fortune in the coming year. In reality, the most celebrated holiday entrées vary in choice ingredients and preparation methods, or by economic and regional conditions.

7.3. Steamed Abalone with Shark's Fin and Fish Maw in Broth (*Fo-tiao-qiang*)

This is arguably the most elaborate and exotic dish from the Fujian (Min) cuisine with numerous exorbitant ingredients. Created in the late 17th century, this dish drew foodies from near and afar. Some insisted that even the Buddha could not resist its aroma and would scale the monastery's walls for it. While mainly served in upscale restaurants today, some most confident home chefs are often tempted to give it a try as a showpiece for their New Year's Day banquet.

Yield: Serves 1

Ingredients
1 oz. skate fish fin (see notes)
½ oz. small abalone
⅓ oz. dry scallop (conpoy)
½ oz. slate cod croaker maw (the dried swim bladders)
½ oz. sea cucumber
½ oz. beef tendon
⅓ oz. winter bamboo shoot
½ oz. shitake mushroom

Note: The previous ingredients are usually in dehydrated form and need to be rehydrated by being soaked in water.

⅔ oz. prawns, peeled and deveined
8 quail eggs, hard boiled
⅔ oz. cooked chicken
2 slices of fresh ginger
3½ tbsp cooking wine
⅔ cup stock (bone broth)
¼ tsp salt
Pinches of white pepper powder

Preparation
1. Layer ingredients in a ceramic jar (with lid) following this order: (1) ginger, (2) bamboo shoot, (3) mushroom, (4) chicken, (5) beef tendon, (6) prawn, (7) scallop, (8) quail eggs, (9) sea cucumber, (10) fish maw, (11) fish fin, and (12) abalone.
2. Pour half of the cooking wine into the jar.
3. Heat a wok, pour in the stock and the other half of the cooking wine, and bring to a boil.
4. Sprinkle in pinches of salt and white pepper powder to flavor.

5. Pour the soup into the jar and cover with lid.
6. Use shrink-wrap to wrap the jar tightly.
7. Place the jar in a large steamer.
8. Steam in medium heat, two hours.
9. Unwrap and open the jar; serve.

Notes: Though the recipe describes making one serving of this dish, types of ingredients and preparation remain the same for making multiple servings. A couple of the ingredients can be substituted or skipped if not available. The rule of thumb is a half-and-half ratio between seafood and meat. Shark fin was substituted by skate fish fin due to a ban on shark fins, but skate fish fin can be substituted with even less endangered fishes such as sole, flounder, halibut, or ocean perch.

Jiaozi (Chinese stuffed dumplings), a favorite in northern China, is particularly important for the New Year's Eve meals. Families would gather and divide the tasks to make the dumpling, from kneading the wheat flour dough to rolling the wrappers, from mixing the fillings to stuffing and wrapping. The dumplings are usually eaten around midnight, in part because the name, *jiao-zi*, is homophonic to the Chinese word "the moment between the old year and the new year" (*Jiao-zi Shi-fen*). Some also argue that the shape of the dumpling resembles the gold ingots that were used as currency during imperial times, so eating it may bring good fortune in the new year.

7.4. *Jiaozi* (Chinese Stuffed Dumplings)

While enjoyed all over China with many regional variations, *jiaozi* is arguably one of the most quintessential staples for just about all holidays and special occasions in northern China. It is also liked by people all over the world. During the 2022 Winter Olympic Games in Beijing, American silver medalist Julia Marino commented that she had fallen in love with the Chinese dumplings, having consumed nearly 200 of them in just a few days.

Yield: Serves 4–6

Ingredients
36 oz. all-purpose wheat flour
1 large napa cabbage

12 oz. (a small bundle) Chinese chives

1 lb. pork (prefer hindquarter cut with moderate amount of fat)

1 Chinese long-stem (bunching) onion; it can be substituted with 5–6 scallions

1 thumb fresh ginger

12 peppercorns

Soy sauce, cooking wine, fresh water, sesame oil, salt, MSG (it can be omitted), quantity as needed

Preparation

Stuffing:

1. Peppercorn water: soak the peppercorns in hot water.
2. Slice and chop the pork to coarse ground (store-bought ground pork can be used).
3. Mince the onion and ginger and mix with ground pork.
4. Add appropriate quantity of salt, sesame oil, cooking oil, soy sauce, and MSG to the ground pork, and mix them together by hand.
5. Add small quantity of peppercorn water to pork and mix clockwise till gooey, then add more water and mix; repeat until all peppercorn water is used.
6. Wash and drain the outer leaves of napa cabbage, mince, and strain in cheesecloth: strain as much water out of the minced cabbage to prevent the stuffing from becoming too soggy.
7. Chop Chinese chive.
8. Add cabbage and chives to the stuffing; mix until it reaches a gooey consistency.

Wrapper:

1. Add water to flour, stir the mix with chopsticks into soft flakes, then knead them into a smooth dough. Wrap the dough with a wet cheesecloth and let stand for 30 minutes.
2. Knead the dough again, then stretch and roll it into 1-inch diameter thick dough strip.
3. Cut the dough strip into 1-inch cubes.
4. Spread flour over the cubes, press each cube flat and roll it into a thin pancake-shaped wrapper, 2½ to 3 inches in diameter. The ideal wrapper should be slightly thicker in the middle.

Dumpling:

1. Add stuffing to the middle of the wrapper.
2. Fold the wrapper.
3. Overlap and press the edge of the wrapper firmly to enclose the stuffing.

Cooking the dumpling:

1. Boil water in a large pot; add some salt to the boiling water.
2. Add the dumplings to the boiling water and stir them gently so that they do not stick to each other or the bottom of the pot. Do not add too many dumplings since they need space to expand.
3. When the water comes to a boil again, turn heat to medium high. Add a little cold water to stop the boiling momentarily; repeat this step three times.
4. The dumplings are fully cooked when they start to puff up and float on top of the boiling water.
5. Cool and serve; popular condiments for the Chinese include black vinegar, soy sauce, chili pepper sauce, and raw garlic.

Notes: The stuffing can be any combination of meat, eggs, tofu, fish and seafood, and just about any vegetables. Various seasonings, herbs, spices and condiments are used to enhance flavors. A key to good *jiaozi* is the wrapper, however. Made with wheat flours, the ideal wrapper, at least to northern Chinese, needs to provide a slightly chewy texture and be complementary to the stuffing. Premade *jiaozi* wrappers can often be found in Asian grocery stores in major metropolitan areas. They are not nearly as good as the homemade fresh ones but may suffice if making them at home appears to be too cumbersome.

In many southern regions, where rice is the preferred staple, *nian-gao* (glutinous rice cake) is the substitute for *jiaozi* as the must-have food for New Year's Eve. Again, people endowed the rice cake with a homophonically auspicious name: eating something that would allow you to move (socioeconomically) higher (*gao*) in the coming year (*nian*)! The rice cake is made of glutinous rice flour, and after being steamed, has a chewy, sticky texture. Typically, the rice cake, in small slices, is stir-fried with any combination of meats, soy products, seafood, and vegetables, such as soybean sprouts and spinach mustard (*Brassica rapa subsp. Narinosa*) called *ta-cai* in Mandarin and *tat-soi* in Cantonese.

Another food for the Spring Festival is a snack of sticky rice balls with sweet stuffing. Called *tang-yuan* in southern China and *yuan-xiao* in northern China, it is a popular snack and dessert year-round but is the food for the Lantern Festival, which is held on the 15th day of January in the Chinese agricultural calendar. With origin dating back to the Song Dynasty (960–1279), *tang-yuan* is a sort of dumpling made with glutinous rice wrappers and stuffing, usually a mix of sweet ingredients and nuts or seeds. Its northern counterpart, *yuan-xiao*, is similar in ingredients and even flavor, but different in the way it's been made. The stuffing for *yuan-xiao* is made with dry fruits, nuts, and sugar; it is hardened and cut into cubes. The stuffing cubes are dipped in water and then dropped into a wicker basket filled with glutinous rice flour. The basket is shaken rigorously to create a snow-bowling effect, and rice flour eventually forms a thick layer outside the stuffing, culminating in white rice balls. Some insist that *tang-yuan* and *yuan-xiao* are two different foods since their preparation and texture differ. One thing they do have in common is that they are both the high-profile, ritualic foods for the Lantern Festival. They also look alike with their mini snowball appearance, resembling the full moon on the day of the festival.

Tang-yuan has many regional varieties. Under "Tang-yuan" in *Baidu Baike* (Baidu Encyclopedia), a Chinese equivalent to Wikipedia, 21 traditional *tang-yuan* were listed in late 2021, most of which were renowned local snacks. *Lai Tangyuan*, named after Master Lai, its inventor, is one of the renowned snack foods in the culinary mecca of Chengdu, Sichuan Province. The stuffing does not have to be sweet; *tang-yuan* in Xing-yi, a municipality in southwestern Guizhou Province, features salty sesame chicken stuffing in chicken broth. As could be expected, there is a fierce debate in Chinese social media over which regional version of *tang-yuan* is superior.

Many traditional main courses for the Spring Festival feasts are no longer that special to the Chinese as more and more of them can afford any dishes at any time during the year. Phenomenal economic growth in the last four decades has brought ample supply of ingredients, eager culinary businesses, and expanding purchasing power. No wonder the older generations that had lived through the materially deprived times often exclaim that everyday dining is like the Spring Festival feasts. While some of the customs for the most important traditional holiday are no longer closely observed, the Chinese still consider sumptuous family meals the centerpiece in celebrating the coming of the New Year.

Pure Brightness Festival (*Qing-ming-jie*; Tomb Sweeping Day)

The Chinese pay tribute to their dead by visiting the gravesites of their loved ones, especially their parents and forebearers, during the peak of the spring. The special occasion is sometimes called Tomb Sweeping Day, and is more popularly known as Pure Brightness Festival (*Qing-ming-jie*) since it coincides with the so-named solar term of the Chinese agricultural calendar. It is celebrated on the 108th day from the Winter Equinox, which usually falls on April 5 (April 4 in a Leap Year) of the Gregorian calendar. Once deemed a feudalistic relic and shunned by the state, Tomb Sweeping Day became an officially sanctioned national holiday in 2007. Two other ancient festivals precede Pure Brightness Festival by a day or two. The first is Double Third Festival (*Shang-si-jie*), which centered on the ritual of spring cleansing by bathing in rivers and, later, by taking field trips. The second is Cold Food Festival (*Han-shi-jie*) dating to the 7th century BCE, which was an ancient ritual of cleaning out and reigniting the fire hearth in the spring. For safety reasons, no fire was allowed during the ritual, and people ate prepared food cold.

As time went on, Double Third and Cold Food festivals faded away, but some of their rituals were absorbed into activities during Pure Brightness Festival, especially field trips and consumption of cold food. Today, during Pure Brightness Festival, family members clean family gravesites and then leave sacrificial items, especially favorite foods and beverages, to their late relatives. For the living, cold food is customarily served, and the selections vary regionally. For example, many southerners still enjoy *qing-tuan*, a sweet or salty rice bun dyed green with Chinese mugwort (*Artemisia argyi*), while northerners would eat *sang-ze*, deep-fried noodles in a twisted pyramid shape. In rural Shandong Province, villagers would eat hard boiled eggs and steamed bread (*man-tou*), while people sell strings of roasted rice balls in Sichuan Province.

Dragon Boat Festival (*Duan-wu-jie*)

The Dragon Boat Festival has gained notoriety beyond China and other Asian societies mainly because of its paddle boat races. It falls on the fifth day of May on the Chinese agricultural calendar, which is usually a day in June on the Gregorian calendar. On this day, teams race in paddle boats adorned with dragon bows and tails. The Dragon Boat Festival bears a mythical origin: Qu Yuan (ca. 340–278 BCE), a renowned poet and exiled court official of the State of Chu, committed suicide by jumping into a river upon hearing that the Chu capital had been sacked by the invading Qin army. Local folks raced to the site and threw rice into the river so that fish would not devour Qu's corpse. The true origin of the festival, however, dates back several hundred years earlier to the Yangzi Delta as part of sacrificial ceremonies for good harvest and health at the beginning of the hot and humid summer. It did not become a popular holiday until the Tang Dynasty (618–907).

In preparation for the festival, families and communities would make *zong-zi*, the specialty food for the occasion. It is made by mixing glutinous rice with stuffing, wrapping the mix in dry reed or bamboo leaves, then steaming. In northern China, cane sugar and other sweet ingredients, such as dry fruits and red bean pastes, plus some seeds and nuts, are common stuffing. There is a much greater variety of stuffing in southern China, and the salty ones are popular, ranging from salted eggs and cured meats to vegetables and seafood.

The festival also carries pragmatic and important functions of promoting health awareness and disease prevention. Medicinal baths, for example, used to be a common ritual during the celebration. The Chinese use mugwort (*Artemisia argyi*) not only in the classic snack *qing-tuan* but also in household decorations for the plant's properties of warding off ailments. Other ingredients with purported exorcising capacity, such as garlic, are also used in food and in rituals. In Beijing, steamed bread with stuffing of honey and dry roses were stamped with five poisonous creatures, namely snake, scorpion, centipede, toad, and spider, and then served to exorcise evil spirits that could cause ailments. Realgar, an arsenic sulfide mineral, was regarded by ancient Chinese to be an antidote to all poisons. A concoction of realgar powder and alcohol (*xiong-huang-jiu*, realgar wine) was consumed during the festival and was rubbed on kids' foreheads to cast magic spells.

The Inseparable Ties Between Food and Medicine

Ancient Chinese believed that food and medicine were intrinsically intertwined: every food was regarded as having medicinal efficacy and, consequently, most medicine could be drawn from food. During the Zhou Dynasty (1,046–256 BCE), there was even a court-appointed official with the title "the food doctor." In practice, however, myths have often overshadowed science in the food–medicine relationship. Indulgence in exotic foods under the pretense of their "health efficacy" has resulted in health problems and ecological crises. The pursuit of aphrodisiac foods, for example, has led to unscrupulous consumption of animal penises, antlers, bones, and bear gallbladders, and endangered many protected species.

Mid-Autumn Festival (*Zhong-qiu-jie*, "The Moon Festival")

This festival may be the second most celebrated traditional holiday in China. It dates to prehistorical times when the ancients practiced rituals to worship celestial events and made sacrifices to the moon. As a regular festival, it became popular about two millennia ago. With a revised calendar emphasizing agricultural seasons, the date of the festival moved from the autumn equinox to August 15 on the Chinese agricultural calendar. It falls sometime between mid-September and early October on the Gregorian calendar. Ancient Chinese regarded August as the height of autumn, the season of harvest and contentment, and the full moon on this day symbolized their yearning for food security and family reunion.

Celebratory activities and foods varied regionally, but the festival's key function was always reinforcing family ties through food, which pairs it well to the Thanksgiving holiday in the United States. Moon gazing was the traditional activity, which was most fitting to the farmers who had gone through a busy harvest season and now had food stored for their families. The fitting finale of the celebration is a plenteous dinner heaped with sumptuous entrées and fresh seasonal fruits. The family meals vary based on the highly seasonal and coveted ingredients, such as ducks and freshwater crabs in the wealthy Yangzi Delta. With booming e-commerce, many regional delicacies can be ordered and promptly delivered fresh to anywhere in the country. The famed, and expensive, freshwater crabs from Yang-cheng Lake in the Yangzi Delta, for example, are hot commodities for the Mid-Autumn Festival in recent years.

The signature food for Mid-Autumn Festival, however, is the famous *yue-bing* (moon cake), a pastry that is usually eaten as a dessert or snack. The progenitor of moon cake might have emerged about a thousand years ago. Today, moon cake enjoys many regional styles, and the top three, according to surveys based on sales, are Guangdong-style, Suzhou-style from the Yangzi Delta, and Beijing-style. Beijing-style moon cakes feature stuffing of dry fruits, jujube paste, and a variety of seeds and nuts. Measured use of sugar and animal fat makes the crust crunchy and light. Suzhou-style moon cakes are known for their lard-infused flaky crust and assorted sweet stuffing with a faint taste of peppercorn salt. Guangdong-style (Cantonese) moon cakes are the most popular in China today, partly due to their reputation for quality and partly due to their moist crust and intricate stuffing. Lotus paste, the most expensive stuffing, takes weeks and numerous steps to make. One interesting feature of Cantonese moon cakes is their use of hard-boiled duck yolks for stuffing. It may take an acquired taste to enjoy it, but the use of the yellow and round duck yolks is symbolic of the full autumn moon and, henceforth, is appropriate to be at the center of moon cake stuffing.

How to Share a Meal

The COVID-19 pandemic has reignited a fierce debate in China about dining etiquette. In the last millennium, the Chinese have been accustomed to congregating around the dining table and sharing dishes with their own chopsticks. The custom poses obvious hygienic concerns, especially in the occasion of social dining. The call to serve food individually has gotten louder since the COVID-19 pandemic, but the pushback has also become stronger since dish-sharing has played a vital social function. Using serving utensils may be a compromise, but some insist on using solely their own chopsticks during meals for swift and flexible food-fetching.

The Lantern Festival (*Yuan-xiao-jie*)

Celebrating the first full moon of the agricultural calendar year, the Lantern Festival may have started during the Western Han Dynasty (202 BCE–8 CE) and became an officially sanctioned festival during the Tang Dynasty (7th–10th centuries). While not an officially designated holiday today largely because of its timing at the end of the Spring Festival, this is a special traditional festival because it is, first all, considered by many as being one of the three major traditional festivals, together with the Spring Festival and the Dragon Boat Festival. Second, it is filled with festivities such as large display of fancy lanterns, riddle games, dragon dance, and, of course, consumption of *tang-yuan* or *yuan-xiao*, the sticky rice balls with their round, white shape mimicking the full moon on this day. The Lantern Festival is also referred to as the traditional China's Valentine's Day. Historically, young men and women had few opportunities to meet and socialize, not to mention courting and dating; the public venues during the festival-related outings created one such rare opportunity for chance encounters.

In addition to sticky rice balls, regional specialty foods are also featured prominently. In the north, *jiaozi* is again a favorite, while some southerners would eat *fa-gao* (steamed sponge cakes) because they sound like "moving up" or "getting promoted." The Cantonese would eat *saung choy* (lettuce), which in their dialect sounds like "getting a fortune." In the northwest, a steamed bun made with the flour of proso millet (*Panicum miliaceum L.*) and jujube stuffing is very popular. Noodle dishes are eaten in many areas because their long stringy shape is considered symbolic to longevity.

7.5. Baby Cabbage in Chicken Soup (*Ji-tang Wa-wa-cai*)

This simple, bland, and soupy dish is a crowd pleaser at banquets and holiday feasts that are heaped with rich and sometimes greasy entrées. Baby Chinese cabbage or baby cabbage has a tenderer texture than its cousin, the napa cabbage.

Yield: Serves 8–10

Ingredients
2 heads baby cabbage
1 preserved duck egg (also known as century egg, thousand-year egg, *pi-dan,* or *song-hua-dan*)
½ red bell pepper
½ green bell pepper
1 head fresh garlic
1 scallion
¼ tsp salt
1 soup bowl chicken stock
1 soup bowl wet starch

Preparation
1. Clean baby cabbage and cut into four equal-length sections.
2. Cube bell pepper and preserved egg, mince the scallion, and thinly slice the garlic.
3. Roast garlic in a wok (or a deep pan) till slightly browned and permeating aroma.
4. Pour in chicken stock and bring to a boil.
5. Place cabbage in wok, cover, and bring to a boil again.
6. Remove cabbage from wok and place on a soup plate.
7. Pour bell pepper and egg in the wok and bring to a boil; add a moderate amount of wet starch to thicken the broth.
8. Top the cabbage with the broth; serve.

Special Social and Cultural Occasions

Traditionally, there are ritualistic special occasions that can be divided into two basic types. The first are those rooted in seasonal changes and agricultural cycles, such as the 24 solar terms in the Chinese calendar, and their rituals were usually related to agricultural cycles. The second type of special occasions had, and still has, social and customary functions, such as weddings, funerals, and birthdays. Food has always been an important part of both of them.

Food ingredients and preparations are consistent with Chinese cosmic views and codes of social behavior; the goal is to achieve harmony between humans and nature, and between families and society, through magic rituals and food sharing. It is important to correlate the food and the cultural significance of each special occasion. Confucius says, do not eat what is out of the season. The Chinese always regard food seasonality as being essential for good health and try to have food appropriate for each of the 24 solar terms (Table 7.1). The second day of February, for example, is regarded as the Spring Plough Day, also known as Dragon Awakening Day. Foods eaten on this day, though not unique, are given dragon-themed names for the occasion. Thin noodles, therefore, become "dragon whisks" (*long-xu*) and spring pancakes (*chun-bing*) are on this day called "dragon scales" (*long-lin*), and so on. Pig head meat is a favorite on this day, when the head is treated as "dragon head" (*long-tou*). Villagers used to roast sugared peanuts and soybeans, but nowadays they buy them from stores.

Chong-yang Festival, also referred to as "Double-Ninth Festival" because it is celebrated on September 9 of the Chinese calendar, is the autumn counterpart of Tomb Sweeping Day. It is considered an auspicious occasion since the Chinese regard the number nine as the number for longevity. Perhaps for this reason, in 2012, the Chinese government proclaimed it "Respect the Aged Day." One traditional activity for this holiday is making physical ascendence, either on a hill or in a tower, to immerse oneself in the refreshing autumn air. Historically, folks would carry a plant called *zhu-yu* (*C. officinalis*, also known as Japanese cornel) on this day to ward off ailments and evil spirits. Another popular activity was to visit chrysanthemum gardens. In Chinese culture, chrysanthemum symbolizes resilience because it blossoms in the fall as most other plants are shedding for the upcoming winter. A favorite beverage for this occasion is "longevity wine," an alcohol beverage brewed from sticky rice and chrysanthemum. Foods for Chong-yang Festival vary regionally, but a cake made with fruits and rice flour is common in the south.

7.6. *Chong-yang* Cake (*Chong-yang-gao*)

A ritual for the Double-Nine Festival was to climb high and pray for better life. The lore about this holiday specialty has it that making and eating a cake (*gao*), which phonetically has the same sound as "high" in Chinese,

Table 7.1 Foods for Wellness During the Solar Terms

Spring		Summer		Autumn		Winter	
Solar Term	**Foods**	**Solar Term**	**Foods**	**Solar Term**	**Foods**	**Solar Term**	**Foods**
Beginning of Spring	Egg rolls (*chun-juan*)	Beginning of Summer	Duck eggs	Beginning of Autumn	Watermelon	Beginning of Winter	Chicken soup
Rain Water	Dragon-beard cakes (*long-xu-gao*)	Grain Full	Bitter vegetables	Limit of Heat	Duck	Slight Snow	Bacon
Waking of Insects	Fried Chop Rice Cake (*lü-da-gun*)	Grain in Ear	Green plums	White Dew	Longan	Great Snow	Mutton
Spring Equinox	Spring vegetables	Summer Solstice	Noodles	Autumn Equinox	Sticky rice dumpling (*tang-yuan*)	Winter Solstice	Dumplings (*jiaozi*)
Pure Brightness	Green rice balls (*qing-tuan*)	Slight Heat	New rice	Cold Dew	Sesame	Slight Cold	Eight treasure porridge (*la-ba-zhou*)
Grain Rain	Cedrela sinensis (*xiang-chun*)	Great Heat	Platostoma palustre (*xiang-cao*)	Frost's Descent	Persimmons	Great Cold	Sticky rice cake (*nian-gao*)

Source: Amiee. "Traditional Chinese Food Menu for 24 Solar Terms." *A Daily Food.* May 12, 2021. https://www.adailyfood.com/traditional-chinese-food-menu-for-24-solar-terms/.

would compensate those who did not have the opportunity to ascend to higher ground.

Yield: Serves 8–10

Ingredients
2 lb. glutinous rice flour
1 lb. long-grain rice flour
½ lb. red beans
3 oz. dry fruit
5 cups cane sugar
¼ cup brown sugar
2 tbsp soybean oil
4 tbsp cooking wine

Preparation
1. Thinly slice dry fruit and set aside.
2. Mix red beans, soybean oil, and 1 cup cane sugar; put aside.
3. Mix brown sugar with ¾ cup of the flour mix; add 2 fl. oz. of water to make a thick batter.
4. Mix the rest of flours and cane sugar, add 1 cup of water, mix and knead to make a dough.
5. Flatten the dough and cut it into two halves of equal thickness.
6. Spread the red bean mix evenly over one half of the dough, and top it with the other half of the dough.
7. Steam on high heat for 10 minutes, spread the batter on top of the cake, and then top it with the dry fruits and steam for another 10 minutes.
8. Cool the cake and then cut it into diamond shape, decorate with small paper flags; serve.

The *Laba* Festival (December 8 of the Chinese agricultural calendar) started over two millennia ago and was a ritual for ancestral worship, prayer for good harvest, and avoidance of evil spirits. It later converged with Bodhi Day, which falls on December 8, that commemorates the day that Gautama Siddhartha is said to have experienced enlightenment. In commemorating the sufferings that the Buddha endured for the salvation of the masses, Buddhist monasteries and temples would cook and share with the masses *laba* congee that includes several grains, dry fruits, nuts, and seeds (lotus seeds are a popular ingredient). The special congee became a ceremonial food that most households would make, and nearly everyone would eat, on this day. There are regional recipes for the congee, and some places substitute other foods for the congee. For example, communities in the Wei River valley in Shaanxi Province eat noodles instead of congee. Villagers in northern China pickle fresh garlic in Chinese (dark) vinegar. The peeled cloves would become greenish in a few weeks, and the potent smell and taste make *laba* garlic a favorite side dish in the winter.

Some special occasions are communal ceremonial events. The most important of these events are weddings and funerals, which are dubbed "the red and white happy events." The family involved would offer a feast to relatives, friends, and the entire community, for instance, the village. Until recently, villagers would be in a celebratory mood when a wedding or a funeral came up, since it meant a feast would be in the offing, which was no small feat in a time when many could barely avoid hunger. Birthdays, especially those for babies and the elderly, are also celebrated with sumptuous meals. In the north, the go-to main course in rural areas was invariably a noodle dish in enough quantity to stuff every diner; noodle dishes were affordable to the hosts and were auspicious to the birthday person because of their long, stringy shape, which is considered analogous to longevity.

China is increasingly exposed to major Western holidays such as Christmas and Valentine's Day. The youth are curious about them, and businesses try to seize upon new commercial opportunities. The government does not sanction them, however, and in some cases bans their celebration outright, such as the case of Christmas on college campuses. What distinguishes the Chinese from many other societies are the rituals and myths they place on the food for holidays and special occasions.

Further Reading

The CLI Team. "A Brief Guide to China's Seven Major Holidays." Chinese Language Institute, updated May 27, 2022. https://studycli.org/chinese-holidays/.

Fong, Xenia. "All the Lunar New Year Dishes That Will Bring You the Best Luck." *Food Network*. https://www.foodnetwork.com/fn-dish/news/2019/02/traditional-lunar-new-year-dishes-to-bring-good-luck-and-prosper (accessed November 1, 2021).

Newman, Jacqueline M. "New Year: Once a Fifteen-Day Holiday." *Flavors & Fortune* 25, no. 1 (2018): 8–13. http://www.flavorandfortune.com/ffdataaccess/article.php?ID=1482.

CHAPTER EIGHT

Street Food and Snacks

We love to snack, munching on tidbits not as much to satiate hunger but to enjoy the provocative flavors and textures of the goodies. Many snacks are the foods for gastronomic fun but can also make full meals. Snacks can be had any time but are usually eaten outside formal, full meals, and are usually ready-to-eat or simple to prepare, small in portion, and not too filling. They use nearly all edible ingredients, can be served hot or cold, and can entail any flavor. Popular snacks today would range from a bag of potato chips mass-produced on assembly lines to homemade sugared walnuts, all which are eaten between meals.

Street foods, on the other hand, are traditionally prepared fresh for order-to-go. Fancy restaurants may make the same small plates of delicacies as street vendors do, but the essence of street foods is that they are quickly and simply prepared at public places such as sidewalks and parks by vendors who pack everything needed for cooking in a cart or a food truck. The vendors tend to cluster together, providing many choices at the same location and benefiting from the subsequent increase of customer traffic. Preparation is usually simple and uses local, fresh ingredients; the portions are small and inexpensive but the choices are many, so that customers can sample various items without getting stuffed or busting their budget. Of course, one can eat street food to satiate hunger; a bowl of noodles or a hot dog may just do that.

There is a broad overlap between snacks and street foods. Both can be eaten without much of the usual dining etiquette associated with formal or even daily meals, and there is little preparation and cleanup. A key difference between them, though, is that street food is usually freshly made on site and accessible to the locals, thence bearing specific local traditions and customs, while snacks may be either locally produced street food or mass-produced products from faraway factories. Street food and local snacks are important introductions to anyone who wants to learn a local culture. The large, fresh soft pretzel must come into mind when we think of what makes New York City unique and vibrant, for example. While street food and snacks can make a full meal, more often they are associated with social and leisure activities. People are attracted to them not to get full but to enjoy refreshments and have some fun.

The Chinese regard all food outside the regular daily meals as snacks, so a bowl of noodles or a plate of dumplings can serve either as a snack or a full meal, depending on the quantity and purpose of eating it. Street foods serve either purpose well, though nowadays they are regarded more often as snacks. The Chinese food culture has a rich tradition in street food and snacks, which are called *xiao-chi* (small eats) and *ling-shi* (extra food), respectively. The Chinese snacks first gained popularity in the wealthy Yangzi Delta region during the Southern Song Dynasty (1127–1279). Snacks became more popular during the Yuan Dynasty (1275–1368), when food of small portion and special flavoring were served in addition to the daily meals. By the mid 1700s, Nanjing, Shanghai, Suzhou of Jiangsu Province, and Changsha of Hunan Province began to emerge as the four leading centers of regionally distinct snacks.

8.1. Nanjing Crispy Flatbread (*Ya-you-su Shao-bing*)

This is one of the eight most renowned snacks from Nanjing, the most ancient cluster of street food in China. It uses duck fat to attain a distinct flavor and a flaky, multilayered texture. This recipe is an adapted version that does not require some of the minor and rare ingredients, hence making it feasible for those at home to give a try.

Yield: Serves 8

Ingredients

Crispy crust:
6 oz. all-purpose flour
⅓ cup lukewarm water
⅕ tsp salt
2½ tsp cane sugar
⅓ tsp yeast
½ oz. duck fat

Flaky inner layers:
2 oz. cake flour
1 oz. duck fat

2 tsp peppercorn salt
1 tsp salt

Fillings:
2 tbsp chopped scallion (green onions)
1 tsp peppercorn salt

Toppings:
⅛ cup beat egg
2 tbsp white sesame

Preparation

Crispy crust:
1. Dissolve the yeast with half of the warm water.
2. Mix in all other ingredients; add more water if necessary.
3. Use chopsticks to blend the flour mix into a fluffy dough.
4. Knead the dough 15–16 times to make it smooth on the surface.
5. Cover the dough with shrink-wrap and place it in a warm spot for 15–20 minutes.
6. Remove the shrink-wrap and knead the dough a few times, then cover it again for 30 minutes.

Flaky inner layers:
1. Mix the ingredients in a dough.

Assembling the flatbread:
1. Divide both the crust dough and the inner layer dough into eight equal portions.
2. Flatten each of the crust doughs with a rolling pin.
3. Tightly wrap the inner layer dough with the crust dough.
4. Flatten the dough combo into oval shape.
5. Fold the flattened dough in the middle, then roll it up (similar to cinnamon rolls).
6. Flattened the roll with palm first, then with the rolling pin, into a pancake.
7. Put fillings (chopped scallion and peppercorn salt) on the pancake, then wrap it up into a dough.
8. Cover with shrink-wrap for 10 minutes.
9. Press the dough with palm first, then with rolling pin, into a pancake.
10. Brush beat egg on the pancakes.
11. Sprinkle white sesame seeds on the pancakes.
12. Place the pancakes in a nonsticking pan and cover with shrink-wrap for 15–30 minutes.
13. Heat the oven to 400 degrees Fahrenheit.

14. After the pancakes are leavened, place the pan in the middle rack of the oven for 22 minutes.
15. Take the flatbread out and serve hot.

Notes: The peppercorn salt for the flaky inner layers can be substituted with cane sugar if the preference is sweet instead of salty flavor. In Nanjing, the sweet version of the bread is in an oval shape and the salty version is in a round shape.

For most Chinese, snacking on tidbits is a great pastime and a common scene in social life. New and provocative snacks are invented all the time, with some gaining cult-like followings. One such new snack is "Northeast BBQ Chilled Noodles" that first became a huge hit in Northeast China (Wang, 2016). Created in the 1990s, it was originally a hurried concoction of ingredients at hand by a food vendor. It can be prepared at home, but many fervent fans insist that the pancake-like "noodle" snack cannot retain the unique and authentic flavors unless it is made by vendors in the dusty, cold streets, where the pancake was infused with the chilly air of China's "Rust Belt" and the rough-and-tumble cooking style typical of the Manchurian frontier. It is inexpensive, relatively easy to make, and ever so reminiscent of its counterpart, the soft, warm pretzel from street vendors in New York City. The following recipe is but one of the countless improvisions, each with a claim to be the most authentic.

8.2. Northeast BBQ Chilled Noodles
(*Dongbei Kao-leng-mian*)

This street food has gained a huge fanbase in Northeast China and beyond. Legend has it that it was inadvertently created when leftover Korean chilled noodles (*Naeng-myeon*) were pressed into thin, doughy pancakes for a quick snack wrap. Most people use factory-made, rectangular-shaped noodle sheets, which are available in grocery stores.

Yield: Serves 2

Ingredients
2 sheets of pancakes ("chilled noodles")
2 eggs

2 Chinese sausage links or hot dogs (cooked)

2 tsp of cooking oil

2 scallions or 1 small red onion

4 tbsp of chopped cilantro

2 tbsp of Chinese paste, substitutable with any BBQ sauce, flavor of choice

Pinches of salt, sugar, and ground cumin, to taste

Preparation
1. Mince the scallions (or onion) and cilantro.
2. Pour 1 tsp of cooking oil in a flat pan on medium heat.
3. After oil is hot, put one sheet of pancake in and bake for 1 minute.
4. Crack one egg on the pancake and spread it evenly using a spatula.
5. Flip the pancake and cook for 1 minute with the egged side down.
6. Spread the Chinese spicy paste or BBQ sauce on the pancake.
7. Put half of minced scallion (or onion) and cilantro on the pancake.
8. Put one sausage link or hot dog on the pancake, together with salt, sugar, and ground cumin.
9. Place the "loaded" pancake on a plate, roll it up, and cut it into 1 or 1½ inch sections; serve hot.
10. Repeat steps 1–9 to make the second serving.

Chinese street food has provided affordable quick eats to the low-income working class, using inferior ingredients and simple, sometimes makeshift, methods. As time went on, some snacks evolved into elaborate, restaurant-quality tidbits for the rich and powerful, while most others remained the dependable food source for the underclass. Their distinctions as unique regional foods are fading away, however, as they are becoming available beyond their geographical origins. One now can have Shanghai-style street food in Beijing, and *vice versa*; some of the well-known street snack foods are shipped frozen to grocery stores all over the country. What remains unchanged, however, is people's obsession with street food and local snacks, which provide not only pleasure to the taste buds but also the delight of cultural experiences.

The Geography of Street Food and Traditional Snacks

Street food and local snacks are integral to regional cultural identities. As the Chinese enjoy much improved living standards, they can afford and do demand both variety and quality of snacks. The Chinese snack industry has, as a result, received a tremendous boost in market demand, and the street food scene is as robust and wide-ranging as ever. Many regional specialty snacks have become an integral part of the popular culture. Foodies argue over the authenticity of their favorite snacks but sometimes forget the essence of street food and snacks is that they must be fully appreciated as part of regional cultures.

There are many well-known regional snacks; most are available as street food, and each has distinct local ingredients and preparation. Snacks in northern China mainly consisted of wheat and coarse grains, while many southern snacks are made with rice and rice flours. Mutton and beef are widely consumed in the north while fish, poultry, and tofu are more common in the south. The renowned *you-zha chou-dou-fu* (deep-fried stinky tofu) may be a huge turn-off for nonlocals but a favorite street snack in the hot and humid south. Sometimes, economic conditions and ease in trade may outweigh environmental influence in regional food cultures. Snacks in the southwest are known to be spicy hot, while snacks from the Yangzi Delta tend to be blander and sweeter though they both have subtropical humid climate. The former has been wealthier and more accessible to interregional trade, and it relished sugar and fresh ingredients in its regional food culture.

Chou-Dou-Fu (Stinky tofu)

While stories of its origin are many, the fact remains that the Chinese have made the most out of making tofu into a delicacy through fermentation. The derived products invariably produce an overwhelming stinky aroma, thus earning their namesake, *Chou-dou-fu* (stinky tofu). The "dry version," *Chou-dou-gan* (stinky dry tofu), has many variations, but it is invariably a popular street snack in Jiangsu, Zhejiang, Anhui, Hunan, Hubei, Guizhou, Fujian, Taiwan, and other southern regions. It is deep-fried and topped with a concoction of condiments, usually chili and garlic sauces. It is indeed an acquired taste to many, while others are thoroughly addicted to it.

The North

The northern regions of China are in temperate climate zones and become progressively more arid from the coast to the western interior. The range of food ingredients is relatively narrow, which translates into a smaller variety of snacks and street food in comparison to those in the south. Many regional snacks are made of cereal grains, primarily wheat but also ancient grains such as millet and sorghum, and other starch ingredients such as bean flours and potatoes. In addition to pork and poultry (mainly chicken), mutton and beef are widely used, but fish and seafood are limited except for the coastal regions. Tofu is a common but not extensively used ingredient due to the lack of variety in soybean products. Many northern fruits are dried and sugared as snacks.

Each region in the north has its unique snacks. The Northeast (*Dongbei*) has relatively fewer distinct snacks, due to partly its later settlement and development by the Chinese, and partly its limited choices of natural ingredients. Influence of Russian and Korean food cultures, on the other hand, is quite pronounced. The northern part of the Northeast was under imperial Russia's influence, where many Russian-styled snacks remain popular, such as Harbin red sausage, rye bread, and ice-cream bars with an amazing array of flavors. The large ethnic Korean population along the Sino–Korean border has contributed Korean cold noodle soup, rice cakes, and, of course, *kimchi* to the repertoire of the Northeast snack food scene.

North China (*Huabei*), which includes much of the North China Plain and eastern Loess Plateau, was the cradle of the Chinese civilization. It may have long lost its status as China's economic core region, but many ancient munchies have survived and are signature snacks today. A street snack from Tianjin, *Jian-bing Guo-zi*, has become an extremely popular snack throughout China. Dubbed by some as "Chinese savory crêpes," it is a rolled thin pancake with a deep-fried dough stick and other ingredients inside. A street vendor would pour and spread mung bean flour batter on a baking pan to make a thin pancake, similar to how the French crêpes are made. He or she would then add an egg (or two), scallions, chili sauce, and a number of other condiments on top and evenly spread them over the pancake. Once the ingredients are cooked, the vendor would use the pancake to wrap a freshly deep-fried dough stick (*you-tiao*) and, *voilà*, a tasty snack or breakfast is done! Tianjin is also known for many other renowned snacks, including its sweet and crunchy pretzels (*ma-hua*) and a bun with a funny name that literally means "dog's dislike" (*Gou-bu-li*). Some years ago, the restaurant hung up an English sign that awkwardly dubbed *Gou-bu-li* "Go Believe," which aroused an outrage among its loyal fans for its futile and irreverent attempt at publicity.

As the national capital for much of the last eight centuries, Beijing has been the converging center for all Chinese regional cuisines and occupies a special place in the northern snack food landscape. Northern Chinese cuisines and those of nomadic (the Mongols) and hunting-gathering (the Manchus) cultures, however, have had the greatest influence on Beijing cuisines, especially its street food and snacks. A popular sweet snack,

Sa-chi-ma, for example, is traced to Manchu origin. It is a pastry made of fried wheat flour noodles, lard (traditionally), and a syrup mix of rock sugar and honey. It was a Manchu favorite and was brought to Beijing after the Manchus conquered China and selected Beijing as their capital. The original *Sa-chi-ma* was hard, sticky, and very sweet; its contemporary, southern renditions, on the other hand, have a softer texture remotely resembling that of Rice Krispies.

Two sometimes overlapping traditions have emerged and evolved in Beijing, one from the court and the elite circles, the other from the under-class that consisted of mainly the rural poor from surrounding regions of the capital. Each tradition is distinct in style and sophistication, and each has devoted chefs endeavoring to achieve perfection with what they must work with. At times, "high-brow" recipes trickled down to the food scene of the commers, and the elites, even the royalty, occasionally took a liking to the street food of the commoners. The best-known Beijing snacks may trace their origins to either the imperial court or street food stalls in the ghettos, but all are bulk-made and available to those who are addicted and those who want to try.

Wan-dou-huang (yellow pea cake) is made of pea flours and used to be made and eaten in the spring. It was a popular street food that was brought to the imperial court, where it became refined in ingredients and flavors, and later found its way back to the streets. It is one of the signature snacks along with sticky rice roll with red bean paste (*Lü-da-gun*), French bean (*Phaseolus vulgaris*) cake (*Yun-dou-gao*), deep fried crispy ring (*Jiao-quan*), and steamed sticky rice buns with sweet stuffing (*Ai-wo-wo*). Legend has it that most of them were made famous by the powerful Empress Dowager Cixi (1835–1908), who enjoyed munching on snacks and side dishes from beyond the palace walls.

Two highly popular street snacks in Beijing are *bing-tang-hu-lu* (ice sugar coated haws on a stick) and roast sweet potato (*kao-bai-shu*). The former is made by dipping hawthorn on a bamboo stick into melted rock sugar. They were sold during the cold months but now are available year-round because of availability of refrigeration. The sweet and sour flavor is a big draw to people of all ages. The latter is a street food that requires a single ingredient, the sweet potato, and a stove, which is nowadays often con-verted from an oil drum. A perfectly roasted sweet potato, however, requires the vendor's mastery in controlling the stove temperature. Legend has it that its popularity started with Emperor Qianlong (1711–1799), who discovered that the humble street food not only tasted royally good but also effectively cured his constipation. It has remained an inexpensive and yummy street snack through the ages.

Some of Beijing's street snacks can be challenging to most nonlocals. They were street foods of the urban poor that used low-quality ingredients and featured flavors that demanded a required taste, such as *zha-guan-chang* (deep-fried flour dough in pig intestine casing) or *chao-gan* (garlic-flavored pig livers). The most infamous of this kind of street food is *lü-dou-zhi* (fermented mung bean milk), which is made with fermented dregs from the process of making mung bean vermicelli. The milk has a pungent smell and taste that is guaranteed to turn off most people but that has made many Beijingers from all walks of life addicted to it.

The *Hui* people, whose ancestors came to China from Islamic Southwest Asia and the Middle East during the Yuan Dynasty, established a subcuisine that infuses traditional Chinese and halal cooking. *Ta-si-mi* (twice-cooked honey lamb), for example, is arguably the top halal dish from the *Hui* community and beloved by everyone. Through time, the *Hui*s have carved out a large share of Beijing's food business and were particularly influential in street snack food, making sheep and oxen offal into various mouth-watering halal snacks. One outstanding example is *bao-du*, quick-fried ox (or sheep) tripes dipped in a special sauce of sesame paste, chili oil, fermented bean curd brines, chopped scallions, and cilantro. Another famous snack is boiled sheep head meat, which was created by a Muslim chef in the mid 19th century. Today, two of the best places for halal street snack food are *Nan-lai-shun*, a famous halal restaurant, and Ox Street, the main drag of the traditional Muslim community in Beijing. Halal street foods are also local cultural landmarks in other historic cities where there are sizable Muslim communities, such as Kaifeng (Henan Province), Xian (Shaanxi Province), and Lanzhou (Gansu Province).

Xian, the ancient capital known for its nearby Terra Cotta army of the First Emperor (*Qin-shi-huang-di*, 259–210 BCE), has long been known for its Muslim Snack Street, which has been a tourist attraction for centuries. As the most famous imperial capital and the eastern terminus of the Silk Road, Xian also became one of the gourmet capitals of its time, which shows a distinct influence from Central Asia and even the Middle East featuring mutton and baked bread. In 2016, five of the most famous local snacks in Xian became listed as Shaanxi Province's nonmaterial historical heritage, and the municipal government issued standards as well as official English names for them. One of them, *rou-jia-mo* (*rou-ga-mo*), has become a national favorite. It is a meat sandwich, or "hamburger" as some in Chinese prefer to call it, that features cured meat in savory sauce stuffed in a baked flatbread, reminiscent of its Central Asian equivalents. Another national favorite, *yang-rou pao-mo* (pita bread soaked in lamb soup), directly reflects influence from the oasis and grassland of Central and Western Asia.

8.3. *Yang-rou Pao-mo* (Pita Bread Soaked in Lamb Soup)

Legend has it that *yang-rou pao-mo* traces its origin to the founding emperor of the Song Dynasty (960–1279), who, exhausted and hungry, hastily soaked stale bread in boiling mutton broth. The recipe later became popular and has long been a signature street food in the northwest.

Yield: Serves 4

Ingredients
1 cup all-purpose wheat flour
1 lb. mutton or lamb (leg meat)
1 lb. sheep bones (for broth)
½ cup water
⅙ tsp yeast

Small quantity based on preference:
¼ cup black fungi (soaked in water to soften)
1 bunch mung bean vermicelli
3 slices fresh ginger
2 bay leaves
1 tsp fennel
2 pieces orange peel
4 pieces star anise
1 stick cassia
2 fresh scallions, chopped
3 cloves fresh garlic, peeled and minced
¼ cup cilantro, chopped
2 heads sweet pickled garlic
Pinches of salt, white pepper powder, chili paste

Preparation
1. Slice the mutton and soak it in cold water for 20 minutes, then drain; repeat this step three times.
2. Wash and clean the sheep bones and put in a pot with cold water.
3. When boiling, put in anise stars, orange peels, cassia stick, bay leaves, scallion, and ginger.
4. Boil for 30 minutes, constantly skimming off the foam at the top of the broth.
5. After 30 minutes, take out the star anise, orange peels, cassia stick, and bay leaves.
6. Pour the broth in a clay pot, put in the mutton, and stew for 3 hours.
7. Dissolve the yeast in warm water and make a dough with ¼ cup of flour; let it leaven for an hour.

8. Make a dough with the remaining ¾ cup of flour and let stand for 30 minutes.
9. Mix the two doughs together and knead it until the surface is smooth.
10. Section the dough and press each piece into quarter-inch flatbread dough with a rolling pin.
11. Bake the flatbread in a pan until each side becomes slightly yellow; let them stand and cool.
12. Break the bread into soybean size crumbs with fingers and put them in 4 deep bowls.
13. Bring the broth to a boil and put in the vermicelli to cook, 2 minutes.
14. Pour the boiling broth into the bowls, topped with salt, white pepper powder, black fungi, cilantro, and minced garlic, and with optional chili paste; serve.
15. Serve sweet pickled garlic as a side.

Notes: The restaurant versions of this dish are a lot more elaborate, but many swear that the street stalls serve an as good, or even better, version of it. In any event, the key ingredients are fresh mutton and sheep bones.

There are many other notable street snack centers in the north, which usually feature specialty noodles, stuffed buns, and baked goods. Shanxi Province (to the east of Shaanxi Province), for example, is renowned for its great variety of noodles made from flours of wheat, millet, soybeans, mung beans, potatoes, and so on. The variety is in part because of the effort by the rural poor to make the starch food more palatable since they could not afford much protein and vegetable ingredients. A few snacks appear to be exotic, such as donkey meat sandwiches. Lanzhou is known for one of the most famous Chinese noodle snacks, *Lanzhou niu-rou la-mian* (Lanzhou stretched beef noodles). It requires two common ingredients, clear beef broth and freshly hand-stretched noodles. The broth is made and then preserved for a long time, perhaps years, by repeatedly refilling the heated pot with balanced input of water and meat. The noodle-making is usually done on site as a way of promotion. Potash (potassium carbonate) is added to the dough to give the noodle a unique flavor and a chewy texture.

The South

The warm and humid south boasts more diverse snack foods and more robust street food scenes than the north. The southerners have a much wider selection of ingredients, and the need to preserve fresh ingredients has also fostered sophisticated preparations and exotic snack flavors. In contrast to snack foods in the north, rice is widely used to make snacks. Regional variations in the south may have more to do with disparities in economic development and living standards rather than environmental differences. Four styles can be identified regarding general characteristics of snacks, namely, those of the Yangzi Delta, the Central South, the Southwest, and the South Coast.

The Yangzi Delta, dubbed as "the land of fish and rice," has plenty of snack delicacies to match its reputation as the richest region in the country. Of the four oldest snack clusters in China, three were in the Yangzi Delta (Nanjing, Suzhou, and Shanghai). Yangzi Delta snacks tend not to be very sweet so as to enhance the savory flavors of fresh local ingredients. Among the famous regional snacks are *zong-zi* (sticky rice dumpling). Dubbed as "Chinese tamale," it is usually stuffed with fresh pork and *ba-bao-fan* (sticky rice with eight treasures). There are many locale-specific noodle and *hun-dun* (wonton) soups, scallion pancakes, and stuffed buns as well as all kind of tofu snacks. One of the most famous and pungent snacks is the regional version of stinky tofu. Stinky tofu is made from marinating fresh tofu curds in age-fermented tofu brines, which has a potent whiff because of the bacteria. The marinated bean curds are then deep-fried (*you-zha*) and topped with condiments of choice. Stinky tofu in the Yangzi Delta is not spicy, which is consistent with the region's cuisines that are bland with a subtle sweetness.

8.4. *Xiang-yang* Beef Noodles (*Xiang-yang Niu-rou-mian*)

This is the hometown snack that General Nie, one of the Chinese astronauts, requested upon completing his space mission in September 2021. It is a local favorite that was previously little known elsewhere but may now have found new fame with the astronaut, regarded as a national hero, as its best promoter. The recipe demands complex ingredients and laborious preparation for the broth. Vendors focus on red-braising beef and tripes, and concocting broth in large quantity for making the noodle soup the next day.

Yield: Serves 1

Ingredients

Red braised beef and tripe:
½ oz. each: beef flank, tendon, shank, tripes (reticulum and omasum)

½ cup regular soy sauce
½ cup dark soy sauce
1 tbsp rock sugar
1 *cao-guo* (*Lanxangia tsaoko*)
2 star anise
1 tsp fennel
1 tsp coriander
1 stick cassia (Chinese cinnamon)
2 pieces sand ginger (*Kaempferia galanga*)
2 pieces orange peel
2 pieces nutmeg
1 piece ocardamon
1 piece *cao-dou-kou* (*Alpinia katsumadai Hayata*)
3–5 thin slices of ginger
3 scallion (green oinion) white

Noodle broth:
2 tbsp beef fat
2 tbsp red chili soy paste
6–10 dry red chili pepper
2 tbsp peppercorn
Small quantity of Chinese allspice, minced ginger, soy sauce and dark soy
   sauce, sugar

Noodles:
2 oz. fresh dietary alkali noodles
1 tsp sesame oil

Toppings:
Small amount of mung bean sprout, chopped cilantro, and scallion

Preparation
1. Half-cook the noodles (2 minutes in boiling water) and mix in sesame
   oil, then spread them out and refrigerate the noodles for use the next day.
   Red braising brine: boil 2 cups of water in a pot and then mix in all spices.
2. Scald the beef and offal and chop them into small pieces.
3. Red braise the beef and offal in the brine for approximately 1 hour; set
   the beef and offal aside to cool; save the brine.
4. Noodle broth: melt the beef fat in a wok, then stir in the seasonings.
5. Pour the red braising brine into the wok, and cook the flank, tendon,
   and shank for 40–50 minutes.
6. Slice the tripes and add them to the wok; cook for 10 more minutes.
7. Boil bean sprout and noodles, approximately 2 minutes.
8. Place the noodles and sprout in a bowl; add the broth, beef, scallion,
   and cilantro; serve.

Snacks in the eastern part of the Central South, such as some areas in Anhui Province, are similar to those in the Yangzi Delta. Food becomes quite pungent in areas further to the west, however, and street snack food in provinces including Jiangxi, Hubei, and Hunan are pungent, though they lack the unique numbing sensation due to not using peppercorn for season-ing. Preserved meat and vegetables are very common, and some are essen-tial ingredients in the region's snacks. The oldest snack hub in Central South is Changsha, Hunan Province, which features more than 300 snacks encom-passing both the historical and the new, including its version of stinky tofu. Xiang-yang beef noodles and Wuhan hot-dry noodles, both nationally pop-ular today, represent the rich food tradition of Hubei Province.

8.5. *Ci-Fan-Tuan* (Fried Sticky Rice Roll)

Ci-fan-tuan is one of the most popular snacks and breakfast entrées in Shanghai. It is a sticky rice rolls filled with flavorful local ingredients, mainly savory pickled vegetables, shredded pork, and either salty or sweet deep-fried dough (*you-tiao*). People in the Yangzi Delta consider glutinous rice as a grain that can soothe the digestive system in the fall and winter, and the fillings make the otherwise bland rice flavorful.

Yield: Serves 4

Ingredients
½ cup glutinous rice
½ cup regular rice
1 tsp salt
⅘ cup cooking oil
2 scallions
Stuffing (e.g., ready-made pickled vegetables and cooked meats)
Sesame seeds for topping

Preparation
1. Soak rice (both kinds) for 2 hours, then drain and rinse clean.
2. Steam-cook the rice.
3. Wash and mince the scallions.
4. Stir and break loose the rice; mix in salt, stuffing, and scallion.
5. Put the rice and salt mix in a plastic bag, and press on the bag with a rolling pin a few times.
6. Line a food container with shrink-wrap, pour in, and press tight the rice. Let it cool to room temperature.

7. Cut the rice cake into 2.5 × 1.0 × 0.6 (inch) cubes, and drizzle on them sesame seeds.
8. Keep the cooking oil in medium heat in a wok or pan, deep fry the rice cubes to golden brown, and serve hot.

The cuisines in the Southwest, which includes Chongqing and Sichuan, bring forth the clashing spicy-hot flavor (chili pepper) and numbing sensations (peppercorn). Every locale can boast its snack specialties, such as Yunnan's *Guo-qiao Mi-xian* ("Crossing-the-Bridge Noodles"), a snack of rice vermicelli cooked in a flavorful boiling soup. Chengdu, the capital of Sichuan, however, is the ultimate capital of Southwest snacks with a most celebrated street food tradition which seduced, among many others, celebrity chefs Anthony Bourdain and Andrew Zimmern. Visitors could find Dandan noodles, *Fu-qi Fei-pian* ("Mr. and Mrs. Smith"), *Ma-po Tofu*, *Yu-xiang Rou-si* (Fish-flavored Shredded Pork), and a strange local snack delicacy, braised rabbit head! Many ethnic minorities have also made their unique contributions to the richness of the region's snacks.

The South Coast, which includes provinces of Fujian, Guangdong, and Guangxi, arguably has the most innovative snack tradition. Having been the main source region for the Chinese diaspora, its snack foods are available and well-known beyond China. The region's snack foods use a wide range of ingredients with strong preference for seafood and poultry. Cantonese *dim sum*, for example, are the Chinese equivalent of *tapas* that can serve as either breakfast or brunch, and are enjoyed as a dinner party for the extended families. The variety of *dim sum* ranges from shrimp rice dumplings to steamed chicken feet, from century egg congee to sauteed asparagus, all of which are expertly prepared either in fancy restaurants or at street vendors. A trip to a large Chinatown in the United States or Western Europe may afford one the opportunity of trying out *dim sum* either as a sit-down full meal or as a quick snack stop.

8.6. Rice Noodle Crêpe
(*Chang-fen*; Cantonese: *Cheong-fan*)

This is one of the most common breakfast foods in the Guangdong (Cantonese) cuisine, which is also enjoyed as a *dim sum* entrée during any meal or for snacking. This recipe is among the simplest to follow, suitable for a homemade breakfast or an *hors d'oeuvre* for family or social gatherings.

Yield: Serves 2

Ingredients

For the crêpe:
½ cup rice flour
⅖ wheat starch
⅕ cup starch (preferably water chestnut, cassava, or sweet potato starch)
1¾ cups of water
¾ tsp salt
Cooking oil, as needed

For the sauce:
¼ cup soy sauce
¾ tsp dark soy sauce
½ cup water
1¼–1⅓ tsp sugar
1⅓ tsp oyster sauce
1½ tsp each of ginger and onion

For egg topping:
2 eggs
¼ tsp wet starch
¼ cup fresh lettuce, chopped

Preparation
1. Mix the flour and starches, then pour in the water.
2. Mix until a smooth batter is made.
3. Oil a baking pan, then spread a thin layer of the batter in the pan.
4. Boil water in a steamer.
5. Put the pan in the steamer, and steam for 30 seconds to make a crêpe.
6. Take the pan out of the steamer and use a spatula to scoop the crêpe out.
7. Mix soy sauce, dark soy sauce, oyster sauce, and water.
8. Add minced scallion and ginger to the sauce.
9. Simmer the sauce for 5 minutes.
10. Crack and beat the eggs in a bowl with a teaspoon of wet starch.
11. Steam the egg for approximately 1 minute.
12. Roll the steamed egg with the crêpe, drizzle sauce over it; serve.

Notes: Stir the batter often to prevent batter from congealing; add water if the batter becomes too thick. Make sure to keep the batter layer in the pan thin to ensure its soft texture.

Commercial promotion has made some local snacks famous in recent decades. Sha-xian, an inland county in Fujian Province, had long nurtured a food culture that reflects an infusion of cuisines from southern and northern Fujian Province. Many of the Sha-xian snacks have preserved the styles and flavors of ancient origins because of the area's isolation. In the late 1990s, the county government began to support local businesses to capitalize the traditional snacks with subsidies, standardization, and nationwide promotions. A trade guild for snack makers was established, and *Sha-xian Xiao-chi* (Sha-xian Snacks) was registered as a trademark. The efforts paid off. Nowadays, there are more than 60,000 Sha-xian Snacks shops in China, and its franchization has reached the rest of the world, known for its inexpensive and tasty varieties.

Traditions and New Trends

While famous snacks usually bear unique historical and regional cultural imprints, there are some snacks that transcend these parameters. Chinese everywhere love munching on seeds and nuts, for example. Sunflower seeds, roasted with salt or soaked in spices and then baked, are the favorite, though pumpkin seeds and watermelon seeds are also popular. A watermelon variety was cultivated solely for its large seeds. It is a great pastime for the Chinese to lounge, crack seeds, drink tea, chat, and watch TV. Peanuts are the most affordable and popular among all nuts, and pine nuts, hazelnuts, and wild walnuts are enjoyed where and when they are available. In recent decades, imported pistachios and almonds have gained popularity among the urbanites. Some of the traditional snacks have turned out to be highly problematic, however, as shown by the cancerous effects of betel nuts that people in south China and many Southeastern Asian countries have loved to chew on for centuries (McSpadden, 2021).

New snacks are being developed to please the insatiable and adventurous Chinese populace. Liuzhou, a city in Guangxi, is home to a new snack sensation, *luo-si-fen* (snail rice noodles), a snack that was invented several decades ago. The main ingredients of *luo-si-fen* are rice vermicelli, soup stock made from river snails and pork bones, tofu skin, and a selection of fungi and pickled vegetables. It has a sweet and sour flavor that is derived from the pickled vegetables; the river snails, a local delicacy, give the soup stock and the noodle snack itself a pungent fishy aroma. People agree that it is an acquired taste to enjoy this snack food, and many indeed have. *Luo-shi-fen* has gone through several ups and downs in the marketplace and has carved out a special niche in China's enormous instant noodle market.

China's burgeoning market economy has not only transformed many traditional snacks into mass-produced commodities but also made popular new snacks. Wheat gluten has long been a substitute to meat and even tofu in poor people's diet. It could be flavored with spices and made into various textures. The humble and inexpensive edible, however, became the key ingredient for a star snack that swept through China.

La-tiao (a spicy wheat gluten stick) was invented in 1998, when a major flood decimated crops in southern China. Villagers in an impoverished area in Hunan Province were forced to substitute dry tofu with wheat gluten in making a popular local snack, spicy dry tofu, because of skyrocketing soybean prices. A local businessman saw the business opportunity in wheat gluten and developed a new snack, *la-tiao*, using wheat gluten, chili, sugar, and MSG. Mass production was then set up further north in Henan Province, where wheat flour was cheap and abundant. *La-tiao* was an instant hit in the burgeoning Chinese snack market with its low price and pungent flavor. It quickly conquered the taste buds and hearts of the Chinese youth. Flavorful and cheap, *la-tiao* was the favorite after-school snack that could be had with pocket change.

La-tiao's commercial success, however, had more to do with shrewd promotion on TV, social media (e.g., Weibo), and even rage comic (trollface), which congealed its association with fun for the youth. Despite controversies and scandals related to food safety and dietary health, *la-tiao* has become China's answer to potato chips and fostered a multi-billion-dollar business. The cottage industry comprised of thousands of small *la-tiao* shops two decades ago has consolidated into several large corporations. The largest of them all, *Wei-long*, sells 30–40 million bags of *la-tiao* a year. In 2021, it received financing from venture capital investors, including Hillhouse Capital Group and Sequoia China Investment Management, and applied for an initial public offering (IPO) on the Stock Exchange of Hong Kong with a total market capitalization of more than US$10 billion!

Chinese street food, varied and adventurous, is an intimate reflection of China's diverse regional cultures. What may unify all of them is the passion for food beyond satiating hunger, and snacks are the perfect venue for them to sample the exotic and to appreciate others' way of life. Commercialization and globalization, accompanied by improved living, would allow the Chinese to explore with their imaginations and appetite for both the old and the new, the familiar and the strange, snacks and street food that please all their senses.

Further Reading

Kane, Jason. "Chinese Snacks—Sweet, Salty, and Savory Adventure of Amazing Treats." *Snack History*. https://www.snackhistory.com/chinese-snacks/.

McSpadden, Kevin. "A 'Cancerous Snack' Is Starting to See Raised Eyebrows from Chinese Government." *South China Morning Post,* October 7, 2021. https://www.scmp.com/news/people-culture/social-welfare/article/3151367/cancerous-snack-starting-see-raised-eyebrows?module=lead_hero_story&pgtype=homepage.

Newman, Jacqueline M. "Dim Sum and Other Snack Foods." *Flavor & Fortune* 10, no. 3 (Fall 2003): 29–31. http://www.flavorandfortune.com/ffdataaccess/article.php?ID=431.

Wang, Tracy. "Street Eats: Grilled Cold Noodles? Not Really, but Still Delicious." *The Beijinger,* May 6, 2016. https://www.thebeijinger.com/blog/2016/05/05/street-eats-grilled-cold-noodles-it-opposite.

CHAPTER NINE

Dining Out

Some scholars conclude that the earliest restaurants, by modern definition, appeared in China (Roos, 2020). By the late 11th century, a dining-out culture had emerged with economic prosperity and urban development during the Song Dynasty (960–1279). Neighborhood partition and night curfew were removed, and people dined out as a form of socialization, as a source for sustaining a robust night life, and as a way to enjoy a wide range of cuisines and street food. Upscale restaurants provided not only gourmet dishes but also enticing ambience and entertainment, while the rustling, bustling street food scene pleased everyone in the city. No wonder even emperors were rumored to sneak out of their palaces and frequent these establishments under disguise.

In the next millennium, however, China's dining out scene remained subdued, partly due to a lack of affordability in a society where the masses were impoverished. When economic reform started in the late 1970s, China was replete with very few restaurants, most of which were owned by the state with short business hours and little ambience. It must be noted that wealthier regions, most of which were in the south, always had a more robust dining out scene than their northern counterparts.

Economic reform ushered in an era of rapidly rising living standards as well as lifestyle transformations. As China began to nurture one of the largest consumer economies in the world, its restaurant industry has become a leading marketplace for investment and innovations. A report in 2022 shows that in 2010, China's food service industry had a market capacity, that is, the potential volume of sale of goods and services, of about 1.34 trillion RMB or US$199 billion (2022 values). By 2019, the sector value had jumped to 4.45 trillion RMB or US$662 billion (2022 values). The Chinese are dining out with an unprecedented eagerness and scale; to most of them, dining out is not only affordable and necessary but also an integral part of social life and pop culture.

Dining Out in China Today

The reasons for the Chinese to dine out are no different from those for Americans and other peoples in the world: convenience, special occasions, socialization, gastronomical pleasures, and a combination of these reasons. These reasons for dining out influence the choice of cuisines and establishments. One way to choose a restaurant is to pick a regional cuisine to enjoy the specialty dishes that bear cultural experience and historical legacy. The recipes in this chapter reflect a survey of the so-called four regional schools of cuisines in China that have been recognized in recent history. At the same time, the much hyped eight regional cuisines are very recent and arbitrary conjuring as a promotional response to the tidal wave of dining out during the reform era. Any regional culinary tradition, nonetheless, has its signature dishes, and the complexity in ingredients and preparation make it impossible to cook them at home.

9.1. Braised Intestines in Brown Sauce (*Jiu-zhuan-da-chang*)

The Shandong cuisine may have the longest history in China. It had perhaps the greatest influence over the court menu in the late imperial epoch, thence became renowned in its selectivity of ingredients and elaborate preparation, which transcended in the best of northern cuisines. Today, there are three or four subregional variations, reflecting environmental and social influence through time. To most Americans, animal intestines are not part of their regular diet. To many other peoples, however, they are. The Chinese are particularly fond of intestines and have made famous dishes from street food to court gourmet. This recipe is one of the most famous dishes from the Shandong cuisine.

Yield: Serves 6–8

Ingredients
35 oz. large pork intestines
For cleaning the intestines: 1¾ tbsp salt, 2¾ tbsp white vinegar
1 thumb ginger
1 stick cinnamon
1 dry bay leaf
15 peppercorns
4 star anise
1 tbsp Chinese hard liquor

2 tbsp rock sugar
1½ tbsp white vinegar
¼ tbsp black vinegar
1¼ soy sauce
1 tbsp oyster sauce
¼ tsp black pepper powder
1 cup starch
5 tbsp cooking oil

Preparation
1. Clean the intestines (the strenuous process is omitted here).
2. Overlap the cleaned intestines twice to form four layers and affix it with toothpicks or pins.
3. Place the intestines in a pressure cooker; add ginger, cinnamon, bay leaf, peppercorns, anise stars, Chinese hard liquor, and some water.
4. Steam for 12–15 minutes in low heat after boiling.
5. Slice the intestines into 1-inch sections and coat them with starch.
6. Fry the intestines to light yellow in wok, then take them out.
7. Leave a little oil in the wok, add rock sugar, and let it melt.
8. Stir-fry intestines with white vinegar, black vinegar, soy sauce, oyster sauce and black pepper power for about 1 minute.
9. Add a cup of water and cook till water is reduced to a thick broth.
10. Sample taste the intestines to see if more sugar or vinegar is needed (this dish tastes slightly sweet and sour).
11. Arrange the intestines on a plate; serve.

Notes: There are numerous versions of this famous dish. It is a signature dish known for its strenuous preparation and high demand on the skills of the chef and a must-have entrée in upscale Shandong-style restaurants.

Until recently, convenience was not a main reason for the Chinese to dine out, mainly because of costs: food expenses comprised a lion's share of income for most Chinese, and dining out cost more than eat in. Furthermore, the vast majority of Chinese peasant farmers struggled in poverty and hunger until recent decades, and simply had no money to eat even at low-cost street vendors. For most Chinese, dining out was considered a luxury that few could afford to have.

Historically, the elites and well-to-do did dine out at fine-dining establishments known for their exorbitant dishes and ambience, often tailor-made for their clients. Some of them are still in business today. Even for those who could afford it, however, dining out was viewed as being contradictory to the virtue of humility and wealth embellishment, both of which were antithetical to the Confucian code of social behavior. Eating in, in contrast, was viewed as being the norm to family life, and meal preparation was a top duty for women as homemakers. The common folks, such as day laborers, had to "dine out" because they needed to "eat on the go," but all they could afford was simple, inexpensive bites at street vendors. To them, "dining out" was not something to brag about because of the inferior quality of street food and the dining environment devoid of any ambience.

Convenience-based dining out has become a norm, however, as a result of changing economy and improving living standards. Most workers, blue-collar or white-collar, find themselves spending long hours working and commuting, with little time and energy left at the end of the day to prepare meals at home. Dining out is, as a result, a coping strategy in terms of sustenance replenishment. This is especially true to supper since breakfast and lunch have become rushed refills. Supper is now the biggest meal of the day, but to the tired and weary workers, preparing it from scratch, as their forebears did for many generations, is simply out of the question. Dining out is increasingly the way to get supper, though ready-to-cook food and restaurant food delivery are poised to overtake dining out as the leading forms for supper. A 2019 survey of over 1,800 people showed that no more than a quarter of the respondents preferred cooking and eating at home, while others preferred dining out (28%) or ordering food delivery (37%). Another survey revealed that, in 2019, about a quarter the respondents stated that they would eat out several times a week, while more than half (53%) indicated that they would dine out once a week or several times a month.

Practical considerations dictate the choices when dining out for convenience. Most people would prefer either Chinese or foreign fast-food, bistros, and no-frill restaurants close to home. What they look for is their own "comfort food," that is, eats that they are familiar with and that are easy to ingest and digest, which is important for those who have just completed a day's hard work and dreadful commuting. This type of dining out is a pragmatic routine, usually informal and quick, by individuals, couples, or in small parties.

Special occasions motivate people to spend money to dine out for dishes and ambience that home cooking and eating cannot replicate. Improved living standards today afford many Chinese the convenience and food quality that dining out offers. The Chinese regard many occasions as being special, with perhaps the biggest ones being weddings and funerals. Known as "red and white" revelries, they are used not only to commemorate the important events themselves but also to reaffirm family ties and rekindle friendships. They usually include either banquets at home or dining out at reputable restaurants. Other special occasions that usually involve dining out include birthdays, engagements, graduations and, of course, admissions to desired colleges. Guest gifting during dining out is a social norm and a highly anticipated way to pool familial and communal resources for the hosts or their children. Dining out of this kind usually takes place at large, fine-dining restaurants, where private dining rooms, sometimes even the entire restaurant, are reserved for the special occasions. Catering is also getting popular, though it is difficult for urbanites, most of whom are living in apartments, to have large gatherings at home.

9.2. Steamed Chinese Cabbage in Supreme Soup (*Kai-shui Bai-cai*)

The Sichuan cuisine has the greatest varieties among all Chinese regional cuisines and is also the most popular. From megacities to small towns, from its birthplace in the humid and hot southwest to the arid northwest or cool northeast, one can always find a Sichuanese restaurant. Sichuan cuisine today is renowned for its *ma-la*, or numbing (peppercorns) and spicy (chili peppers), sensations on our taste buds, but such pungency is a relative recent acquisition in southwestern cooking, considering chili pepper was introduced no earlier than the late 16th century into China. Even for its modern reputation, the Sichuan cuisine actually boasts some of its most delicate and delicious dishes that are not spicy, or even bland. This dish, one of the 10 best Sichuanese dishes popular in many upscale restaurants, is a prime example of the versatility and diversity of the Sichuan cuisine.

Yield: Serves 8–10

Ingredients
4–5 Chinese (Napa) cabbage heart (the innermost 6–8 leaves), or 4–5 Chinese baby cabbage
1 free-range old hen
½ lb. pork hocks
½ lb. pork bones
2 tbsp cooking wine
2 tbsp salt
1 thumb fresh ginger (2 tbsp minced)
3 scallions
1 tbsp white pepper powder

Preparation

Chicken stock:

1. Clean the meat: scald the chicken in boiling water for a few minutes; soak the pork bones and hocks in cold water for 20–30 minutes.
2. Fill a large pot with water, chicken, pork bones, and hocks, half of the cooking wine, ginger, and scallions.
3. Bring the pot to a boil, then simmer for 3 hours.
4. Scald napa cabbages, then run them through cold water; place napa cabbage in a large soup bowl.
5. Fill a ceramic pot with the stock, the other half of cooking wine, white pepper powder, and salt; bring to a boil.
6. Pour the stock into the soup bowl with napa cabbage, steam for 30 minutes; serve.

Notes: There are many versions of this dish with various ingredients. The key is to prepare a superior stock, which requires the skills, experience, and patience of the chef. Do not add salt and cold water when preparing the stock to prevent animal protein from solidifying. Skim off the froth when boiling chicken and pork hocks, which is critical in making a clean and rich stock.

Dining out as socialization is as common and popular for the Chinese as it is for the Americans to go to a bar. A 2013 survey showed that 62% of respondents said that their reason for dining out was to meet up with friends. Research in 2017 profiled dining out activities of college students, based on a 2014 survey in Chongqing, and revealed that 56% of respondents stated that meeting friends was the main reason for them to dine out. Social dining out appears to favor places that serve specialty and experimental dishes, which by themselves may become topics of casual conversations, even entertainment. Social dining out is particularly popular with the younger generations, who may have little interests in preparing for a meal from scratch and want the convenience and experience that dining out provides.

The Chinese enjoy gastronomical undertakings as much as any other peoples in the world. When more and more Chinese are becoming able to afford this most favored pastime, the food service industry, especially its fine-dining segment, gets a tremendous business boost. Many specialty dishes, be they unique in terms of regions, ingredients, or preparation, are impossible to prepare at home. First, there are special ingredients that are only available to commercial businesses, such as the special duck for the famed Peking Roast Duck. Second, only restaurants can afford to have special cooking equipment, such as the burners that can generate extraordinary heat, creating the so-called "Maillard reaction" that imparts special flavors to the stir-fried ingredients. In addition, only restaurants can afford to maintain wide-ranging condiments, spices, herbs, seasonings, and stocks. Third, and the most important reason, is the chefs, each of whom is an artist of his or her own character, who can create unique and different gastronomical experience for the diners.

Today, dining out in China presents an all-possible world. In the era of reform and globalization, China has transitioned from an insulated and impoverished country to one where a swelling middle class is eagerly seeking exposure to world cultures. In the cities, dining out presents the dilemma of too many choices, from humble street food stalls to upscale or themed restaurants, and from Chinese regional specialties to endless international flavors, be they American fast food, French bistros, or Brazilian churrascaria. The international eateries operate very much like they do in their respective home countries but often with some added features that cater to China's customs or dining preferences. The most striking example may be how KFC China transformed: it has adopted a menu that blends both classic American and traditional Chinese items. It serves, for example, *you-tiao*, the popular Chinese deep-fried dough and soy milk, alongside hash brown and egg cheese sandwiches for breakfast.

Dining out at upscale and fancy places is a way to embellish wealth or power, or both. Until about a decade ago, dining out on exorbitant meals was an easy way for public officials to indulge themselves on public coffers, and for businesses to curry favors from the government officials. The restaurant industry profited from the rampant corruption, which helped sustain many fancy dining establishments. This era came to a screeching end in 2012, however, when the Chinese government began to crack down on government spending on dining out, which was followed by an anti-corruption campaign. Many luxury restaurants had to either adapt by abandoning menus full of overpriced fancy entrées or close shop for good.

9.3. Sliced Boiled Chicken Served with Sauce (*Bai-qie-ji*; Cantonese: *Bak-chit-gai*)

Of all chicken recipes in Chinese cooking, this one may be the most popular. While its various versions are featured in some southern regional cuisines, it is a signature dish in the Guangdong cuisine and a must-have dish when the Cantonese dine out. The key to this recipe, like to many other Cantonese dishes, is the selectivity and quality of the ingredients, especially the chicken. All chickens are not the same. This recipe requires a specific broiler chicken, the so-called "Three-Yellow," that is, chickens with yellow beak, yellow feet, and yellow feathers, which includes numerous chicken breeds that are native to China and are generally grouped under "Yellow Feather" chickens. It is said that this chicken tastes a lot better than the "White-Feather" broiler chickens that are most common in the United States; the former takes an average 120 days to raise versus no more than 50 days for the latter. In the United States, some Cantonese-style restaurants may serve the "Three-Yellow" chicken as a cold dish.

Yield: Serves 4–5

Ingredients
1 "Three-Yellow" chicken (2.0–2.5 lb.), cleaned
1 bunching onion
1 small thumb ginger
6 cloves fresh garlic
2 tsp sesame oil
1 tsp salt
½ tsp sugar
2 tsp black vinegar
½ tsp MSG

Preparation
1. Bring water in a large pot to a boil, then immerse the cleaned whole chicken completely in the boiling water, cook for 30 minutes.
2. In a small sauce bowl, add minced ginger and scallion with sugar, salt, vinegar, and sesame oil, then add some of the broth in which the chicken was soaked; stir and mix well to make the sauce.
3. Chop the chicken into bite-size pieces and arrange on a plate.
4. Pour the sauce over the chicken; serve.

Dining Out Etiquette

Dining out for specific purposes or occasions accords specific rituals and etiquette. Unlike eating in, when dining out, the Chinese want to focus on dishes with meat and seafood, tofu varieties, poultry and vegetables, which are referred to as *cai*, also called *fu-shi* ("accompanying food") because their function was to aid the ingestion of starch staples, or *zhu-shi* ("main food") in the traditional Chinese diet. When dining out, appetizers or cold dishes are the first course, served along with tea or other beverages. The main courses, or *zhu-cai*, mostly hot specialty dishes, are served next as the highlight of dining out. Starch food, usually steamed rice, noodles, or steamed and baked bread, is served when diners finish up with the main courses. Sometimes sweet snacks are also served at this time. Some believe that starch food is served toward the end of the meal to make sure that everyone would leave with a full stomach, and indeed many diners skip it. The last course is usually a light soup, which can be supplemented or substituted with seasonal fresh fruits. The serving order is designed to let the diners focus on the main courses (*zhu-cai*), which are limited in variety, quality, and quantity in regular daily meals.

One of the most important matters to take note of when dining out in China, in contrast to that in the United States, is that all ordered items are meant to be shared by everyone at the table. Group dining out has been made convenient with the round table topped with a smaller, integrated turntable, similar to a "Lazy Susan," for sharing dishes. The etiquette is to spin the turntable clockwise slowly once entrées are served, so that every diner would have access and time to sample the food. Sometimes, ordering is shared decision-making among the diners, while other times a particular person is designated to do the job, if he or she is supposed to know more about the restaurant or the type of food. The dishes ordered, from appetizers to main entrées, should take into consideration everyone's needs and preference. Usually, the number of main entrées matches that of the diners, and even numbers of both are considered more appropriate.

Another important matter to note when dining out in China is who is responsible for the expenses at the conclusion of the meal. This is a delicate and ritualistic matter due to the complex cultural and social significance of Chinese food culture (Eagan and Weiner, 2011). Customarily, one party would declare that the dining out is his or her treat in advance, and there would be no argument who would pay the bill at the end. The host of a special occasion, for example, most definitely would cover the costs of dining out. There would be a ritualistic tug of war among the diners to pick up the tab when the dining out is a shared decision with no preannounced payer. Often someone would grab the bill before it reaches the table or pay for it at the cashier before anyone else attempts it. It was unimaginable and unacceptable for the Chinese to "go Dutch," or "go AA" ("Algebraic Average") as the Chinese call it. This is still the case for most Chinese, especially the older generations. To them, splitting the bill defeats the very purpose of dining out, which is a ritual to reinforce familial and social relationships. The norm is that diners belonging to the same social or familial circles would take turns paying for the dining out so in the long run the financial cost evens out for everyone. For family dining out, on the other hand, it is the most senior, sometimes the well-to-do working adults, who would pay the bill.

It must be pointed out that "going AA" has gained a social and cultural foothold in recent years, especially among young, white-color profession-als who want to shed the bind of old social norms and who can afford dining out frequently at restaurants of their choice. Social dining out has become a leisure activity for the urban middle class and no longer carries the same ritualistic significance as it did traditionally. To them it is all about being practical and independent, not at all about being proper in traditional ways, to enjoy a good meal with companions and then split the tab evenly.

9.4. Sliced Lamb Quick-Fried with Scallion (*Cong-bao Yang-rou*)

This is a very popular dish in north and northwest regions, where there are large Chinese Muslim communities that feature a wide range of halal specialties.

Yield: Serves 3–4

Ingredients
12 oz. mutton, preferably leg meat
2 tsp baking soda
½ cup cooking oil
3 bunching onion (*Allium fistulosum*)
2 cloves of fresh garlic
3 *Xiaomila* pepper (*Capsicum frutescens*), similar to Tabasco pepper
Marinate: ¼ tsp salt, ½ tsp dark soy sauce, 1 egg white, 1 tbsp potato starch, ¾ tbsp canola oil
Sauce: ⅛ tsp salt, ⅛ tsp black pepper powder, 2 tbsp cooking wine, 1½ tbsp soy sauce, ⅓ tbsp dark soy sauce, ½ tbsp sesame oil

Preparation
1. Thinly slice the mutton against its grains; clean out fat and tissues.
2. Add baking soda to cold water; rinse sliced mutton for about one minute.
3. Rinse mutton in water several times to get rid of baking soda taste.
4. Cut the white section of bunching onion and *Xiaomila* pepper perpen-dicularly; mince the garlic.

5. Marinate: (1) add salt and dark soy sauce to the mutton, mix clockwise till the mutton feels sticky, (2) add and mix the egg white with the mutton, then the potato starch, then cooking oil.
6. Make the sauce by mixing ingredients for the sauce in the order they were listed.
7. Heat the ½ cup cooking oil to about 300 degrees Fahrenheit.
8. Remove the wok from stove and add marinated mutton; stir to separate.
9. Remove mutton from wok when it turns opaque.
10. Pour out most of the hot cooking oil, then heat the remaining oil to about 350 degrees Fahrenheit.
11. Stir-fry *Xiaomila* pepper till aroma is generated.
12. Stir-fry bunching onion for a few seconds, then add mutton.
13. Drizzle in sauce along the side of the wok; stir-fry for about 8 seconds.
14. Place mutton on a plate; serve hot.

Notes: This is a dish to dine out for. The most discriminating chefs prefer leg or tenderloin for this dish; the former is more flavorful and the latter tenderer; the key to success for this dish, however, lies in stir-frying the marinated meat briefly in high heat (*bao*, or "explosive" quick stir-fry), which is nearly impossible to obtain even with the most powerful gas stoves at home.

Seating custom is the third etiquette point for dining out. Traditionally, it was the most important of Chinese dining etiquette rules because it was a real-life manifestation of the Confucian code, which emphasizes familial and social hierarchy, the foundation of order and stability. Today, the traditional seating arrangement may not be as strictly observed as it used to be, but it is definitely followed at more formal or multigenerational family dining out events (Xin, 2015). As a general rule, the seat facing the door, or the main entrance, is the seat of honor and reserved for the most senior member of the family or highest-ranking person of the dining party. Others are seated from the seat of honor based on their seniority in the family or status among the diners.

One traditional dining etiquette can be annoying to Westerners. The Chinese hosts and seniors always pay close attention to making sure that everyone gets enough food, and each would get more from his or her favorite dishes. For such purposes, they often pick out and "chopsticks over" food for others since the guests and juniors are not supposed to "help themselves." "Help yourself" as the American expression of hospitality implies almost the opposite in the Chinese dining etiquette. Henry Kissinger, President Nixon's National Security Advisor who secretly visited China in 1971, certain got his first-hand experience of the Chinse dining etiquette (NCUSCR, 2022). Film footage shows that Kissinger was treated with a banquet, in which occasion the Chinese Premier picked up food from a dish and placed it on his plate. The Premier did the same for President Nixon himself at the state banquet in Beijing in 1972 (Perlez, 2022). This practice is certainly taboo in the West, but we must remember the motto, "in China, do what the Chinese do." To our relief, the younger generations appear to be abandoning the "chopsticks over" part of the ritual even though they are still verbally attentive to others during a meal.

Traditionally, it was not common to have serving utensils for the purposes of fetching food from the shared dishes—the Chinese mostly used their own chopsticks to do so. This practice has obvious public health ramifications, especially when dining out with friends and acquaintances who otherwise would not be in such close physical contact with each other. Lately, there has been an effort to promote use of communal serving utensils for food sharing purposes, which appears to have gotten a big boost after the outbreak of the COVID-19 pandemic because of the conspicuous correlations between public hygiene and infectious diseases. The devastating pandemic finally struck a chord in public awareness and resulted in local regulations mandating provision and use of shared serving utensils at restaurants.

Table setup for each diner at a decent restaurant consists of a plate, a pair of chopsticks on a rest in a vertical direction, a teacup, a liquor shot glass, a soup bowl and Chinese soup spoon, and napkins (cloth ones in upscale restaurants). Knives and forks may be available in upscale or international restaurants, usually upon request. Once seated, the waitstaff would bring the menu to the host, serve free tea of mediocre quality, and, in some upscale restaurants, offer warm towels for guests to freshen up. In China, cold tap water is not automatically served for both digestive and sanitation reasons. Tea is traditionally the most common beverage during the meal, but alcohol beverages, from Chinese hard liquor to beer, are always popular drinks at dining out. Chinese hard liquor is the traditional favorite, but beer is the most common. Chinese rice wine (*huang-jiu*) is still consumed in some regions, especially the Yangzi Delta. Wines are quickly becoming the choice alcohol beverage among young white-collar professionals in fine-dining and upscale restaurants.

Hot Pot Nation

The earliest known hot pot was excavated from the tomb of a former emperor of the Han Dynasty whose reign lasted 27 days in 74 BCE. Hot pot became a regular restaurant cuisine during the Song Dynasty (960–1267) and gained great popularity during the Ming and Qing dynasties (1368–1911). It is the top culinary choice for dining out in China today. In 2018, for example, hot pot accounted for 22%, or more than US$120 billion, of the total revenue of China's food service industry. The most famous hot pot may be Instant Boiled Mutton, but Sichuan/Chongqing hot pot is arguably the most popular.

The Chinese prefer to consume alcohol with food as a health measure, and the best time to drink is during dining out. Toasting can be not only typical but also exhaustive during dining out. People frequently stand up and toast to each other, and *gan-bei* ("bottom up") is both a rally cry and a real act. Diners try to trick others into drinking more while staying sober themselves. Sometimes, the dining scene can get rowdy when friends and close acquaintances start playing finger games, and the losers would have to drink more alcohol. One needs not worry too much about excessive drinking at most family dining out events since being rowdy is not socially acceptable.

With or without consultation, the host(s) would place the order. Yet another etiquette for dining out is the amount of food ordered. To the host, it is imperative that plenty of food be ordered because it is a social disgrace if the dishes are completely consumed during the meal. Dishes are usually heaped up on the table; it is better to have a lot of leftovers, which means the hosts have fully displayed their generosity and hospitality, and collectively everyone has triumphed over the enduring food insecurity at a meal of plenty. By the same token, it used to be considered a stingy act if the host took leftovers home, and an insult if any guests dared to do so. This practice resulted in enormous waste as dining out has become a regular activity. It is a relief to see more and more people, especially the young, moving away from over-ordering and wasting leftovers when dining out, as a result of public campaigns and exposure to Western dining out etiquettes.

9.5. Sautéed Shelled River Shrimp (*Shui-jing Xia-ren*)

This is a signature dish in the Shanghai cuisine, which gained unique characteristics and reputation as Shanghai became an international city in the late 1800s. This dish was selected as one of the 10 most famous Shanghai dishes in 2018 and is a must-order entrée at a Shanghainese restaurant. Its most special feature is also its main ingredient: the freshwater shrimp (*Macrobranchium nipponense*) that is particularly plentiful in the Yangzi Delta. Notwithstanding the special nutritional value that many locals insist it possesses, the freshwater shrimp does carry a unique flavor that other types of shrimp cannot replicate in this and other Yangzi Delta dishes.

Yield: Serves 4–6

Ingredients
1 lb. large river shrimps, shelled and deveined
1 egg white
⅔ tbsp yellow cooking wine (Shaoxing brand)
2⅛ tbsp starch
2⅔ tbsp salt
⅕ tsp granulated sugar
Pinch of baking soda
7¼ cups peanut oil

Preparation
1. Wash the shrimp in cold water, then marinate them with the cooking wine, half of the salt and baking soda—mix with hands until the shrimps feel sticky.
2. Put the shrimp in a refrigerator for about an hour, then rinse off the marinade and pat dry with paper towels.
3. Coat the shrimp with the other half of salt and baking soda, egg white, and starch.
4. Heat peanut oil in a wok to about 300 degrees Fahrenheit, stir-fry the shrimp till they turn light yellow, then ladle them out to a plate with a skimmer; serve.

Notes: Make sure to pat the shrimp dry after marinating and rinsing them so that they can be well coated in step 3. Some recipe variations call for cooking the shrimp with delicate vegetables such as fresh lily pads (*bai-he*) or asparagus to add refreshing flavor and pleasing color to the dish.

Until now, tipping is not expected when dining out in China, and there is no separate sales tax added to the bill. It can make the final tab significantly smaller than what would be the case in the United States. Some upscale restaurants, especially those that cater to an international business clientele or the local elites, may add gratuity or "service fees" to the tab, however.

Notwithstanding all the talk about traditional dining out etiquette, it is reassuring that today's China is becoming much less uptight with rigid traditions since the socioeconomic conditions have fundamentally changed, and the changes have transcended many customs and rules. There is a set of rules for using chopsticks properly, for example, but a Westerner only needs to remember not to use the chopsticks in ways that he or she would not do with forks and knives. The Chinese are generally very easy-going with those who are expected to be ignorant of traditional Chinese dining etiquettes. At the worst, "bad behavior" by the innocents would elicit a frown from the elders or stubborn traditionalists, as portrayed in the acclaimed American film, *Joy Luck Club*. Meanwhile, the young generations are eager to learn and follow Western dining etiquette!

9.6. Beijing Grilled Meat (*Beijing Kao-rou*)

A famous restaurant specialty in Beijing today, its origin was the true "Mongolian Barbecue" that was brought to Beijing in the late 17th century after the Manchu–Mongol alliance conquered China and made Beijing the capital of the Manchu Qing Dynasty (1644–1911). As time went on, the meaty nomadic specialty became a favorite staple for all groups and developed specific etiquette and styles fitting to the socioeconomic and ethnic mosaic of an imperial capital. The centerpiece, so to speak, of this dish is the grill made of cast iron strips, which allows fat and juice to drip off. The meat, usually mutton and beef, is sliced to thin pieces and marinated before being grilled.

Yield: Serves 3–4

Ingredients
2 lb. mutton (lamb) or beef, thinly sliced
1 onion, sliced
2 dry chili pepper, chopped
2 bunching onions, sliced
2 tbsp granulated sugar
½ cup cooking wine
1 cup soy sauce
1 thumb fresh ginger, minced
1 tsp white pepper powder
1 tsp cumin powder
1 tbsp roasted white sesame seeds
1 bunch cilantro, sectioned

Preparation
1. Fire up the grill.
2. Marinate the meat with onion, chili pepper, bunching onion, sugar, cooking wine, soy sauce, cumin, salt, and white pepper powder, 10–15 minutes.
3. Spread marinated meat on the hot grill, and flip when the meat color starts getting darker.
4. When the second side of the meat starts to change color, put onion from the marinade on, and grill for another 10–15 seconds.
5. Take the meat off the grill, top it with cilantro and sesame seeds, and self-serve.

Notes: The special grills are provided in restaurants serving this specialty, but any grills or cast-iron cooking utensils can substitute if one were to make this dish at home. Korean BBQ in the United States may be the closest equivalent to this dish, though the flavors diverge with their own distinct marinades.

The COVID-19 pandemic took a toll on most people and almost every aspect of life. The robust Chinese restaurant industry was hit particularly hard. The 2020 market capacity of food service industries declined to 3.78 trillion RMB or US$563 billion from 4.45 trillion RMB or US$662 billion in 2019 (2022 values). China's "Zero-COVID" policy, which triggered community or even city-wide lockdowns because of a few positive cases, had a disproportionate impact on dining out, which had been a center-piece of the emerging consumer culture in China. In addition to pandemic-induced business shuttering, dining out is one of the first items to be cut back as consumers retrench their spending. Fortunately, dining out also appears to be one of the first activities to roar back when lockdowns are lifted, as the Chinese are being reminded how invaluable the greatest Chinese pastime really is: it is a freedom to savor when dining out with family, friends, or even acquaintances.

In the long run, what may dampen dining out activities and devastate the robust growth of the restaurant industry may be the so-called "ceiling effect": the increasing costs of rent, labor, and ingredients can no longer be offset by price increases and cutbacks in labor cost. The impact of the pandemic may have helped accelerate a new food trend that is redefining food service industries and impacting dining out in China. The market share of ready-to-cook dishes (*yu-zhi-cai*), also known as "ready-made dishes" or "semi-finished dishes," has been surging (Xia, 2022) thanks to advances in food processing and development of cold chain logistics. The market capacity of ready-to-cook dishes reached 345.9 billion RMB (approximately US$51 billion) in 2021 and is projected to reach 517 billion RMB (US$76 billion) in 2023. All segments of food service industries are racing to meet the demand, and the sky seems to be the limit for this new business venture. It would be interesting to see how the burgeoning dining out activities are impacted.

Further Reading

Eagan, Angie, and Rebecca Weiner. *CultureShock! China: A Survival Guide to Customs and Etiquette,* 2nd ed. Tarrytown, NY: Marshall Cavendish, 2011.

National Committee on US-China Relations (NCUSCR). "The Trip that Changed the World: Commemorating Kissinger's 1971 Secret Visit to China." July 8, 2022. https://www.ncuscr.org/event/kissinger-1971-secret-visit-china/.

Perlez, Jane. "Nixon in China: Are There Lessons for Today's Leaders?" *Financial Times,* February 10, 2022. https://www.ft.com/content/aa0192f4-6ec3-465a-83fc-fe046a8b1882.

Roos, Dave. "When Did People Start Eating in Restaurants?" History.com, May 18, 2020. https://www.history.com/news/first-restaurants-china-france.

Xin, Diana. "Chinese Dining Etiquette Survival Guide." YoyoChinese.com, January 13, 2015. https://yoyochinese.com/blog/learn-mandarin-chinese-dining-etiquette-chopstick-manners-paying-the-bill-toast-phrases-seating-arrangement.

Zhong, Xia. "Booming Semi-Finished Food Market and Appetite of Young Chinese." *CGTN,* January 18, 2022. https://news.cgtn.com/news/2022-01-18/Booming-semi-finished-food-market-and-appetite-of-young-Chinese-16T2qYZDBAs/index.html.

CHAPTER TEN

Food Issues and Dietary Concerns

We face a wide range of food issues and dietary concerns. Some in the world have to cope with the consequences of gluttony while many others suffer from hunger. Malnutrition is a persistent impediment for hundreds of millions of children, while high fat and sugar diets have worsened diabetes and cardiovascular illnesses to epidemic proportions. People in wealthy societies are likely to pay more attention to the health effects of ingredients, while safe food and drinking water are hard to come by in many poor countries. In the era of unprecedented globalization, traditional food cultures are facing both pressures to change and opportunities to reinvent. What, then, are the challenges that China faces regarding these critical food issues and dietary concerns? New challenges have risen from mounting pressure on China's agricultural resources, a new diet more dependent on animal protein, and concerns with food safety and public health, commercialization, and loss of food cultural heritage.

Food Security

"One cannot govern without the people; the people cannot be governed without food." This ancient adage remains the principle for governance for Chinese leaders ever since an advisor counseled Liu Bang (256–195 BCE), the founding emperor of the Han Dynasty (202 BCE–220 CE), in such words. Liu, in a desperate campaign against his main rival, heeded the advice to seize control of state grain stockpile and subsequently won a decisive victory. For millennia, the main mandate for the Chinese rulers was to see to it that their subjects were well fed, but too often failed to do so. The Chinese people suffered from frequent famines and perennial malnourishment through much of their history.

In 1942–1943, Henan Province, in the heart of the North China Plain, suffered from droughts and locust attack, and government failure to deliver relief triggered severe famine; the toll was covered by *Time* Magazine (Yarrow, 2022). Between 1959 and 1961, China suffered widespread crop failure, international isolation, and ill-fated government policies that led to national famine in which tens of millions of people perished (Great Famines of China during the Great Leap Forward).

China came to bear the image of a perilous land where people were always on the verge of starvation. "Don't you know the Chinese kids are starving?!" became a *cliché* for American parents to push kids to finish their meals. Lester R. Brown, a prominent environmentalist, warned his audience of "overpopulation" with a shout-out: "Who will feed China?" (Brown, 1995).

China must feed itself, which is a daunting task. At the outbreak of the COVID-19 pandemic, the first instinct for many Chinese was to stock up food, and the government had to saturate all communications channels with the promise that the country had the strategic reserve of cereal grains to feed the entire population for at least a year. The Chinese government has furthered its resolve to enhance China's food security as the world faces great uncertainties wrought by the COVID-19 pandemic, Russia–Ukraine conflict, and dramatic environmental changes.

10.1. Iceberg Lettuce in Oyster Sauce (*Hao-you-ban-sheng-cai*)

Lettuce did not become popular in China until recent years. The Chinese figured out that a quick stir-fry in oyster sauce was a good way to eat lettuce, since it is delicate, bland, and easily overcooked. This recipe requires a little more work, but the result is a refreshing and flavorful vegetable dish that can serve as either an appetizer or a side dish to a variety of main courses. This simple recipe using common ingredients can be very popular at a meal that is overloaded with meat and other heavy main courses.

Yield: Serve as needed

Ingredients
1 iceberg lettuce (about a pound; other types of lettuces would also work, but iceberg lettuce is the best for this recipe for its crunchy texture)
1 average size red bell pepper
6 cloves of fresh garlic
Oyster sauce, soy sauce, starch, cooking oil, and cane sugar

Preparation

1. Wash and hand-break the lettuce to 1-inch pieces.
2. Chop the red bell pepper to small cubes (approximately 0.2 inch).
3. Peel and mince the garlic.
4. Dissolve ½ teaspoon of starch in 4–5 tablespoons of water.
5. Fill a pot with water, add pinches of salt and drops of cooking oil, and bring it to a boil.
6. Blanch the lettuce and drain it thoroughly; the lettuce should now be softer and translucent.
7. Arrange the lettuce loosely in a shallow bowl or deep plate.
8. In a wok, add 4–5 tablespoons of cooking oil, and sauté the minced garlic.
9. When the garlic becomes aromatic, add 3–4 tablespoons of oyster sauce and 2–3 tablespoons of soy sauce, with pinches of sugar.
10. Add the dissolved starch to the wok; stir and mix the ingredients for 10–15 seconds.
11. Add the chopped bell pepper to the wok and stir-mix well with other ingredients, 10–15 seconds.
12. Top the lettuce with the sauce; serve.

In recent decades, significant progress has been made in China's food production, which has greatly improved China's food security. China is a top producer of rice, wheat, and most coarse grains, roots and tubers, fruits, meat, poultry, and eggs. It also tops the world by a large margin in vegetable and aquatic productions. Per capita grain production also increased in the past decades, from about 200 kilograms (440 lb.) per person at the beginning of the 1980s to about 600 lb. two decades later. This number jumped to 1,064 lb. in 2021, higher than the internationally recommended 880 lb. per person per year (Zhang, Xu, and Xiao, 2022).

A close look at the statistics, however, shows that China's domestic cereal grain production has not kept up with domestic consumption, mainly due to increasing demand for animal feed. Specifically, China's total food (including cereal grains, potatoes and sweet potatoes, soybeans, and other legumes) production could only satisfy 86–87% of domestic needs in recent years. The gap between domestic production and demand is mainly caused by increasing consumption of animal feed, as the Chinese diet has been shifting to greater animal protein intake and domestic animal husbandry has skyrocketed. As a result, China has become a major importer of feed, especially corn and soybeans, in the international market. In 2020, 85% of China's domestic soybean consumption came from imports, about 100 million tons or 60% of the total international soybean trade. As the home of soybean domestication, China's soybean farming has been decimated by international competition in recent decades. The cheap GMO soybeans flooded in while China resisted adopting high-yield seeds from international corporations for security and health considerations.

Food security remains a paramount challenge for China. First, conditions of agricultural resources constrain the potential of food production increase. China feeds 18% of the world population with 8–9% of world's arable land. Furthermore, China has been losing arable land due to unsustainable agricultural operations, industrial pollution, urban sprawl, and climate change. China has a small margin for error in terms of its food security without long-term, sustainable solutions.

Taking it as the national priority, the Chinese government has endeavored on multiple fronts to confront food insecurity. Every year, China's central authorities would issue a number of policy directives that are dubbed "central documents." Since 2004, the first such directive, or "No. 1 central document," has been on the priorities and support for agriculture, the countryside, and the farmers (*san-nong*). The 2023 No. 1 central document, for example, outlines nine tasks for countryside vitalization, and the first task is "to stabilize production and ensure supply of grain and important agricultural products" (Xinhua, 2023).

China has eagerly invested in new technology and introduced innovations in agriculture and food sectors. Decades of intensive scientific research has yielded new crop varieties that have much higher yield and are more durable to natural hazards, the most notable of which is the hybrid rice by Yuan Long-ping (Wu, 2021). In September 2021, Chinese scientists announced that they had succeeded in turning carbon dioxide into starch in the laboratory environment (Xinhua, 2021). Chinese scientists have also succeeded in breeding perennial rice, which is cost-efficient for the farmers and has a higher yield than its annual counterparts. In late 2022, Chinese scientists announced that they had discovered a gene variant in wild corn that could boost corn's protein content from about 10% to 30% (Huang et al., 2022).

China has also made great strides in conservation. Farmland conservation includes nationwide soil erosion programs and the so-called "Three-North" afforestation project (Ding, 2018), which was designed to slow down and eventually stop rapid desertification in northern China. The Chinese government has set the so-called "redline" for the minimum acreage of farmland, about 120 million hectares (nearly 300 million acres), with 103 million hectares dedicated to grain production. The threshold is in line with the government's goal of producing 650 million tons of cereal grains and 89 million tons of meat annually, and not crossing it is no small task as urban sprawl and industrial expansion, two driving engines for China's economic growth, exert enormous pressure on the best farmland near urban centers. Even if China succeeds in holding this redline, the per capita farmland is only 0.2 acres for China, in contrast to more than one acre for the United States.

China has been tiptoeing in one crucial area of food technology, namely, genetically modified organisms (GMOs). On the one hand, ordinary Chinese are cautious about the unknown health effects of GMO food; at the same time, the Chinese government considers the lack of control over GMO seeds' supply and modification as a breach of national food security. The imported soybeans and corn are almost exclusively used as animal feed, while their domestic equivalents are used for direct human consumption, such as making soy food and cooking oil. There are signs that the Chinese government is giving a closer look at GMOs and has made substantial progress in developing its own GMO seeds. It is doubtful, however, whether China would fully embrace foreign GMOs if doing so may jeopardize its absolute control over the entire chain of food production and consumption.

10.2. Hot and Sour Soup (*Suan-la-tang*)

Sweet and sour soup, a less spicy and sweeter version of this recipe, is served in many Chinese restaurants in the United States. In China, it is usually spiced up with white pepper powder. It has various regional versions and names but is always popular as an appetizer with its enticing tangy taste, which the Chinese believe would help digestion.

Yield: Serves 6–8

Ingredients
3.5 oz. tofu
1.8 oz. lean meat
2 eggs
0.4 oz. vermicelli
8 wood ears
3 shitake mushrooms
1½ tbsp vinegar
1 tbsp soy sauce
2 tsp white pepper powder
1 tsp MSG (it can be omitted)
⅛ cup cilantro

4 cups meat bone stock
Amount as needed: cooking oil, salt, green onion, fresh ginger, starch,
    sesame oil

Preparation
1. Soak the wood ears and vermicelli in lukewarm water for 30–40 minutes.
2. Slice the meat, tofu, and wood ears; cut vermicelli to 4-inch sections.
3. Mince the onion and ginger.
4. Crack and beat the eggs in a bowl.
5. Wash and cut the cilantro.
6. Heat a tablespoon of cooking oil in a wok; stir-fry ginger and onion till aromatic.
7. Stir fry meat till its color turns opaque.
8. Stir fry mushrooms till softened.
9. Pour in the stock; water can be added to increase volume or dilute pungency.
10. Bring the soup to a boil, then add tofu, wood ears, and vermicelli.
11. Dissolve starch with some water.
12. Pour wet starch into the wok and get the soup to desired thickness.
13. Add soy sauce, salt, vinegar, and egg, in this order.
14. Bring the soup to a boil.
15. Add white pepper powder, MSG, cilantro, and sesame oil; mix and remove from stove; serve.

Notes: Add white pepper powder to the soup no more than 30 seconds before removing the wok/pot from the stove. Meat bone stock can be substituted with chicken stock or even water to avoid greasy texture. Do not make the vermicelli too soft.

An increase in crop production in recent decades has been attributed to heavy uses of agricultural chemicals such as fertilizers, herbicides, and pesticides. China used 12 million tons of chemical fertilizers in 1980s, and more than quadrupled the amount to 56 million tons 30 years later. Data show that China's chemical fertilizer use accounts for one-third of the world total but only produces 25% of starch food in the world. Excessive use of agricultural chemicals has caused serious environmental and health problems such as declining nutrient utilization rate, deteriorating soil fertility, environmental pollution, and crop contamination. All these problems post long-term threats to food security and negative impacts on food safety and public health. The Chinese government began to curb agricultural chemical use in recent years with technology guidelines and farmer assistance to minimize adverse impact on agricultural output. After peaking at over 60 million tons in 2015, China's chemical fertilizer use began to decrease precipitously. In 2020, China's total chemical fertilizer use was 52.5 million tons, and the 2021 figure went further down to 51.9 million tons.

China's food imports have outpaced exports since the early 1990s, and it is now a major food importer. In 2021, China imported 28 million tons of corn, marking a 152% increase over 2020 (11.3 million tons). Wheat imports also hit a record 9.77 million tons, an increase of 16.6% over 2020. In the same year, China bought roughly 60% of soybeans, 13% of corn, and 4.6% of wheat available on the world market. These numbers appeared to go up in 2022 as geopolitical uncertainties and environmental changes prompted the Chinese government to shore up strategic grain reserves. During the first half of 2022, for example, China's reserve of key grains exceeded half of the world total, that is, 69% of corn, 61% of rice, and 51% of wheat, while its soybean reserve was 30% of the world's total. China's international buying spree and insatiable stockpile have caused consternation as global grain prices continued to rise.

Another controversial approach to enhancing food security is China's investment in farming operations overseas. In recent years, China has joined the ranks of countries in leasing large tracts of farmland in Africa, Latin America, and Europe (Ukraine) to produce grains and other food for Chinese domestic market. While some in the United States have sounded alarms that Chinese companies were buying up American agricultural resources, the Chinese count for less than 1% of total foreign owned land in the United States, far below the Netherlands (13%), Italy (7%), the United Kingdom (6%), and Germany (5%). In contrast, China has bought much larger acreage of land in some African and Asian countries, such as Myanmar, Russia, Belarus, Cambodia, and Venezuela. In 2013, China, through Xinjiang Production and Construction Corps (XPCC), acquired nearly 9% of all farmlands in Ukraine. Chinese investment in international food business is not limited to farmland acquisitions. It may come as a surprise that many Chinese investors in overseas food businesses sell their products at the host countries instead of to the Chinese market (Gooch and Gale, 2018). It may be reasonable to conclude that Chinese overseas investment in food and agriculture does not contribute significantly to China's food supply but may have long-term strategic ramifications in world food supply.

A peculiar phenomenon is enormous food waste in China in recent years, considering how deeply food insecurity has become imbedded in its national psyche. It is estimated that the wasted food every year is enough to feed 200 million Chinese! According to the *Food Waste Index Report 2021* by the United Nations Environmental Programme (UNEP), China generated the largest quantity of food waste, though the top five countries in terms of per capita food waste are the United States, Australia, New Zealand, Ireland, and Canada (Douglas and Groom, 2022). The waste comes from several main sources. First, an average of 350 million tons of grains are lost every year due to deficiencies in the country's infrastructure and management systems for processing, transportation, and storage. This source of waste accounts for more than one-third of the total food waste, based on the estimates by UNEP.

Second, the Chinese appear to be more wasteful when they dine out. This is an unexpected downside of China's burgeoning dining out culture. People tend to overorder, perhaps due in part to vanity and in part to overcompensation of food scarcity from which they and their forebears suffered. Surveys show that up to 38% of food at large banquets is wasted, and school students discard almost one-third of their meals. The waste is real and stunning. Data show that, in 2018, every diner wasted almost 12% of the food ordered on average. In total, roughly 20 million tons of food were wasted each year. Some Chinese have also taken gluttony for fun; eating competitions on social media have a big fan base. In response, the government has countered with public awareness campaigns and even passed laws to curb food waste. As early as 2012, a "clean your plate" campaign promoted food frugality as a moral code and to improve national food security. In 2021, the Standing Committee of National People's Congress passed "Anti-food Waste Law of the People's Republic of China" as the legal basis for reducing food waste. Food waste remains a major problem, however.

Food Safety

China's food safety has become a major concern ("Tainted and Poisoned Foods in China," 2015). The country is confronted by, first, increasing commercialization and mass production that have taken food procurement out of the hands of individuals and families. Mishaps and scandals are the results of intertwined factors such as material contamination and use of harmful additives, lack of industrial hygiene and lax quality control, poor management, and insufficient regulatory enforcement. A major culprit to food safety is the horrendous environmental pollution induced by rapid industrial and urbanization. It is estimated that nearly 20% of China's farmland is polluted. Many farmers even refuse to eat the foods they produce, knowing how toxic they are.

Food safety has also been compromised by substandard industrial operations, including poor quality and sanitation control, and widespread business malpractice. These problems permeate all stages of the food supply chain, including food processing and packaging, handling and storage, distribution and retailing, and consumption. By the early 21st century, food scares had become frequent news headlines, such as use of the so-called Sudan Red, a toxic red dye, in making certain products appear more enticing. A widespread shady business operation involved collecting and reusing used cooking oil, or "gutter oil" as it was aptly called. Illegal liquor under bogus labels had, and still has, its own nationwide supply chain. None of the food safety scandals was worse than the 2008 milk formula catastrophe, however, in which a major dairy processor, Sanlu Group, was found to have added melamine to its milk and infant formula, ostensibly to enhance the protein content. Up to 300,000 infants, mostly from low-income families, suffered from kidney damage. The local government, at the same time, tried to cover it up. After the incident became a national, even international, scandal in September 2008, the central government intervened, and punishments were meted out swiftly to those who were directly responsible. Further probes showed, however, adulterating formula was a widespread industrial practice in the fiercely competitive formula market. The scandal prompted the Chinese government to pass the Food Safety Law the next year (2009). Repercussions of the scandal were long-lasting: in the years to come, the Chinese shunned all domestic formula brands and rushed to purchase imported formula (Huang, 2018).

While overall food safety has improved since then, it continues to pose a major concern with new scandals and incidents. China has a robust cottage food industry that churns out tens of millions of tons of mainstream or off-beat snacks with little or no regulatory oversight. Large companies often outsource production to them to save costs and jack up profit, while providing little or no quality control. In 2022, it was exposed that pickled sour cabbage (the Chinese equivalent to sauerkraut), a key ingredient in a flavor-branded instant noodle, was prepared under extremely unsanitary conditions by villagers who were under contract with Hunan Chaqi, a corporate supplier to other large food producers (Qi, 2022). After media exposure, companies using sour cabbage from Hunan Chaqi removed all their products from store shelves, but the incident further weakened public confidence in the food industry and food safety in general.

A silver lining of heightened sensitivity toward food safety is the rising support for "green" food, innovative food collectives, and fledgling community-supported agriculture (CSA), especially among the well-heeled urban middle class that has both the demand and wherewithal for healthy and safe food.

Efforts in improving food safety have run into entrenched roadblocks due to some of the traditional dietary preferences and dining etiquette. First, certain aspects of food tradition persist even though they can no longer be legitimized as coping strategies for severe food insecurity; they have come to bear negative consequences to public health and environmental damage on a much larger scale. The lack of regulation over the wildlife trade results in a health and food safety nightmare. There was some scientific evidence, for example, that the 2003 SARS (severe acute respiratory syndrome) outbreak was related to civets, a mammal that was considered a delicacy in the Cantonese cuisine. Some research has hypothesized that the original source of COVID-19 outbreak was linked to a so-called wet market in Wuhan, where wildlife, live and dead, was traded with little oversight. Appetite for wildlife presents major concerns to food safety and ecological conservation. Curtailing wildlife consumption, however, has met stiff resistance in China. Many eager consumers are willing to pay hefty prices not only for the exotic gastronomical experience but also for the concomitant socioeconomic status.

In addition to wildlife, another controversial culinary tradition is consumption of dog meat in some regions. Unlike the case in Korea, where dogs are raised for meat, dog meat in China comes mostly from pet and guard dogs that are either abandoned by their owners or ensnared by criminals. Notwithstanding mounting public loathing in China, dog meat consumption is first and foremost a real threat to food safety and public health because there is no regulation, not to say standards, over the sources and health conditions of the dogs. Amid increasing public outcry, the government appears reluctant to pass legislation to ban or at least restrict dog meat consumption, perhaps because most Chinese are indifferent toward this issue even if they themselves do not eat dog meat.

Dietary Changes and Health Concerns

A common pleasantry in China went like this: "Wow, you've gained some weight!" No longer used today, it was meant to flatter someone for having more than plenty to eat, which was no small feat for most common folks throughout Chinese history marred by food insecurity. Rapid economic development has afforded most Chinese adequate basic foodstuff, and many have started to indulge and have zeroed in on meat and seafood. The Chinese per capita annual meat consumption jumped from 32 lb. in 1980 to 110 lb. in 2000. After peaking in 2017 at 136 lb. in

2017, the figure dropped to 98 lb. in 2020, in part due to drastic increases in pork prices. The projected per capita meat consumption in 2022 is 115 lb., according to the Food and Agriculture Organization of the United Nations (FAO). Meanwhile, other forms of animal protein, such as eggs, seafood, and dairy products, have substantially increased during the same period.

Meat Consumption

Until recent decades, the Chinese ate little meat. In 1961, China's per capita annual meat consumption was only 17–18 pounds. This number jumped to 50 pounds in 1990, as China's economic reform began to accelerate. In 2019, China's per capita annual meat consumption rose to 106 pounds. Between 1975 and 2018, China's total meat consumption increased from 7 million tons to 86.5 million tons, the highest of any country. While America's per capita meat consumption is still more than twice as much as China's, the astronomical increase of Chinese total meat consumption bears great environmental and geopolitical ramifications.

While carbohydrate intake declined in recent years, the Chinese are eating more fat than ever. In 2020, fat accounted for 35% of energy intake through food and beverages, exceeding the recommended range of 20% to 30%. Changes in dietary structure have been accompanied by the introduction of "fast food." Nowadays, American-style fast food has a strong presence in the Chinese diet, especially among the urban middle class and the young. Chinese-style fast food has also become very popular, especially in the form of prepared food such as instant noodles. Large quantity and regular consumption of fast foods carry health risks due not only to their high sodium and fat content, as well as other artificial additives, but also their inducement for fast and irregular eating.

Consciously or not, the Chinese seem to be overcompensating their cravings for fat and protein that they lacked in the previous generations. They prefer deep fried or grilled meat, soy, and seafood and shun fiber-rich, carbohydrate-heavy traditional staples. The dietary changes appear to accelerate with little public awareness of their unhealthy consequences that are exacerbated by an increasingly stationary lifestyle (Zhang et al., 2015). The prevalent Chinese diet today posts serious national health challenges as diet-related diseases are spiking. Research shows that the changing diet is a major contributor to the rising cases of obesity, cancer, cardiovascular diseases, hypertension, and diabetes, which are the leading causes of mortality. China had a stunning number of 140 million diabetes patients in 2021, more than a quarter of the world's total. Treating them cost nearly US$10 billion. The number of patients and cost are expected to go up drastically in the next several decades if the current trajectory continues unabated.

Children have fallen victim to overindulgence of high-sugar, high-fat, and additive-laced diets. This is especially the case in the cities. A 2015 Nestlé-sponsored study found that most infants and toddlers in the sample group got their daily calories from five sources: milk, rice, noodles, pork, and eggs. Such a narrow and unbalanced diet subjects them to deficient intake of essential vitamins and minerals. The Chinese children also consume disproportionally large amounts of fast food, unhealthy snacks, and sugary soft drinks. As a result, the child obesity rate among Chinese children increased from about 5% in 1995 to about 20% in 2014 (Dong et al., 2019). A 2021 report on the development of Chinese children revealed that more than 24% of K–12 children and adolescents were obese. Weight-losing summer camps have become a booming business in the cities, but it takes both intensified physical education and a healthy family diet to achieve sustainable improvement in obese children.

Health-oriented changes in the traditional diet have been slow, which has led to public health problems. The traditional diet rooted in an agrarian culture is high sodium, which was necessary for high-intensity manual work but is antiquated today as lifestyles have changed for most Chinese. The traditional high sodium intake might have been appropriate for manual laborers, but not so for the white-color office workers of today. The average salt intake among the Chinese is one of the highest in the world and is at a very unhealthy level. The daily per person salt intake in China hovers above 10 grams in 2019, more than double the goal set by the Chinese government in "Healthy China 2030" to reduce it to 5 grams by 2030, which could theoretically lead to tens of millions fewer cardiac events.

China's per capita sugar and oil intakes have also become high, reaching a daily intake of 30 grams free sugars in 2019, in comparison to 25 grams daily sugar intake set in Healthy China; the per person daily intake of edible oil was 42 grams in 2019, also significantly higher than the 25–30 grams goal set for 2030. Added sugar and edible oil were historically luxuries; it must have been liberating for most Chinese to be able to indulge in their abundance and affordability. By the way, they do make the dishes tastier. Some traditional foods and snacks have proven to have adverse health effects, including smoked meat and pickled vegetables that have been linked to localized high cancer rates. Also, any advice for transitioning to a healthier diet is often met with strong and stubborn pushback; traditional food cultures may be the most resistant to change. It is very popular for folks in certain southern regions such as Hunan Province to chew betel nuts, for example, which is linked to mouth cancer. The government had to launch a public awareness campaign to try to help locals abandon the habit, but so far it has yielded only limited success.

Changing Food Culture

Among all the changes in China's culinary landscape, the ascendance of premade food has to be the most stunning. Premade food can be divided into two general categories: commercially prepared food and ready-to-cook dishes. Commercially prepared food is manufactured in large quantity and in anticipation of consumer purchase and consumption, it can be canned, frozen, and air packaged. While commercially prepared food has long been common in the daily food scene, the Chinese are among those in the world who strongly prefer food that is or resembles being freshly prepared. Such a preference, however, collides with today's hectic lifestyle, which has made the traditional "start-from-scratch" food preparation untenable for many people, especially urban white-collar professionals. Ready-to-cook meals, henceforth, have come to meet the new and swelling market demand.

10.3. Instant-Boiled Pork with Bunching Onion and Vegetables (*Shuan-zhu-rou-pian Pei-da-cong-xiao-cai*; a ready-to-cook dish)

This dish does not involve stir-fry and is very easy to prepare, which may be appreciated by the young professionals who do not know how to cook. Cooking instructions on the kit read as follows.

Suggested preparation time
10 minutes

Freshness retention
3–4 days in refrigeration
Yield: Serves 2

Ingredients (in the packet)
10 oz. pork, sliced
½ Welsh (bunching) onion
1 bag enoki mushroom

Seasoning (not included in the packet):
2–3 tbsp flavored soy sauce
½ tbsp sesame oil
1 tsp cooking wine
Pinch of salt

Preparation
1. Take contents out of the package.
2. Clean the mushrooms.
3. Bevel the onion into thin slices, drizzle salt, and press on them; let marinate for 5 minutes, then rinse with water.
4. Add hot water to a pan, add some salt and the cooking wine, then pour in pork and mushroom.
5. Stir to keep the content loose; boil for 1–2 minutes.
6. Scoop out the contents into a colander to drain broth.
7. In a bowl, mix pork, onion, mushroom, soy sauce and sesame oil; serve.

Here comes ready-to-cook entrées. More aptly called *yu-zhi-cai* ("pre-assembled dishes") in China, they have the potential to fundamentally alter the way the Chinese prepare and eat food, threatening cooking as a form of art and relegating dining out to special occasions. Ready-to-cook entrées are made with paired main ingredients based on known recipes and can be cooked and eaten with minimal preparation. The ingredient kit is often made after a specific order is placed, and then is either picked up by the customer or delivered quickly so that all ingredients remain fresh. Ready-to-cook entrées feature three specific subcategories based on their targeted market segments. The first is precooked meals that need only heating before consumption. The second provides paired ingredients based on classic recipes that can be prepared with minimal skills and little time to cook. The third includes meal kits that come with all main ingredients of a recipe that would require more preparation, providing the consumer, especially someone who fancies to be an amateur chef, to improvise and enjoy the experience of cooking.

Japan has been a leader in making and consuming ready-to-cook food on an industrial scale since the 1930s. China, on the other hand, is catching up quickly with its immense and growing market in recent years. Skipping the time-consuming and laborious shopping and cleaning steps, a person with rudimentary cooking skills can prepare a multiple-course meal quickly by ordering specific ready-to-cook kits, then cooking, heating, or simply opening them up, and *voilà*, a presentable dinner is ready. Upscale restaurants can now deliver complete, ready-to-cook meals for holiday banquets to one's doorsteps, and the outcome is said to be of such fine quality that it has delighted even many foodies.

The COVID-19 pandemic has given ready-to-cook food a huge boost as lockdowns in the early stages of the pandemic trapped tens of millions of Chinese in their condos and apartments. Innovative, even adventurous, cooking provided solace and became a favorite pastime. More and more Chinese seem to accept that, going forward, ready-to-cook food is the way to go for home cooking, even after nationwide lockdowns were lifted, because of the convenience and affordability of the ready-to-cook entrées. Ready-to-cook food competes well for an increasing share of the food market in China with its vast selections, quick delivery or pick up, and quality guarantee. Venture capital has moved in, funding many startups and fueling the already fierce competition among businesses and locales that want to become the leaders and logistic centers of the burgeoning business sector of ready-to-cook food.

10.4. Minced Chicken and Tofu Casserole (*Ji-rou-dou-fu-bao*; a ready-to-cook dish)

This hearty Cantonese dish now comes in a ready-to-cook kit with simple steps for preparation. The original recipe includes salted fish, an ingredient that the kit's manufacturer decided to skip. Cooking instructions on the kit read as follows.

Suggested preparation time
20 minutes

Freshness retention
4–5 days under refrigeration
Yield: Serves 2

Ingredients (in the packet)
7 oz. fully cooked, minced chicken
2 oz. tofu dregs (a residue from tofu making)

2 eggs
2 oz. broccoli

Seasoning (not included in the packet)
1 tbsp miso paste
Salt and pepper, olive oil, as needed

Preparation
1. Shrink-wrap the broccoli and microwave for 1 minute (to reduce its moisture).
2. In a deep dish, mix the chicken with miso paste, pinches of salt and pepper (salt may be omitted since miso is usually very salty).
3. Mix the chicken well with egg and tofu; lightly pound the mix to squeeze out air.
4. Coat a microwave-safe deep dish with olive oil, put in chicken and tofu mix and flatten, then put the broccoli on top.
5. Let stand for 5 minutes, then microwave for 5–6 minutes or until heated through; serve.

Is the surging popularity of the ready-to-cook food sector merely a fad or the harbinger of a sea change in Chinese food culture? A more immediate impact may be on the restaurant industry. It is hard for most casual dining establishments to compete with ready-to-cook sector in terms of the quality and selection of ingredients; upscale restaurants, at the same time, feel pressure from the growing offerings of ready-to-cook entrées, which are significantly cheaper and are rapidly improving in quality. In desperation, some restaurants have resorted to serving entrées using read-to-cook kits and employing *cooks* rather than *chefs*, which has triggered great controversy and outraged the foodies. Can read-to-cook entrées match "the real thing," that is, dishes with expertly selected ingredients and cooked onsite by trained chefs? There is a likelihood that they can. People who have tried *Fo-tiao-qiang* (steamed abalone with shark's fin and fish maw in broth), an upscale classic dish in the Fujian cuisine, swore that it tasted almost as good as the version freshly prepared at fine restaurants. The kit only needs to be heated, either by steaming or boiling, for 20–30 minutes before serving, and it is a lot more affordable. It is amazing that the ready-to-cook kit can achieve such high marks since it substitutes shark fins, now banned in China, with vermicelli. In the long run, some fear that the popularization of ready-to-cook food may subvert the essence of Chinese cooking, which emphasizes start-from-scratch preparation and individualized artistic renditions.

10.5. Salmon with Colorful Vegetables (*Sheng-san-wen-yu Pei-duo-cai-shu-cai*; a ready-to-cook dish)

This newly created dish in a package is particularly popular among the young, white-collar professionals who in recent years have flocked to salmon for its health benefits. Cooking instructions on the kit read as follows.

Suggested preparation time
15 minutes

Freshness retention
3–4 days under refrigeration
Yield: Serves 2

Ingredients (in the packet)
2 fillets raw salmon
½ stem celery
6 cherry tomatoes
1 yellow bell pepper
1 oz. butter cheese

Seasoning (not included in the packet)
Salt and pepper, as needed
1 tbsp vinegar
2 tsp olive oil

Preparation
1. Bevel the celery, halve the tomatoes, and cut the bell pepper into eight equal sized pieces.
2. In a microwave-safe container, place celery at the bottom, then lay salmon on top, with tomatoes and bell pepper filling the gaps.
3. Cut the cheese into small pieces and spread them on top; drizzle vinegar and olive oil over the contents.
4. Shrink-wrap the container and microwave for 5 minutes; serve.

China is experiencing a proliferation of hot and spicy food. Sichuan and Hunan cuisines, infused with hot and spicy chili pepper, have swept through the country and can be easily found in every corner of the land. Some regional cuisines have moved away from their mild flavors and become spiced-up with chili pepper as seasoning and condiment. Sichuan (or Chongqing) hot pot, known for its red-chili broth, is the most popular choice for dining out, as droves of diners descend on food joints and street vendors, scalding all kinds of ingredients through red hot spicy broth before gobbling them down. The hot pot craze is by no means a boon to Sichuan or Hunan cuisines, which have developed artful ways to use hot chili to bring out the rich flavors of many ingredients that may remain hidden otherwise. The use of hot chili is not to mask the good or bad tastes and flavors of food ingredients, not to say the dishes.

The national food "spice-up" may be attributed to several reasons. First, large emigrations from Sichuan and other poorer southwest regions may have spurred the spread of hot spicy food throughout the country. Second, the masses, especially the young, may have become hooked to hot spicy food because of the endorphin-induced exhilaration. Third, hot pot is particularly popular among the low-income and the young because, for the former, it is more affordable than the conventional sit-down meals, and, for the young, it is more relaxing for social dining out with its self-serving etiquette and snack-oriented ingredients.

The proliferation of hot spicy food may also be attributable to ulterior business motives. It is one thing as a way for run-of-the-mill restaurants to attract customers by serving food that generates an addictive, endorphin-induced euphoria; it is quite another matter, unethical and even illegal, when restaurants spice up ingredients that are inferior, stale, or even spoiled. The hot spicy flavor is the easiest way to mask meats and seafood of questionable quality at many low-cost food joints. The shady practice may increase business profitability and would most definitely put the diners at risk and expose the general public to health threats.

Crawfish Craze

Crawfish were introduced to the Yangzi Delta in the 1930s. They quickly took over the natural habitat. Attempts to eat them were deterred by the cumbersome cleaning process. In 1993, a restaurant in Jiangsu concocted a spicy-sweet crawfish recipe that became an instant regional favorite and generated a craze throughout China. It is, for instance, the most popular entrée in Beijing's famed "Ghost Street" nightly dining scene. Crawfish farms are concentrated in the lower Yangzi River valley, from where the miniature crustacean is shipped to every corner of China thanks to a highly developed supply chain.

Nationwide popularity of hot spicy food also has far-reaching implications for Chinese food traditions. Some observers have noted that many restaurants are reducing their menus of stir-fry entrées, which have been the cornerstone of Chinese cooking, and which can achieve the highest form of culinary art when prepared by chefs and served immediately out of the wok. It is very tempting to turn a restaurant into a hot pot haven to generate higher profitability by adopting assembly line preparation and by hiring fewer highly paid chefs.

The surging popularity of ready-to-cook and hot spicy foods are but two of the challenges facing traditional Chinese food culture. The Chinese food culture has always been evolving, and the Chinese have always been eager to embrace the new in their pursuit of adequate food and tasty food. Today, China is braving a far-reaching transformation, and the issues and concerns are many and often intersecting. While the Chinese must put food security as their first national priority, they are also keenly aware of the challenges that they face in food safety and dietary changes. In addition, they face the challenge of how to preserve the essence of tradition, a cultural heritage, while embracing changes that are inevitable but ambiguous in terms of their long-term social and cultural ramifications. The future is now, so are the Chinese ready to take on the challenges that their most cherished cultural heritage is facing?

Further Reading

Brown, Lester R. *Who Will Feed China?: Wake-Up Call for a Small Planet.* New York: W. W. Norton & Company, 1995.

China Power Team. "How Is China Feeding Its Population of 1.4 Billion?" *China Power*, January 25, 2017. Updated August 26, 2020. https://chinapower .csis.org/china-food-security/.

Ding, Qian. "China Releases 40-year Assessment of the Green Great Wall." *CGTN*, December 24, 2018. https://news.cgtn.com/news/3d3d514e304d544e31 457a6333566d54/share_p.html.

Dong, Yanhui, Catherine Jan, Yinghua Ma, Bin Dong, Zhiyong Zou, Yide Yang, Rongbin Xu, et al. "Economic Development and the Nutritional Status of Chinese School-aged Children and Adolescents from 1995 to 2014: An Analysis of Five Successive National Surveys." *The Lancet Diabetes and Endocrinology* 7, no. 4 (April 2019):288–299. https://doi.org/10.1016 /S2213-8587(19)30075-0.

Douglas, Leah and Nichola Groom. "World Making Little Progress on Food Waste, A Big Climate Problem." *Reuters*, November 14, 2022. https:// www.reuters.com/article/climate-un-usa-foodwaste-idAFKBN2S5094.

Gooch, Elizabeth and Fred Gale. "China's Foreign Agriculture Investments." *USDA Economic Information Bulletin*, 192, April 2018. https://www.ers .usda.gov/webdocs/publications/88572/eib-192.pdf.

"Great Famine of China during the Great Leap Forward." *Facts and Details.* https://factsanddetails.com/china/cat2/sub6/item2854.html (accessed August 16, 2022).

Huang, Echo. "Ten Years After China's Infant Milk Tragedy, Parents Still Won't Trust Their Babies to Local Formula." *Quartz,* July 15, 2018. Last updated July 20, 2022. https://qz.com/1323471/ten-years-after-chinas-melamine-laced-infant-milk-tragedy-deep-distrust-remains/.

Huang, Yongcai, Haihai Wang, Yidong Zhu, Xing Huang, Shuai Li, Xingguo Wu, Yao Zhao, et al. "THP9 Enhances Seed Protein Content and Nitrogen-use Efficiency in Maize." *Nature,* November 16, 2022. https://doi.org/10.1038/s41586-022-05441-2.

Qi, Xijia. "Chinese Consumers Urge Harsh Punishment for Food Safety Violations amid Anger over Revelations." *Global Times,* March 16, 2022. https://www.globaltimes.cn/page/202203/1255042.shtml.

"Tainted and Poisoned Foods in China." *Facts and Details.* Last updated July 2015. https://factsanddetails.com/china/cat11/sub73/item144.html.

Wu, Shellen X. "Yuan Longping (1930–2021): Crop Scientist Whose High-yield Hybrid Rice Fed Billions." *Nature,* 24 June 2021. https://www.nature.com/articles/d41586-021-01732-2.

Xie, Echo. "China Urges Farmers to Consider New Variety of Perennial Rice." *South China Morning Post,* October 19, 2022. https://www.scmp.com/news/china/science/article/3196436/china-urges-farmers-consider-new-variety-perennial-rice.

Xinhua. "Survey Shows Eating Habit Change Among Chinese During COVID-19 Epidemic." August 20, 2020. http://en.people.cn/n3/2020/0820/c90000-9736827.html.

Xinhua. "Chinese Scientists for the First Time Synthesize Starch from Carbon Dioxide." September 24, 2021. http://en.people.cn/n3/2021/0924/c90000-9900197.html.

Xinhua. "China Issues No. 1 Central Document for 2023, Highlights Rural Vitalization Tasks." February 13, 2023. http://english.www.gov.cn/policies/latestreleases/202302/13/content_WS63ea2efcc6d0a757729e6b4b.html.

Yarrow, Richard. "Theodore White's Reporting of Famine in Henan Saved Lives." *SupChina,* March 31, 2022. https://supchina.com/2022/03/31/theodore-whites-reporting-of-famine-in-henan-saved-lives/.

Zhang, Yuan, Tengfei Xu and Jingxin Xiao. "How Has China Maintained Domestic Food Stability amid Global Food Crises?" *World Economic Forum,* November 7, 2022. https://www.weforum.org/agenda/2022/11/china-domestic-food-stability-amid-global-food-crises/.

Zhen, Shihan, Yanan Ma, Zhongyi Zhao, Xuelian Yang and Deliang Wen. "Dietary Pattern Is Associated with Obesity in Chinese Children and Adolescents: Data from China Health and Nutrition Survey (CHNS)." *Nutrition Journal* 17, no. 68 (2018). https://doi.org/10.1186/s12937-018-0372-8.

Glossary

The glossary is organized by the Chinese food terms in six categories: (1) cooking methods and tools; (2) common food terms; (3) sample foods and dishes; (4) seasonings, condiments, spices, and herbs; (5) beverages; and (6) dining facilities and etiquette. The Chinese terms are alphabetized based on their Romanized spellings, followed by their English translations, if available, in parentheses, or explanatory phrases.

COOKING METHODS AND TOOLS

Ao (Decoction)
Very slow cooking technique that uses heat to extract all the possible nutrients from the ingredients.

Ba
A cooking method that involves boiling, then stir-frying or deep-frying, and finally braising. It is usually used for making meat dishes.

Ban (Blend)
Mixing various ingredients with seasonings and spices.

Bao
Two distinct cooking methods: (1) high-heat, quick stir-fry, (2) low-heat simmer in pot.

Bao-chao (Stir-frying in high heat)
A cooking technique similar to stir-frying but with a much larger amount of cooking oil to bring a deep-fry flavor to the dish.

Cai Dao (Chinese cleaver)
A large, rectangular blade bound by a wooden handle without a pointed tip and heavier than the Western cleaver.

Chao (Chāo, first tone in Chinese spelling; scalding)
Mixing ingredients in boiling or hot water briefly to get rid of blood (meat) or certain flavors (vegetables). It is not a cooking method *per se*, but one step in preparing a specific dish.

Chao (Chǎo, third tone in Chinese spelling; stir-frying)

Fry cooking in pans that requires constant stirring so that food can be cooked more easily. The most common technique in Chinese cooking that includes plain stir-frying, dry stir-frying, and stir-frying in high heat.

Chao-guo (Wok)

Traditional Chinese saucepan that has a bowl-shaped bottom and is usually deeper than its Western counterpart. It is also called *cai-guo* (wok for dishes) or *chao-cai-guo* (wok for stir-frying dishes).

Ding

Bronze cauldrons used in ceremonial rituals and cooking during the Classical Epoch (30th–3rd centuries BCE).

Dong

Chilling slow-simmered meat in original broth until the mixture becomes jellified.

Dun (Stewing in low heat)

A slow-cooking method usually after bringing the content to a boil. It can be used to make a stew or meat in brown sauce.

Gan-mian-zhang (Rolling pin)

a smooth wooden dowel for making Chinese flour wrappers (for dumplings and wontons), noodle sheets, and pancakes.

Gou-qian

Thickening a dish with wet starch.

Guo-chan (Wok spatula)

An essential cooking tool designed for stir-frying, scraping, and serving dishes in a wok.

Hong-shao (Red-cooking)

Cooking over prolonged heat with the ingredients completely immersed in a soy sauce–based broth. This style of cooking is commonly used for beef and eggs. Slow red cooking (*lu*)—Prolonged cooking under constant heat where ingredients are strongly flavored by soy sauce–based broth.

Hui

Quickly precooking ingredients in hot water, then stir-frying them.

Huo-qi

Also referred to as *guo-qi* (Cantonese: *wok hei*), it refers to the chemical reaction during high-heat stir-frying that can impart special flavors to the dishes. It is scientifically similar to the so-called Maillard reaction. Extensive training and special fire hearth are needed to achieve *huo-qi* in stir-frying.

Jian (Pan-frying)

Frying in pans that have more oil or liquid present, and covering when ingredients are semi-cooked to hold heat and moisture in order to obtain crispiness on one side and fluffiness on the other (e.g., potstickers).

Jiao-ye (*Jiao-zhi*)
Glazing by drizzling broth over a dish.

Kuai-zi (**Chopsticks**)
Sticks used in shaped pairs of equal length for cooking, serving, and eating in East and Southeast Asia. Most chopsticks are made of wood or bamboo but can be of bone or metal.

Liang-ban
Making a salad with vegetables either chilled or at room temperature, topped with condiments such as salt, vinegar, sesame oil, and granulated sugar.

Liu
A double-cooking method: deep frying until meat or fish is semi-cooked and then lightly braising food while adding additional ingredients.

Men (**Simmer**)
Processing something by braising, frying, or parboiling and then simmering in the original broth until ingredients are fully cooked.

Shao (**Braising**)
Mix of both frying and cooking in liquid that is heated to medium heat.

Shao (**Second tone in Chinese spelling**)
General term for spoons and ladles.

Shao-kao (**Roast**)
Chinese roasting method which involves marinating/seasoning meat or seafood and then grilling or barbecuing it on an open fire or in an oven.

Tang
Pouring boiling water over ingredients, sometimes repeatedly, to get them cooked.

Wei
Cooking something with a surrounding heat source, either in cinders or in broth. It is a cooking method common in central southern China.

Xun (**Smoking**)
Cooking by heating the food ingredients by allowing them to come in direct contact with hot smoke that is produced either by sugar or tea leaves. The method preserves the smoked food and imparts special flavors to it.

Yan
Marinating or pickling with different spices, condiments, or herbs such as salt, soy sauce, soy pastes, fresh green onion, ginger, or garlic.

Zha (**Deep-frying**)
Traditional immersion frying using oils or fats.

Zheng (**Steam**)
Cooking using heat from steam that is produced by boiling water. Any ingredients or their combinations can be cooked with this method.

Zheng-long (Steamer)

The traditional Chinese steamer is usually made of bamboo, which is called *zheng-long* ("steamer box"); it is also made of aluminum or stainless steel today, which is referred to as *zheng-guo* ("steamer pot").

Zhuo

Different from boiling, this method gets ingredients barely cooked in boiling water, then adds special sauces to them. It is popular in Guangdong (Cantonese) cuisine.

COMMON FOOD TERMS

Cai

The generic term for dishes that are non-starch entrées or a type of cuisine (e.g., Sichuan *cai*).

Da-mi

General term for rice.

Dan-lei

Eggs of any kind, with chicken eggs being the most common.

Dian-xin

Literally meaning "touch of the heart," these are tidbits that are mostly served as snacks or desserts. They can be made into a meal if consumed in multiple servings and large varieties, as is in the case in the Guangdong cuisine (Cantonese for *dian-xin*: dim sum).

Dou-zhi-pin (Soy products)

Soy products have great variety in texture, flavor, and shape. *Dou-fu* (tofu), the most common and least expensive soy product, is a soft white protein-rich food made from soymilk curds.

Fan

The generic term for (1) meals, (2) starch food which are traditionally referred to as "main food" (*zhu-shi*), or (3) cooked whole grains such as steamed rice (*mi-fan*).

Gai-fan ("Covered rice")

Rice served with meat/seafood and vegetables of choice. It is a popular lunch choice that is a type of Chinese fast food.

Hai-xian

Seafood of any kind, usually including saltwater fish.

Jian-bing Guo-zi

Pancakes made with mung bean flour and eggs

Kai-wei-cai

Appetizers. They are sometimes called *leng-pan* ("cold plates") and *tou-tai* (in Cantonese cuisine), or *liang-cai* ("chilled dishes").

Mai-yang-tang
Maltose or malt sugar, a natural sweetener.

Mian-fen
Wheat flour.

Rou-lei
Meat of any kind, including poultry meat.
    Ji rou: chicken meat.
    Niu-rou: beef.
    Yang-rou: mutton.
    Zhu-rou: pork.

Shu-cai
Vegetables of any kind.

Suan-nai
Yogurt.

Tang
Soup or any soupy liquid.

Tian-dian
Sweet snacks that can also serve as desserts.

Wan-fan
Supper or dinner, also called *wan-can*.

Wu-fan
Lunch, also called *wu-can*.

Xiao-chi
Tidbits, snacks, or street food.

Xiao-mi
Millet.

Ye-xiao
Night snacks, usually soupy light fares.

Yu-lei
Fish (*yu*) of any variety.

Yu-zhi-cai
Commercially premade, ready-to-cook dish kits.

Zao-fan
Breakfast, also called *zao-can*.

Zhou
A porridge made of rice or other grains.

Zhu-sun
Any kind of bamboo shoots (young sprouts).

SAMPLE FOODS AND DISHES

Ai-wo-wo
A famous Beijing snack: a dough made from glutinous rice flour and sweet red bean paste.

Ba-bao-fan (**Eight treasures rice**)
A sweet dish that uses glutinous rice, lard, and several dry fruits, nuts, or seeds. It is popular throughout China but especially in the Yangzi Delta.

Bao-du
Quick-fried tripe with Welch onion, garlic, and dry chili pepper.

Bao-zi
Steamed buns with fillings.

Beijing kao-ya (**Peking roast duck**)
Ducks roasted whole in ovens and sliced to serve with special sauce and side dishes. The trademark dish of Beijing.

Bing-tang Hu-lu
Candied haws on a stick.

Cha-ye-dan (**Tea eggs**)
Hard-boiled eggs flavored by being stewed in tea leaves and soy sauce.

Chao-fan (**Fried rice**)
Cooked rice quickly stir-fried in hot oil with a selection of meats, shrimp, vegetables, and eggs.

Chao-mian (**Fried noodles**)
Cooked noodles quickly stir-fried in hot oil with a selection of meats, shrimp, vegetables, and eggs. Similar to *chao-fan* in cooking method.

Char-siu (**Mandarin:** *cha-shao*)
Cantonese style barbecued pork.

Chou-dou-fu
Stinky tofu, often a popular deep-fried street snack.

Chua'r
Skews of meat, seafood, soy, or vegetables or any combo of them.

Chun-juan (**Spring rolls**)
Seasonal appetizers or snacks using thin wrappers or pancakes to roll up meat, soy, or vegetables. They are traditionally consumed during the spring and vary greatly from region to region. The so-called egg rolls, on the other hand, were invented as a Chinese restaurant appetizer in the United States.

Dim sum (Mandarin: *dian-xin*)

It literally means "heart's delight"; a traditional meal featuring a variety of small dumplings, buns, rolls, balls, pastries, and finger food, served with tea in the late morning or afternoon.

Gong-bao-ji-ding (Kung Pao chicken)

A dry stir-fried dish of cubed chicken, peanuts, and vegetables with a strongly pungent flavor. The version served in Chinese restaurants outside China is not nearly as pungent and often has a sweet and sour flavor.

Guo-tie (Potstickers)

Chinese dumplings pan-fried on one side and then steamed with lid on.

Hong-shao-qie-zi

Eggplant stir-fried in oil and then cooked in "red sauce," that is, a sauce made of soy sauce, garlic, ginger, and sugar. It is a popular vegetarian dish.

Hong-shao-rou

Braised pork belly (side pork) allegedly conjured up by Su Shi (1037–1101).

Hun-dun (Wonton)

A soup dish with dumplings stuffed with selective minced meat, seafood, or vegetables in thin wheat flour wrappers.

Huo-guo (Hot pot)

One or more soup broths cooked in a special pot, in which diners scald or briefly boil a variety of food ingredients, then dip them into various sauces to flavor and eat.

Jiang-cai

Pickled vegetables.

Jiaozi (Chinese stuffed dumplings)

Chinese dumplings filled with a mixture of meat and vegetables, and also seafood, eggs, soy, and vermicelli. They are boiled-cooked. Also refers to *guo-tie* (potstickers) and wontons.

Man-tou

Steamed buns; those made of wheat flours are the staple in northern China.

Mapo Tofu

A famous Sichuanese dish of tofu and minced meat cooked in a spicy fermented paste.

Mi-jian

Moist and flavorful candied fruits made using the method of maceration.

Nian-gao

Glutinous rice cake, usually with various stuffing or topping and served steamed or stir-fried.

Pi-dan (Century eggs or thousand-year-old eggs)
Chicken, duck, or goose eggs preserved in ashes, lime, and salt. It is called *song-hua-dan* (pine flake eggs) in some regions.

Rou-jia-mo
Sliced flat bread filled with shredded meat, usually pork belly, cooked in a special sauce. It has recently become known as the Chinese hamburger, but it resembles Sloppy Joe a lot more.

Shao-bing
Flat bread made in a clay oven.

Suan-la-tang (Hot and sour soup)
A soup with regional variations that usually contains ingredients such as wood ear fungus, bamboo shoots, vegetables, meat, and tofu. The hot and spicy taste comes from white pepper powder, and the sour flavor from dark vinegar. It is sometimes referred to as *hu-la-tang* (hot black pepper soup) in some regions.

Tang-yuan
A traditional Chinese dessert or snack made by making ball-shaped dumplings with fillings and glutinous rice flour wrappers; the rice balls are boiled and served in their original hot broth. It is more popular in the south and serves as a special food during the Lantern Festival. See also *Yuan-xiao*.

Tong sui (Mandarin: *tang-shui*)
Sweet, soupy Cantonese dessert.

Xiao-cai
Side dishes that literally mean "little dishes."

Yan-wo-tang (Bird's nest soup)
A soup thickened and flavored with the nests of cliff-dwelling swallows. It is considered a rare delicacy.

Yin-er-tang
Snow fungus soup made with a species of fungi (*Tremella fuciformis*) and rock sugar.

You-tiao
Deep-fried dough stick, also known as Chinese crullers.

Yu-chi-tang (Shark fin soup)
Soup thickened and flavored with the cartilage of shark's fins, which provides a protein-rich gelatin.

Yuan-xiao
A traditional Chinese dessert or snack made by "snowballing" cubed fillings in damp glutinous rice flour; the rice balls are then boiled and served in their original hot broth. It is more popular in the north and serves as a special food during the Lantern Festival. See also *Tang-yuan*.

Yue-bing (Moon cake)

A Chinese pastry, usually in round shape, that is a specialty food for the Mid-Autumn Festival.

Zhang-cha duck

Tea-smoked duck.

Zong-zi

A special snack for the Dragon Boat Festival; it is made of glutinous rice and savory or sweet fillings wrapped in dried bamboo or reed leaves.

SEASONINGS, CONDIMENTS, SPICES, AND HERBS

Ba-jiao

Star anise (*Illicium verum*). Also known as *hua-jiao* or *da-liao*.

Cao-guo

Also spelled Tsaoko (*Amomum tsao-ko*), it is a ginger-like plant; the dried fruit is used in cooking to suppress gamy tastes of meat.

Chen-pi

Dried tangerine peel usually used as a seasoning for meat stew.

Cong

In Chinese cooking, the term most commonly refers to either *da cong* (*allium fistulosum l. var. gigantum mankino*), which is called Chinese long-stem onion, scallion, bunching onion or Welsh onion in the West, or spring onion (*allium fistulosum l.var caespitosum makino*).

Da-suan

Fresh garlic, often simply called *suan*.

Dou-ban-jiang

Fermented bean paste made with broad beans, chili pepper, soybeans, salt, and sugar.

Dou-chi (Tempeh)

Fermented, salty black beans or soybeans used as a seasoning in certain southern cuisines.

Dou-kou

Cambodian cardamom.

Huang-dou-jiang

Soybean paste, including yellow soybean paste and sweet soybean paste.

Fan-qie-jiang

Ketchup.

Fu-ru

Fermented bean curd, including red, white, and cyan bean curds. It can be used either as a seasoning or a side dish.

Hao-you
Oyster sauce.

Hu-jiao
Black pepper.

Hua-jiao
Sichuan pepper, prickly ash. The key spice for the numbing taste in the Sichuan cuisines. It is not related to species of the pepper family.

Hui-xiang
Fennel.

Jiang-you (Soy sauce)
A dark liquid made from fermented soybeans that is used as marinate, seasoning and condiment.

Jie-mo-jiang
Green mustard paste, similar to wasabi.

La-jiao
Any variety of spicy chili peppers.

La-jiao-jiang
Chili pepper sauce.

Liao-jiu
Cooking wine, also known as *Huang-jiu* (yellow wine), including the famous *Shaoxing* rice wine.

Ma-la-jiang
A paste made of chili and Sichuan peppercorn that gives a "numbing-spicy" (*ma-la*) taste, which is the essential taste for the Sichuan cuisine.

Rou-dou-kou
Nutmeg.

Rou-gui
Also called *Gui-pi,* the bark of Chinese cinnamon (*Cinnamomum cassia*); it is commonly used for stewing meat, especially in southern cuisines.

Sheng-jiang
Fresh ginger, the most common form of ginger in Chinese cooking.

Shi-tang
Sugar for cooking. It can be either cane sugar or beet sugar, either granulated ("white") or crystalized ("rock"). *Hong-tang* ("red sugar") is the so-called "Chinese brown sugar" that is made from raw sugar cane juice containing molasses.

Shi-cu (Vinegar)

Chinese vinegar is made from glutinous rice, sorghum, wheat, or a combination of them. Rice vinegar includes white, red, and black versions. Sorghum-based vinegar, more popular in the north, is the most full-bodied version of Chinese vinegar.

Shi-yan

Edible salt, commonly referred to as *yan*.

Shi-yong-you (Cooking oil)

Edible oil used in Chinese cooking. For stir-fry, the most popular include vegetable oil (*cai-you*), peanut oil (*hua-sheng-you*), soybean oil (*da-dou-you*), sunflower seed oil (*kui-hua-zi-you*), corn oil (*yu-mi-you*), and light olive oil (*gan-lan-you*). Sesame oil (*xiang-you* or *ma-you*), as well as other flavored oil such as chili oil, is used as condiment or seasoning.

Wei-jing (MSG)

Monosodium glutamate, a flavor enhancer.

Wu-xiang-fen (Five-spice powder)

A spice mix of five or more spices used in many Chinese recipes. The most common five spices are star anise (*ba-jiao*), cloves (*ding-xiang*), Chinese cinnamon (*rou-gui*), Sichuan pepper (*hua-jiao*), and fennel seeds (*xiao-hui-xiang*).

Xia-you

Shrimp sauce. Important seasoning in some southern cuisines.

Xiang-cai

Coriander or cilantro (*Coriandrum sativum*). The fresh leaves are known as cilantro or Chinese parsley, and are used as an herb for adding unique tastes to soups, salads, and meat stews, and for garnishing. The seeds are a spice better known as *yan-sui* (*yan-qian* in Cantonese) and are often ground up and added to spice mixes.

Xiang-ye

Bay leaf.

Xiang-you

Sesame oil, used mainly as a condiment to many entrées.

Zhi-ma-jiang

Sesame paste used as condiments.

Zi-ran

Cumin.

BEVERAGES

Bai-jiu

Chinese hard liquor.
> *Mao-tai* (*Moutai*): the most famous Chinese hard liquor.
> *Wu-liang-ye*: the best known in the "strong aroma" variety

Cha
Tea.
>   *Hong-cha* (Black tea)
>   *Lü-cha* (Green tea)
>   *Jü-hua-cha* (Chrysanthemum tea)
>   *Mo-li-hua-cha* (Jasmine tea)
>   *Nai-cha* (Milk tea/bubble tea)
>   *Wu-long-cha* (Oolong tea)

Dou-jiang (Dou-zhi)
Soymilk.

Guo-zhi
General term for fruit juice.

Ka-fei
Coffee.

Mi-jiu
Rice wine.
>   *Shao-xing-hua-diao* (Shaoxing rice wine)

Niu-nai
Cow's milk.

Pi-jiu
Beer.

Pu-tao-jiu
Wine.
>   *Bai-pu-tao-jiu* (White wine)
>   *Hong-pu-tao-jiu* (Red wine)

Ruan-yin-liao (or Yin-liao)
General term for soft drinks.

Shui **(Water)**
>   *Bing-shui* (ice water)
>   *Kai-shui* (boiled water)
>   *Re-shui* (hot water)

DINING FACILITIES AND ETIQUETTE

Bao-le
Full; having enjoyed the meal.

Bu-ke-qi
You are welcome; not at all.

Can-ting
Dining room, like those in a dorm, a workplace, or a hotel.

Cha-guan
Chinese tea house.

Fan-dian
A large, upscale restaurant.

Fan-guan
A small, low-key restaurant.

Fu-wu-yuan
A restaurant server.

Gan-bei
Standard Chinese toast meaning "cheers!" or "bottom-up."

Jiu-guan
Chinese pub or bar; the Western-styled equivalent is called *jiu-ba* in mimicking "bar."

Jiu-dian
Hotels with restaurant(s).

Ka-fei-shi
Barista.

Kuai-can-dian
Fast food restaurants.

Qing . . .
"Please . . . " e.g., "*qing-yong*" (please try it), "*qing-zuo*" (please be seated).

Shi-chang
Market, usually referring to *nong-mao-shi-chang* (farmer's market).

Tiao-jiu-shi
Bartender.

Xiao-chi-dian
Snacks shop.

Xie-xie
Thanks; appreciate it.

Ye-zong-hui
Night clubs.

Zi-bian
Help oneself.

Zong-tai
Front/hotel reception. Also referred to as *fu-wu-tai*.

Selected Bibliography

Ahuja, Kabir, Vishwa Chandra, Victoria Lord, and Curtis Peens. "Ordering In: The Rapid Evolution of Food Delivery." McKinsey & Company, September 22, 2021. https://www.mckinsey.com/industries/technology-media-and-telecommunications/our-insights/ordering-in-the-rapid-evolution-of-food-delivery.

Anderson, Eugene N. *The Food of China*. New Haven, CT: Yale University Press, 1988.

Aoyagi, Akiko, and William Shurtleff. *History of Fermented Black Soybeans (165 B.C. to 2011)*. Lafayette, CA: Soyinfo Center, 2011.

Arnstein, Tom. "Exploring the Chilies of China." *The Beijinger*, May 1, 2018. https://www.thebeijinger.com/blog/2018/05/01/exploring-chilies-china.

Bloomberg News. "Farming the World: China's Epic Race to Avoid a Food Crisis." May 22, 2017. https://www.bloomberg.com/graphics/2017-feeding-china/.

Brewer, Lauren. "Profiling Food Consumption: A Comparison Between China and America." A Research Project through the Borlaug-Ruan Internship, 2012. https://www.worldfoodprize.org/documents/filelibrary/images/youth_programs/2012_interns/BrewerLauren_5CEB97BDB75F7.pdf.

Brown, Lester R. *Who Will Feed China?: Wake-Up Call for a Small Planet*. New York: W.W. Norton & Company, 1995.

Buell, Paul David, Eugene N. Anderson, Montserrat de Pablo Moya, and Moldir Oskenbay. *Crossroads of Cuisine: The Eurasian Heartland, the Silk Roads and Food*. Series: History of Interactions Across the Silk Routes, vol. 2. Leiden, Netherlands: Brill Publishers, 2020.

Cai, Tao, Hongbin Sun, Jing Qiao, Leilei Zhou, Fan Zhang, Jie Zhang, Zijing Tang, et al. "Cell-free Chemoenzymatic Starch Synthesis from Carbon Dioxide." *Science* 373, no. 6562 (September 24, 2021): 1523–1527. https://doi.org/10.1126/science.abh4049.

Cao, L. J., Wei-Ming Tian, Jimin Wang, and Bill Malcom. "Recent Food Consumption Trends in China and Trade Implications to 2020." *Australian Agribusiness Review* 21 (2013): 15–44. https://www.researchgate.net

/publication/304394950_Recent_food_consumption_trends_in_China
_and_trade_implications_to_2020.

Chang, K. C. *Food in Chinese Culture: Anthropological and Historical Perspectives.* New Haven, CT: Yale University Press, 1977.

Chao, Buwei Y. *How to Cook and Eat in Chinese*, 3rd ed. New York: Random House, Incorporated, 1972.

Chen, Aiqi, Huaxiang He, Jin Wang, Mu Li, Qingchun Guan, and Jinmin Hao. "A Study on the Arable Land Demand for Food Security in China." *Sustainability* 11 (2019): 4769. https://doi:10.3390/su11174769.

Chen, Shuo, and James Kai-Sing Kung. "Of Maize and Men: The Effect of a New World Crop on Population and Economic Growth in China." Social Science Research Network, November 1, 2013. https://ssrn.com /abstract=2102295 or http://dx.doi.org/10.2139/ssrn.2102295.

Chen, Yuanyuan, and Changhe Lu. "Future Grain Consumption Trends and Implications on Grain Security in China." *Sustainability* 11 (2019): 5165. https://doi.org/10.3390/su11195165.

Cheung, Christina. "Why Did Chinese Farmers Switch to Wheat?" *Sapiens*, November 20, 2019. https://www.sapiens.org/archaeology/chinese-farmers/.

China Global Television Network (CGTN). "Why China Can Feed Its 1.4 Billion People." September 23, 2019. https://news.cgtn.com/news/2019-09-23 /Why-China-can-feed-its-1-4-billion-people-Ke0zkqhd2U/index.html.

China Power Team. "How Is China Feeding Its Population of 1.4 Billion?" Center for Strategic and International Studies (CSIS). January 25, 2017. Updated June 11, 2020. https://chinapower.csis.org/china-food-security/.

"Chinese Food." CCHATT (Learn Chinese for Beginners Online). https://www .cchatty.com/g/chinese-food.

Crosby, Alfred W., Jr. "New World Foods and Old World Demography," Chapter 5 in *The Columbian Exchange: Biological and Cultural Consequences of 1492.* 30th Anniversary Edition, 165–207. Westport, CT: Praeger Publishers, 2003.

Crump, Marty, and Danté Bruce Fenolio. *Eye of Newt and Toe of Frog, Adder's Fork and Lizard's Leg: The Lore and Mythology of Amphibians and Reptiles.* Chicago: University of Chicago Press, 2015.

Cui, Kai, and Sharon P. Shoemaker. "A Look at Food Security in China." *NPJ /Science of Food* 2 (2018). https://doi.org/10.1038/s41538-018-0012-x.

Dong, Yanhui, Catherine Jan, Yinghua Ma, Bin Dong, Zhiyong Zou, Yide Yang, Rongbin Xu, et al. "Economic Development and the Nutritional Status of Chinese School-aged Children and Adolescents from 1995 to 2014: An Analysis of Five Successive National Surveys." *The Lancet Diabetes and Endocrinology* 7, no. 4 (April 2019): 288–299. https://doi.org/10.1016 /S2213-8587(19)30075-0.

Dott, Brian R. *The Chile Pepper in China: A Cultural Biography.* New York: Columbia University Press, 2020.

Drew, Liam. "The Growth of Tea." *Nature* 566 (2019): S2–S4 (2019). https://doi
    .org/10.1038/d41586-019-00395-4.

Dunlop, Fuchsia. *Land of Plenty: A Treasury of Authentic Sichuan Cooking.* New
    York: W. W. Norton & Company, 2003.

Dunlop, Fuchsia. *Revolutionary Chinese Cookbook: Recipes from Hunan Province.*
    New York: W. W. Norton & Company, 2007.

Dunlop, Fuchsia. "Barbarian Heads and Turkish Dumplings: The Chinese Word
    Mantou." In *Wrapped & Stuffed Foods: Proceedings of the Oxford Symposium
    on Food and Cookery* 2012. Edited by Mark McWilliams, 128–143. Totnes,
    Devon, England: Prospect Books, 2013.

Dunlop, Fuchsia. *Land of Fish and Rice: Recipes from the Culinary Heart of China.*
    New York: W. W. Norton & Company, 2016.

Dunlop, Fuchsia. *Every Grain of Rice: Simple Chinese Home Cooking.* London:
    Bloomsbury Publishing, 2019.

Dunlop, Fuchsia. *The Food of Sichuan.* New York: W. W. Norton & Company,
    2019.

Dunlop, Fuchsia. *Shark's Fin and Sichuan Pepper*, 2nd ed. New York: W. W. Norton
    & Company, 2019.

Eagan, Angie, and Rebecca Weiner. *CultureShock! China: A Survival Guide to Cus-
    toms and Etiquette*, 2nd ed. Tarrytown, NY: Marshall Cavendish, 2011

Flavors and Fortune. Institute for the Advancement of the Science and Art of Chi-
    nese Cuisine. http://www.flavorandfortune.com/index.html.

"Food Safety in China: A Mapping of Problems, Governance and Research." Forum
    on Health, Environment and Development (FORHEAD), February 2014,
    http://webarchive.ssrc.org/cehi/PDFs/Food-Safety-in-China-Web.pdf.

Foreign Affairs Office, Beijing Municipal People's Government. *Enjoying Culinary
    Delights: The English Translation of Chinese Menus.* Beijing: World Knowl-
    edge Publishing House, 2012.

García-Cortijo, María, Emiliano Villanueva, Juan Castillo, and Yuanbo Li. "Wine
    Consumption in China: Profiling the 21st Century Chinese Wine
    Consumer. *Ciência e Técnica Vitivinícola* 34 (2019): 71–83. https:/doi.org
    /10.1051/ctv/20193402071

Guo, Danying, and Jianrong Wang. *The Art of Tea in China.* Beijing: The Foreign
    Language Press, 2007.

Han, Aixi, Tianhao Sun, Jing Ming, Li Chai, and Xiawei Liao. "Are the Chinese
    Moving toward a Healthy Diet? Evidence from Macro Data from 1961 to
    2017." *International Journal of Environmental Research and Public Health* 17,
    no. 15 (2020): 5294. https://doi.org/10.3390/ijerph17155294.

He, Guohua, Chenfan Geng, Jiaqi Zhai, YongZhao, Qingming Wang, Shan Jiang,
    Yongnan Zhu, Lizhen Wang. "Impact of Food Consumption Patterns
    Change on Agricultural Water Requirements: An Urban–Rural Compari-
    son in China." *Agricultural Water Management* 243, no. 1 (2021): 106504.
    https://doi.org/10.1016/j.agwat.2020.106504.

He, Yu-na, Yanping Li, Xiaoguang Yang, Elena C. Hemler, Yuehui Fang, Liyun Zhao, Jian Zhang, et al. "The Dietary Transition and Its Association with Cardiometabolic Mortality Among Chinese Adults, 1982–2012: A Cross-sectional Population-based Study." *The Lancet Diabetes & Endocrinology* 7, no. 7 (2019): 540–548. https://doi.org/10.1016/S2213-8587(19)30152-4.

History of Chinese Food. http://www.chinesefoodhistory.com.

Höllmann, Thomas O. *The Land of the Five Flavors: A Cultural History of Chinese Cuisine.* Translated by Karen Margolis. New York: Columbia University Press, 2014. https://doi.org/10.7312/holl16186.

Holzman, Donald. "The Cold Food Festival in Early Medieval China." *Harvard Journal of Asiatic Studies* 46, no. 1 (1986): 51–79.

Hu, Ping, Tingting Wu, Fan Zhang, Yan Zhang, Lu Lu, Huan Zeng, Zu-min Shi, Manoj Sharma, Lei Xun, and Yong Zhao. "Association Between Eating Out and Socio-Demographic Factors of University Students in Chongqing, China." *International Journal of Environmental Research and Public Health* 14, no. 11 (2017): 1322. https://doi.org/10.3390/ijerph14111322.

Hu, Shine. "2021 China Food Consumption and Innovation Trends." Chemlinked, December 17, 2020. https://food.chemlinked.com/report/2021-china-food -consumption-and-innovation-trends.

Huang, Jikun, Wei Wei, Qi Cui, and Wei Xie. "The Prospects for China's Food Security and Imports: Will China Starve the World via Imports?" *Journal of Integrative Agriculture* 16, no. 12 (2017): 2933–2944. https://doi .org/10.1016/S2095-3119(17)61756-8.

Huang, Yongcai, Haihai Wang, Yidong Zhu, Xing Huang, Shuai Li, Xingguo Wu, Yao Zhao, et al. "THP9 Enhances Seed Protein Content and Nitrogen-use Efficiency in Maize." *Nature* 612, 292–300 (2022). https://doi .org/10.1038/s41586-022-05441-2.

Jiang, Hui. "China: Evolving Demand in the World's Largest Agricultural Import Market." International Agricultural Trade Report September 29, 2020. Foreign Agricultural Service, USDA. https://www.fas.usda.gov/data/china -evolving-demand-world-s-largest-agricultural-import-market.

Knechtges, David R. "Gradually Entering the Realm of Delight: Food and Drink in Early Medieval China." *Journal of the American Oriental Society* 117, no. 2 (1997): 229–240.

Lam, Hon-Ming, Justin Remais, Ming-Chiu Fung, Liqing Xu, and Samuel Sai-Ming Sun. "Food Supply and Food Safety Issues in China." *The Lancet* 381 (9882): 2044–2053. https://doi.org/10.1016/S0140-6736(13)60776-X.

Latsch, Marie-Luise. *Chinese Traditional Festivals.* Beijing, China: New World Press, 1984.

Leonard, Andrew. "Why Revolutionaries Love Spicy Food: How the Chili Pepper Got to China." *NAUTILUS* 35, April 14, 2016. https://nautil.us/issue/35 /boundaries/why-revolutionaries-love-spicy-food.

Li, Anlan. "China's 'Vegetarian Cheese' has Health Benefits." *Shine,* August 15, 2018. https://www.shine.cn/feature/taste/1808150505/.

Liao, Yan. *Food and Festivals of China*. Philadelphia: Mason Crest Publishers, 2006.

Li, Ming, Michael J. Dibley, David W. Sibbritt, and Hong Yan. "Dietary Habits and Overweight/Obesity in Adolescents in Xi'an City, China." *Asia Pacific Journal of Clinical Nutrition* 19, no. 1 (2010): 76–82. PMID: 20199990.

Lin-Liu, Jen. *On the Noodle Road: From Beijing to Rome, With Love and Pasta*. New York: Penguin Random House.

Liu, Zhe, Anthony N. Mutukumira, and Hongjun Chen. "Food Safety Governance in China: From Supervision to Coregulation." *Food Science & Nutrition* 7, no. 12 (2019): 4127–4139. https://doi.org/10.1002/fsn3.1281.

Lo, Kenneth H. C. *The World of Food: China*. New York: Thomas Y. Crowell Company, 1973. https://archive.org/details/worldoffoodchina00loke/page/n5/mode/2up.

Lu, Houyuan, Xiaoyan Yang, Maolin Ye, Kam-Biu Liu, Zhengkai Xia, Xiaoyan Ren, Linhai Cai, Naiqin Wu, and Tung-Sheng Liu. "Culinary Archaeology: Millet Noodles in Late Neolithic China." *Nature* 437, no. 7061 (2005): 967–968. https://doi.org/10.1038/437967a.

Lu, Houyuan, Jianping Zhang, Kam-biu Liu, Naiqin Wu, Yumei Li, Kunshu Zhou, Maolin Ye, et al. "Earliest Domestication of Common Millet (Panicum miliaceum) in East Asia Extended to 10,000 years ago." *Proceedings of the National Academy of Sciences* 106, no. 18 (May 2009): 7367–7372. https://doi.org/10.1073/pnas.0900158106.

Mann, C. Charles. *1493: Uncovering the New World Columbus Created*. Knopf, 2011

Maron, Dina Fine. "'Wet Markets' Likely Launched the Coronavirus. Here's What You Need to Know." *National Geographic*, April 15, 2020. https://www.nationalgeographic.com/animals/2020/04/coronavirus-linked-to-chinese-wet-markets/.

Moey, S. C. *Chinese Feasts and Festivals: A Cookbook*. Periplus Editions (HK), Ltd., 2006.

Newman, Jacqueline M. *Food Culture in China*. Westport, CT: Greenwood Press, 2004.

Newman, Jacqueline M. "Early Chinese Food: Neolithic to Now." *Food in History* 23, no. 1 (Spring 2016): 27–30. http://www.flavorandfortune.com/ffdataaccess/article.php?ID=1392.

Organization on Economic Cooperation and Development (OECD). Meat Consumption (indicator). https://doi.org/10.1787/fa290fd0-en (accessed on 26 November 2022).

Phillips, Carolyn. *All Under Heaven: Recipes from the 35 Cuisines of China*. Berkeley, CA: Ten Speed Press/San Francisco, CA: McSweeney's, 2016.

Phillips, Carolyn. "Dividing and Conquering the Cuisines of China." *Vice*, April 27, 2017. https://www.vice.com/en/article/z4dg4j/dividing-and-conquering-the-cuisines-of-china.

Pirazzoli-t'Serstevens, Michèle. "The Art of Dining in the Han Period: Food Vessels from Tomb No. 1 at Mawangdui." *Food and Foodways* 4 (1991): 209–219. https://doi.org/10.1080/07409710.1991.9961982.

Rawson, Katie, and Elliott Shore. *Dining Out: A Global History of Restaurants.* Islington, London: Reaktion Books, 2019.

Ren, Guangpeng, Xu Zhang, Ying Li, Kate Ridout, Martha L. Serrano-Serrano, Yongzhi Yang, Ai Liu, et al. "Large-scale Whole-genome Resequencing Unravels the Domestication History of *Cannabis Sativa.*" *Science Advances* 7, no. 29 (July 16, 2021): eabg2286. https://doi.org/10.1126/sciadv.abg2286.

Riley, Christopher. *One Cup, A Thousand Stories.* London: BBC Studios, 2021. https://www.skygo.co.nz/show/mac_sh_133038.

Ritchie, Hannah. "Which Countries Eat the Most Meat?" *BBC*, February 4, 2019. https://www.bbc.com/news/health-47057341.

Sedivy, Eric, Faqiang Wu, and Yoshie, Hanzawa. "Soybean Domestication: The Origin, Genetic Architecture and Molecular Bases." *The New Phytologist* 214, no. 2 (January 2017). https://doi.org/10.1111/nph.14418.

Si, Zhenzhong, and Steffanie Scott. "China's Changing Food Habits and Their Global Implications." *Dialogo Chino*, January 23, 2019. https://dialogochino.net/en/agriculture/21163-chinas-changing-food-habits-and-their-global-implications/.

Simonds, Nina, and Leslie Swartz. *Moonbeams, Dumplings & Dragon Boats: A Treasury of Chinese Holiday Tales, Activities & Recipes.* San Diego, CA: Houghton Mifflin Harcourt Publishing Company, 2002

Spindler, Audrey A., and Janice D. Schultz. "Comparison of Dietary Variety and Ethnic Food Consumption Among Chinese, Chinese-American, and White American Women." *Agriculture and Human Values* 13 (1996): 64–73. https://doi.org/10.1007/BF01538228.

State Council Information Office of the People's Republic of China. *Food Security in China*, October 2019. http://www.scio.gov.cn/zfbps/32832/Document/1666228/1666228.htm

Stepanchuk, Carol. *Red Eggs & Dragon Boats: Celebrating Chinese Festivals.* Berkeley, CA: Pacific View Press, 1994.

Sun, Dianjianyi, Jun Lv, Wei Chen, Shengxu Li, Yu Guo, Zheng Bian, Canqing Yu, et al. "Spicy Food Consumption Is Associated with Adiposity Measures Among Half a Million Chinese People: The China Kadoorie Biobank Study." *BMC Public Health* 14, no. 1293 (2014). https://doi.org/10.1186/1471-2458-14-1293.

Tian, Robert Guang, and Camilla Hong Wang. "Cross-Cultural Customer Satisfaction at a Chinese Restaurant: The Implications to China Foodservice Marketing." *International Journal of China Marketing* 1, no. 1 (2010): 60–72. http://www.na-businesspress.com/ijcm/RTianWeb.pdf.

United Nations in China. "Advancing Food Safety in China." Office of the United Nations Resident Coordinator in China, 2008. https://archive.org/details/365292-advancing-food-safety-in-china/page/n1/mode/2up.

Wang, Hongjie. "Hot Peppers, Sichuan Cuisine and the Revolutions in Modern China." World History Connected 12, no. 3 (2015). https://worldhistoryconnected.press.uillinois.edu/12.3/wang.html.

Wang, Q. Edward. *Chopsticks: A Cultural and Culinary History*. Cambridge University Press, 2015.

Wang, Q. Edward. "The Global Appeal of Pungency: Sichuanese Food as Chinese Food." *Chinese Food & History*, December 27, 2019. https://www.chinesefoodhistory.org/post/the-global-appeal-of-pungency-sichuanese-food-as-chinese-food.

Wang, Zhiqiong June, Mingxia Zhu, and Andrew Terry. "The Development of Franchising in China." *Journal of Marketing Channels* 15, no. 2/3 (2005): 167–184. https://doi.org/10.1080/10466690802014021.

Watson, James L. "China's Big Mac Attack." *Foreign Affairs* 79, no. 3 (2000): 120–134.

Weng, Weijian, and Junshi Chen. "The Eastern Perspective on Functional Foods Based on Traditional Chinese Medicine." *Nutrition Reviews* 54, no. 11 (1996): 11–17. https://doi.org/10.1111/j.1753-4887.1996.tb03811.x.

World Health Organization (WHO). *Healthy Diet in China*. https://www.who.int/china/health-topics/healthy-diet (accessed July 10, 2021).

Wright, Jeni. *Chinese Food & Folklore*. San Diego, CA: Laurel Glenn Publishing, 1999.

Xiang, Hai, Jianqiang Gao, Dawei Cai, Yunbing Luo, Baoquan Yu, Langqing Liu, Ranran Liu. "Origin and Dispersal of Early Domestic Pigs in Northern China." *Scientific Reports* 7 (2017): 5602. https://doi.org/10.1038/s41598-017-06056-8.

Xiao, Xiao, Chris Newman, Christina D. Buesching, David W. Macdonald, and Zhao-Min Zhou. "Animal Sales from Wuhan Wet Markets Immediately Prior to the COVID-19 Pandemic." *Scientific Reports* 11 (2021): 11898. https://doi.org/10.1038/s41598-021-91470-2.

Yang, Song, Xuemei Li, and Lishi Zhang. "Food Safety Issues in China." *Iranian Journal of Public Health* 43, no. 9 (2014): 1299–1300. https://www.ncbi.nlm.nih.gov/pmc/articles/PMC4500434/.

Yang, Xiaoling. "Study on Translation of Chinese Food Dishes." *Open Journal of Modern Linguistics* 7 (2017): 1–7. https://doi.org/10.4236/ojml.2017.71001.

Young, Grace. *The Wisdom of the Chinese Kitchen: Classic Family Recipes for Celebration and Healing*. New York: Simon & Schuster, 1999.

Young, Grace. *Stir-Frying to the Sky's Edge: The Ultimate Guide to Mastery, with Authentic Recipes and Stories*. Newtown, CT: Taunton Press, 2011.

Yü, Ying-Shih. "Food in Chinese Culture: The Han Period (206 B.C.E.–220 C.E.)," Chapter 5, "The Seating Order at the Hong Men Banquet," Chapter 6 in *Chinese History and Culture: Sixth Century B.C.E. to Seventeenth Century*. Columbia University Press, 2016.

Yuan, Mei. *Recipes from the Garden of Contentment: Yuan Mei's Manual of Gastronomy*. Translated by Sean J. S. Chen. Great Barrington, MA: Berkshire Publishing Group, 2018 [1792].

Zhang, Ronghua, Zhaopin Wang, Ying Fei, Biao Zhou, Shuangshuang Zheng, Lijuan Wang, Lichun Huang, et al. "The Difference in Nutrient Intakes between Chinese and Mediterranean, Japanese and American Diets." *Nutrients* 7, no. 6: 4661–4688. https://doi.org/10.3390/nu7064661.

Zhang, Yuan, Tengfei Xu and Jingxin Xiao. "How Has China Maintained Domestic Food Stability amid Global Food Crises?" *World Economic Forum,* November 7, 2022. https://www.weforum.org/agenda/2022/11/china-domestic-food-stability-amid-global-food-crises/.

Zhao, Zhiyun, Mian Li, Chao Li, Tiange Wang, Yu Xu, Zhizheng Zhan, Weishan Dong, et al. "Dietary Preferences and Diabetic Risk in China: A Large-Scale Nationwide Internet Data-Based Study." *Journal of Diabetes* 12, no. 4 (2020): 270–278. https://doi.org/10.1111/1753-0407.12967.

Zhen, Shihan, Yanan Ma, Zhongyi Zhao, Xuelian Yang, and Deliang Wen. "Dietary Pattern is Associated with Obesity in Chinese Children and Adolescents: Data from China Health and Nutrition Survey (CHNS)." *Nutrition Journal* 17, no. 68 (2018). https://doi.org/10.1186/s12937-018-0372-8.

Zhong, Yongping, Segu Oh, and Hee Cheol Moon. "What Can Drive Consumers' Dining-Out Behavior in China and Korea during the COVID-19 Pandemic?" *Sustainability* 13 (2021): 1724. https://doi.org/10.3390/su13041724.

Zhou, Zhang-yue, W. Tian, Ji-min Wang, Hongbo Liu, and L. Cao. "Food Consumption Trends in China." Report submitted to the Australian Government Department of Agriculture, Fisheries and Forestry, 2012. https://www.agriculture.gov.au/ag-farm-food/food/publications/food-consumption-trends-in-china.

Index

ABOUT THE AUTHOR

Qian Guo is an associate professor in the Department of Geography and Environment at San Francisco State University. He teaches courses in urban and regional geography and geopolitics. His research interests include sustainable development and China's western frontiers. Guo is the author of *Beijing: Geography, History, and Culture* (ABC-CLIO, 2020).